The School as a Work Environment: Implications for Reform

Sharon C. Conley
University of Arizona

Bruce S. Cooper
Fordham University

Editors

Allyn and Bacon

Boston London Toronto Sydney Tokyo Singapore

A Division of Simon & Schuster, Inc.
160 Gould Street
Needham Heights, Massachusetts 02194

Library of Congress Cataloging-in-Publication Data

The School as a work environment : implications for reform / Sharon C. Conley and Bruce S. Cooper, editors.
p. cm.
Includes bibliographical references and index.
ISBN 0-205-12787-8
1. Teacher participation in administration--United States. 2. Teachers--United States--Job satisfaction. 3. Work environment--United States. I. Conley, Sharon C. II. Cooper, Bruce S.
LB2806.45.S36 1991
371.1′06--dc20 90-48691
CIP

Printed in the United States of America

10 9 8 7 6 5 4 3 2 1 95 94 93 92 91

Contents

Preface

The introductory chapter of this book, entitled, "From Blame to Empowerment: Critical Issues in the Teacher Work Environment," contrasts the first and second phases of this country's educational reform movement. The first wave of reform lambasted teachers for the nation's educational shortcomings; the second wave empowers them as the key change agents in education. The chapters contained in this book suggest that it is time to progress beyond the abstract debate of blame versus empowerment and begin to identify specific areas of the school work environment that could serve as a basis of change in schools. Teachers are willing to experiment with new practices and roles but can do so only within a context of organizational support, collegial networks, and resources.

Areas that may serve as a focus of change in schools include the managerial style of principals, the influence structure of schools, teacher collegiality, and teacher participation in decision making. Other areas ripe for change are how teachers are inducted into schools, how teachers move into leadership roles, how teachers and administrators construct new collective bargaining agreements, and how teachers are promoted and evaluated.

The current reform movement has placed a great deal of emphasis on decentralization and site-based control. However, new management structures will have little impact if they are not collectively developed and managed through the participation of all the professional teachers in the school. Our introductory chapter explores this issue in greater detail, maintaining that well-prepared teachers will only be frustrated in a work environment that disregards their expertise. The chapters in this book—addressing, for example, classroom management, teacher induction, school university collaboration, and new collective bargaining arrangements—offer different perspectives on the image of the professional teacher working in the school.

Teachers know their craft; reformers may not. Hence, a conflict emerges between external pressures to improve and teachers' own beliefs and practices about teaching. The lessons from these chapters seem to be that reformers must understand the culture of teaching, which is immediate, dynamic, and pressured; work closely with teachers in reforming schools; and place teachers in a central role when formulating reforms. These seem to be the roads to improved teaching and learning.

The first wave of this country's reform movement clearly deprofessionalized teachers in the workplace. This second wave of reform has introduced a broader set of concerns regarding teachers and the educational system. Four goals seem critical: (1) quality teachers must be recruited, (2) teachers must be retained in the profession, (3) teachers must be motivated to perform, and (4) the school system as a whole must be effective. The architects of reform have thus far paid the most attention to the first three goals and relatively less to the fourth. Ensuring that teachers will be recruited to the workplace, retained in the profession, and motivated to perform are necessary but insufficient criteria for ensuring quality education. Reformers must also consider the inner workings of the organizational system, including the relationships that emerge among teachers (teacher collegiality), between teachers and administrators (managerial practice), and between teachers and students (classroom environment). This book will hopefully assist in addressing this fourth concern by offering a diversity of perspectives on changing the teacher work environment as a way of changing schools.

ACKNOWLEDGMENTS

We wish to acknowledge the assistance of Yvonne Cano and Peggy Placier for providing technical assistance and help with drafting the chapter abstracts. We are grateful to our colleague Samuel Bacharach for his guidance; to Ray Short, Mylan Jaixen, Sean Wakely, and Carol Craig at Allyn and Bacon for their assistance and support; and to Mike Sacken for his counsel. Carolyn Cormier was indispensable for her clerical assistance and calmness. Appreciation is also owed to publishers for permission to cite materials from their publications.

Contributors

Samuel B. Bacharach is Professor of Organizational Behavior and Education Administration at Cornell University. He is also currently a Senior Research Consultant with Organizational Analysis Practice in Ithaca, New York. In education, he has written on such topics as merit pay, school administrative evaluation, and school-based management.

Kathy Carter is Associate Professor in Teaching and Teacher Education at the University of Arizona. She is Advisory Editor of the *Elementary School Journal* and the *American Educational Research Journal.* She currently serves as Vice President of Division K of the American Educational Research Association. Her current work is focused on studies of teachers' knowledge and on the development of a case literature for teacher education.

Sharon C. Conley received her Ph.D. from the University of Michigan. She is Associate Professor of Educational Administration in the College of Education at the University of Arizona. Her writing and research interests are in the general areas of organizational behavior in education, the managerial work environment of teachers, and teacher evaluation.

Bruce S. Cooper has a Ph.D. from the University of Chicago and has taught at Dartmouth College, the University of Pennsylvania, and the University of London. He is currently Professor of Education Administration in the School of Education at Fordham University and a research fellow at Hudson Institute.

William A. Firestone received his Ph.D. from the University of Chicago. He currently teaches educational administration at the Rutgers University Graduate School of Education where he is also a senior research fellow at the Center for Policy Research in Education. His current research is on the professionalizing of teaching.

H. Jerome Freiberg is Professor of Education in the College of Education at the University of Houston and Associate Chair of the Department of Curriculum and Instruction. He is also the editor of the *Journal of Classroom Interaction.* His research interests include the general areas of school mission and effectiveness, classroom observation, and teacher education.

Naftaly S. Glasman is Professor of Education and teaches graduate seminars in educational administration and leadership at the University of California, Santa Barbara, and at UCLA. He is the former dean of the Graduate School of Education at Santa Barbara. He has written extensively on the leadership of the school principal and the achievement levels of the students. Professor Glasman is the former editor of *Review of Educational Research.*

Suzanne R. Hajnik received her Ph.D. in the program of Educational Policy and Organization at the University of California, Santa Barbara. She is a teacher in the Orchutt Union School district in California and currently an administrative intern in the district.

Charles Taylor Kerchner received his Ph.D. from Northwestern University and his MBA from University of Illinois at Urbana. He is Professor of Education at the Claremont Graduate School and director of the school's educational administration programs.

Stephanie L. Knight is Assistant Professor of Curriculum and Instruction at Texas A & M University. Her research interests include school climate as it relates to teacher development and cognitive strategies for problem solving and critical thinking.

Julia E. Koppich received her Ph.D. from the University of California at Berkeley, where she is currently Associate Director, Policy Analysis for California Education (PACE). Her writing and research interests focus on labor relations and school reform.

Virginia Richardson received her Ph.D. in Comparative Education from Syracuse University. She is Professor of Teaching and Teacher Education in the College of Education at the University of Arizona. Her scholarly interests include research on classroom processes, teacher education and educational change, qualitative methodology, and the relationship between research and practice. She is also past editor of the *American Educational Research Journal.*

Susan Stavert Roper is Director of the School of Education and Psychology at Southern Oregon State College. She received her Ph.D. in Sociology of Education from Stanford University where she worked as a coordinator for the Stanford Teacher Corps project before coming to Oregon. Her areas of specialization include partnerships between higher education and public schools, designing graduate teacher education programs, and the preparation of new deans of education.

John Mahaffy received his Ph.D. in adult education and has gone on to focus his professional career on faculty development. He is currently affiliated with the Northwest Regional Educational Laboratory. His professional activities have ranged from working with medical school faculty to helping teachers learn to mentor their neophyte colleagues. **Burl Brim** is Professor of Education at Southern Oregon State College. His interests are in multicultural education, school restructuring, and beginning teachers. **Neil McDowell** is former chair of the Education Department at Southern Oregon State College. His professional activities have included establishing a learning disabilities clinic, developing an interest in teachers in one-room schools, and designing new fifth-year teacher education programs. **Charles Barker** is a district administrator with Josephine County in southern Oregon.

Richard L. Schwab is Chair of the Department of Educational Administration at Drake University. His research interests are in the general areas of extended teacher education programs, occupational stress, teacher evaluation, and educational administration. He is also the Associate Editor of the *Journal of Personnel Evaluation in Education.*

Mark A. Smylie is Assistant Professor of Education at the University of Illinois at Chicago. He received his Ph.D. in Educational Leadership from Peabody College of Vanderbilt University. His research addresses issues concerning the organizational contexts of teachers' work and professional development, teachers' work roles, and collegial relationships.

Roberta Trachtman is an Associate Professor of Educational Administration at Fordham University in New York City. Her research focuses on education reform, including the reengagement of the private sector with the public schools and the restructuring of school leadership.

Bruce L. Wilson is Co-Director of the Applied Research Project at Research for Better Schools in Philadelphia. His current research focuses on how contextual influences impact the implementation of educational policies, programs, and practices at the local level.

Chapter One

In this introductory chapter, the editors set out the guiding assumptions of this book. They contrast treatment of teachers during the two recent waves of educational reform. While first-wave reformers blamed teachers for the system's problems and punished them through external controls, second-wave reformers argue that teachers must be recognized as key decision makers and empowered to construct school-level solutions. States and districts that have instituted both first- and second-wave reforms send teachers contradictory messages, which entail both a loss of their professional autonomy and a recognition of their professional status. The authors explain that the focus of this book is on teachers and the work environment of the school*—the "middle zone" between the classroom and the central office, where teachers are most likely to gain control over their work and their status as professionals. Through collaboration at the school level, teachers are creating a central role for themselves in the reform of schooling.*

From Blame to Empowerment: Critical Issues in the Teacher Work Environment

Bruce S. Cooper
Fordham University
School of Education

Sharon C. Conley
University of Arizona
College of Education

> I have been a teacher for 29 years—it is not getting any easier, either in the classroom or from the [legislative] point of view. Teachers today are not appreciated and their worth cannot and never will be measured on a computer. Teaching is a profession of the heart. It is a profession of caring, not only for the knowledge to be imparted but a caring for the child you see every day. Teaching goes beyond dollars and cents. A good teacher's worth will never be measured or valued on this earth. It is discouraging at this late date for me to read about merit pay for those with a master's degree—I guess we should only go to a doctor or a dentist with the most degrees, because that makes them better. I've been teaching 29 years. . . . I have 14 more to go for retirement—[a] total [of] 43 years—think I'll make it? You bet I will!
>
> —Arizona teacher

The United States has never known quite how to treat its teachers. It has alternated between "loving" teachers and feeling sorry for them, "fawning" over them and blaming them. Some observers proclaim that teachers hold the future of society in their hands, may qualify for sainthood, and live forever in the hearts and minds of their grateful students. Others argue that teachers may be doing only a mediocre job at best and qualify only as low-status, poorly paid semi-professionals (see Lortie, 1969).

The recent era of educational reform reflects a confusing image of the U.S. teacher. The first wave of reform, ushered in by the publication of *A Nation at Risk* in 1983, victimized teachers and held them responsible for the education shortcomings of this nation. The second wave "empowered" teachers as key educational decision makers and made them the driving force in reform; that is, professionals who work at the center of the educational universe.

This book brings to the forefront teachers, their work world, and the school work environment. Since Waller's (1932) and Lortie's (1975) seminal sociological work on the occupation of teaching, significant advances have been made in studying classrooms and schools. Yet little has been done to provide a synthesis of those aspects of the school work environment that could serve as the impetus for change in schools.

The work world of teachers includes what they do in the classroom as well as in the school as a whole. More fundamentally, the teacher work environment involves the relationships teachers have with other organizational members and how those relationships are structured and managed in the schools in which they work. It involves the commitments of teachers to their jobs, their belief systems concerning their work, and the structures in the school organization that facilitate or impede those various commitments and beliefs. As such, it includes the reform strategies (such as career ladders) that may change teachers' work lives.

Our book has little to say about those who teach and go home. But where teachers interact with other teachers, supervisors, parents, unions, and legislators, hoping to define their work, we become more interested. We do little with teaching techniques; we have no chapters on new pedagogical methods, team teaching, computers, or other technology in the classrooms. We are not trying to analyze instructional strategies per se, but rather those strategies and activities that are part of the teacher's work life in the school.

This introductory chapter focuses on the context of reform, the debate over whether or not teachers are professionals, and the school work environment as the focus of reform. These consistent issues are woven throughout the chapters in this book.

TRENDS IN REFORM

The Reform Context

The "rising tide of mediocrity" which made the United States "a nation at risk" (National Commission on Excellence in Education, 1983) tarred and feathered teachers for their poor knowledge and preparation, low motivation, and lackluster performance. The solution in many states was to raise standards of entry into teaching, institute statewide testing of teachers (before entry and during their careers), and have undergraduate majors in education include courses in liberal arts and sciences (see Holmes Group, 1986). Other measures included devising state and locally mandated objectives, setting curriculum standards, requiring grade-level tests, and raising school graduation requirements. Most of these reforms were formulated by state legislators, governors, and private citizens, with relatively little teacher input. It was not surprising that teachers and their representatives felt slighted by these early proposals.

The "tide of mediocrity" was thus met by a new tide of centralization, accountability, and externally imposed standards. Bureaucratic accountability made teachers appear less like professionals and more like victims. They seemed to be getting it from all sides: during preservice training, at entry into the ranks, in their classrooms, in the writing and teaching of curriculum, and in the testing of the "products" of their labors—the students. If teachers had ever dreamed of taking control of their lives, work, and profession, it seemed to dim with the early reform movement.

Taking a dramatic 180-degree turn, educational policy makers, legislators, and administrators called for teachers as full partners in the education enterprise. Task forces of the National Governors' Association (1986) called for giving teachers "a real voice in decision [making]." Similar calls were issued in the reports of the Holmes Group (1986) and the California Commission on the Teaching Profession (1985). The National Association of Secondary School Principals and the National Education Association (1986) jointly developed and publicized a "cooperative model" that heavily emphasized teacher participation. The Carnegie Forum (1986) called for teachers having the "ability to make—or at least strongly to influence—decisions." The nation suddenly wanted, earnestly, for teachers to be partners in educational improvement. *Teacher participation, professional autonomy,* and *empowerment* became watchwords of the new phase of school reform.

A consistent theme running through these second-wave reforms was that reform should be decentralized. Rather than being prescribed by higher-level state and federal policy makers or administrators, reforms initiated at the local level would be tailored to the specific needs and problems of districts and schools. However, as Bacharach (1988) argues, considerable ambiguity existed concerning where exactly the local level was—the school or the district. Some observers suggested that it was the district: "The district is also an important actor in local school reform. While education improvement occurs school by school, the appropriate unit for analyzing the local site improvement process is the school district . . ." (Kirst, 1988, p. 322). Others suggested that it was the school: "One of the primary benefits of school site discretion is the ability of the school, within the context of state and local goals, to shape a unique and coherent school mission and culture that responds to the needs of its particular clientele" (Cohen, 1988, p. 16).

Some advocates of school-site reform went a step further and argued that reform should not only originate at the school level but that the school itself should operate as a decentralized system (Cooper, 1989). In a decentralized school, decision-making control would be placed as close to the client and the core activity as possible (i.e., the teachers, clients [students], and the clients' representatives [parents]) (Cooper, 1989). A centralized school, by contrast, would place primary decision-making control at higher administrative levels (Blau and Scott, 1963) (i.e., with the principal).

However, there are two caveats to the general assertion that school and district decentralization will create a new participative agenda in schools. First, decentralization of the district may not automatically ensure decentralization of the school (Cooper; Conley and Bacharach, this volume). Indeed, it is not difficult to envision a centralized *school* in a decentralized *district* being run by one person—the principal (Conley and Bacharach, this volume). Such a context of school management may still deny teachers a meaningful role in determining school goals, programs, and policies. Indeed, it is not yet clear whether school-based control will mean schoolwide participation.

Second, it is important to note that while the ink is still drying on "second-wave" reform reports calling for participation and decentralization, in many states the centralized prescriptions of the first wave are still being implemented. Indeed, some policy makers appear unable to distinguish which "wave" they are riding: whether they are instituting reforms that create greater centralization, standards, and control;[1] or whether they are trying to decentralize resources, devolve authority to schools, and empower teachers. Teachers seem to have been told, "Yes, go forward, use your professional skills and understanding; and no, we don't trust you, so you must take these examinations, teach this state-approved curriculum, and subject your students to more tests." We argue in the following section that it is how we view the professional work of teachers that may well determine which wave we ride.

Teacher involvement in an expanded agenda of school decision making is a primary thread running through many of the chapters of this volume (Glasman and Hajnik; Conley and Bacharach; Wilson; Cooper; this volume). Alternatively, chapters focus on the problems and obstacles that occur when teachers are *not* active partners in school-level decision making (Carter; Richardson; Freiberg and Knight; this volume).

Teachers as Professionals

A key debate in the current reform movement is whether or not teachers are professionals. Indeed, early sociological research on teaching, such as that by Lortie and Waller, cast teaching as a semiprofession, characterized by relatively low status, easy access, the absence of an arcane body of knowledge, and a low degree of self-regulation. More recent studies of the teaching profession suggest, however, that the concept of professionalism needs some reexamination. Bacharach and Conley (1989), for example, describe three traditional characteristics of a profession (citing Hall):

1. *Structural criteria:* The degree to which there is a formalized code of ethics and a prescribed and lengthy training process in certified training institutes or the like.
2. *Attitudinal attributes of members:* The degree to which the members believe in service to the public, self-regulation, autonomy, and similar professional values.
3. *Societal recognition:* The degree to which society in general views the occupation as a profession.

With regard to these characteristics, it is clear that the Holmes Group (1986) and the Carnegie Forum (1986) attend significantly to the formal preparation of teachers. Second, a number of observers now argue that teachers and their representatives are more actively engaged in setting (or helping to set) their own conditions of work and policing their own ranks (Shedd, 1988; Kerchner and Mitchell, 1986). For example, teachers and their representatives show an increased interest in negotiating contracts that set ground rules for joint decision making to be conducted away from the bargaining table, that is, at the school site (Shedd, 1988). And third, salary gains and reform initiatives providing for more active teacher involvement in school management and decision making appear to be according teachers greater public status.

However, we would argue that more important than all of these traditional criteria is the criterion of whether or not teachers are treated as professionals in the *work place* (Bacharach and Conley, 1989). As mentioned previously, more than anything else, the second wave of reform underscored the fact that schools are *work organizations;* how schools are managed organizationally became a critical issue. Indications of professional management and treatment in schools include how much autonomy teachers receive, the degree of control over their work that they enjoy, and the extent to which they are involved in schoolwide decisions. In this sense, professionalism is more than a matter of preparation or public status; rather, it is a state of mind that is created and enhanced in the school organization.

As such, teacher professionalism greatly depends on such factors as level of discretion, control over work, ability to mobilize resources, and inclusion in school decisions. If teachers are controlled as "factory workers" in schools, then it matters little what kind of preparation they have, what kind of information is available to them (arcane or pedestrian), or what credentials they hold. Analogously, if physicians were placed in large public bureaucracies and stripped of the authority to make decisions, the argument that "doctors are professionals" would mean little.

Indeed, first-wave reform prescriptions served to bureaucratize the teacher work environment: policies formulated at the top of the system were translated by administrators into rules for teachers to follow. Consequently, teachers were encouraged simply to apply "rules and procedures (class schedules, curricula, textbooks, rules for promotion and assignment of students, etc.)" and process students according to them (Darling-Hammond, 1986, p. 11). In this context, critics maintain, teachers became little more than a bureaucratic extension of school systems, reminiscent of a return to "teacher-proof curriculum."

The preceding observations suggest that teachers' work may be characterized by two different models: professional and bureaucratic (Bacharach and Conley, 1986). The *professional* model allows teachers individual responsibility for identifying client needs and for choosing particular techniques designed to meet those needs. That is, as professionals, teachers are expected to make numerous decisions and deal with uncertainty. The *bureaucratic* model, by contrast, expects teachers to implement rules and procedures determined by others. In this sense, teachers are simply technicians implementing routine solutions to clear and predictable problems. Within a bureaucratic mode of management, the organization is constantly concerned with reducing uncertainty for teachers as well as the number of decisions teachers have to make.

Whether we adhere to the bureaucratic or professional model in part determines how we manage teachers. For example, administrators and policy makers who view teachers as professionals tend to favor reducing standardization of teachers' work activities, whereas those who view teachers in a bureaucratic mode favor standardizing teachers' work. Some chapters in this volume deal directly with the issue of teachers as professionals (Conley and Bacharach); others implicitly argue that teachers' work activities cannot be bureaucratized or standardized (Smylie; Carter; Richardson; this volume).

The School Work Environment as the Focus of Reform

Thus far, we have examined several related themes: teachers and reform, centralization versus decentralization, and teachers' status as professionals. We now examine the question of where the logical starting point of reform should be.

The first wave of reform focused primarily on changing teachers' level of motivation, through such mechanisms as merit pay and career ladders. This concern was predicted on the dual assumptions that problems in education could be attributed at least partially to school systems' failure to motivate teachers, and that changes in the teacher compensation structure would enhance teacher motivation. It was hoped that through the use of such mechanisms as merit pay and career ladders teachers would have an opportunity to be rewarded for their efforts and in turn would be more motivated in their jobs and more committed to their careers. However, in focusing primarily on the structure of compensation as a way of motivating teachers, the early stages of the reform movement ignored some basic premises of organizational theory.

A basic tenet of organizational theory, and one that is consistent with many chapters in this book, is that one needs to be as concerned with examining the *work* of individuals as with individuals themselves. Researchers and practitioners in organizational science have long recognized that problems in job performance can be due as much to the design of work and the work context as to the efforts of the individual. But in the field of education, primary emphasis has been placed on examining individual competence with only little emphasis placed on examining the design of teachers' work.

It was with the publication of the reports of the Carnegie Forum and the Holmes Group in 1986 that we have seen an increasing emphasis on changing the work environment as a way of changing schools. The chapters in this volume focus on identifying those work environment factors that are critical to improving the motivation, commitment, effectiveness, and professionalization of the teacher work force.

Some may argue that, by placing primary emphasis on teachers and their workplace, this book overlooks other important issues such as teacher preparation and recruitment. Although teacher preparation is important, if we prepare and recruit the best and the brightest teachers but do not provide them with a work environment where they can be successful, it will not matter how many degrees they hold or how many tests they pass. Likewise, if we attempt to motivate teachers through providing merit and career ladder rewards but fail to provide a work environment where they can achieve these rewards, we will surely fail. The question then becomes: Where do we begin reform? The chapters in this volume implicitly maintain that teachers and their work life are the logical starting points of school reform. However, within this general assumption, several different focuses are proposed; for example, teachers' problem solving and "justifications" for practice (Carter; Richardson), teacher commitment (Firestone), teacher participation (Glasman; Conley and Bacharach), teacher induction (Schwab; Roper and colleagues), and teacher reward systems and leadership (Freiberg and Knight; Kerchner and Koppich; Trachtman).

In conclusion, we have attempted to outline some of the more provocative issues dealing with teachers and the school work environment. Although we have divided the volume into three sections, these issues are interwoven throughout the chapters. For example, our knowledge of the teacher as a professional can only be understood as that role is embedded in the work environment in schools. This theme will appear in virtually every chapter, in slightly different form. For example, in his chapter, Cooper focuses primarily on the formal qualities of the work environment, whereas Smylie treats the environment in a more cultural sense. Whatever the definition, the concept of the work environment is essential to this inquiry.

CONTENT OF THE VOLUME

Chapters have been selected that represent the diversity of the growing field of inquiry—teachers gaining control over their work and their status as professionals. Each chapter addresses a particular area of the school work environment and is grouped into one of three topical areas: teachers' work cultures and contexts, teachers and the school organization, and changing the school work environment. Taken together, the chapters in this collection bring into sharper focus certain issues and themes concerning the relationship between teachers and the school work environment. They illustrate the range of methods and approaches employed by professionals as they collaborate at the school level, enabling teachers to create a central role for themselves in the reform of schooling. We acknowledge that one volume cannot do justice to all the theory and research, and thus we have chosen topics we feel are the most significant ones in the field at this time.

Part I: Teachers' Work Cultures and Contexts

Part I of the book focuses primarily on teachers' work lives in the classroom and the school. The chapters underscore the need for teachers to exercise professional judgment, initiative, and problem solving in their work, and a school context that supports the critical work activities of the professional teacher. Chapter Two, written by Smylie, examines the culture of schools and maintains that restructuring initiatives will be successful only if they are compatible with existing school cultures. According to Smylie, teachers' beliefs and practices must evolve within the cultural context of the school. Summarizing the literature on planned change and cultural influence, Smylie maintains that teachers play the key role in creating any lasting reform in schools.

Chapter Three, written by Carter, focuses on teachers as problem solvers and reflective practitioners in classrooms. Using a case, it outlines obstacles teachers may confront in their work. Like Smylie, Carter suggests that when work context factors facilitate change and allow teachers to become critical evaluators of their own practices and beliefs, teachers are not only willing but eager to experiment with teaching practices.

Chapter Four, written by Richardson, summarizes the immense literature on teachers and change. Richardson counters a prevailing belief that teachers are resistant to change: "Getting teachers to do what someone else wants them to do may be a problem; and very often there is good reason for resistance to this type of change." She maintains that teachers, in fact, change all the time—they continually adapt their techniques and strategies to the classroom situations they face. Richardson sets forth an interesting tension between teaching as an intensely personal experience that is thus based partly on individual idiosyncrasies versus teaching as rooted in a commonly understood professional language and set of standards.

Part II: Teachers and the School Organization

Within the larger organizational context, Part Two begins with the obvious issue: How do the influence patterns between teachers and administrators affect teachers' work behavior and attitudes? Chapter Five, written by Wilson, examines influence and goal consensus processes in schools. Influence, not authority, is the critical variable in understanding the organization of a professional work environment. Drawing on a study of over 380 schools nationwide, Wilson examines the consensus teachers have concerning the amount of influence they wield over principals. For example, teachers report more consensus in settings where principals are supportive of their professional work activities.

Chapter Six, written by Glasman and Hajnik, describes a component of school culture—the opportunities principals afford teachers for participation in decision making. The authors specifically examine how teachers and principals interact on a daily basis. Data from a study of 13 principals suggest that out of hundreds of interactions between teachers and principals, only a small minority are devoted to discussing schoolwide issues (i.e., participation in schoolwide decisions). Indeed, principals more frequently announce decisions to teachers than solicit input or delegate decisions. Further, only selected teachers (termed repeaters) may be regularly involved in decision making. Although much is being made in the reform debate about involving teachers in decisions, these data suggest that teacher involvement in school decisions may be the exception rather than the rule.

Chapter Seven, written by Conley and Bacharach, examines teacher participation within the context of school-site management. To manage teachers as professionals, administrators must adopt a collegial management model that is based on a participatory managerial philosophy. The success of a school-site management program, according to the authors, will first and foremost depend on administrators' view of teachers as professionals.

Chapter Eight, written by Firestone, examines the issue of teacher commitment in the workplace. Drawing on two case studies of urban high schools, the author examines how the school organization facilitates or inhibits teachers' instrinsic work commitments. Differentiating between macrocommitments to the organization as a whole and microcommitments to student learning and self-esteem, Firestone examines school practices affecting commitment. Teachers are more committed under conditions where they frequently interact with both teachers and administrators, receive support from administrators and colleagues, have a sense of clear goals, and exert influence on school decisions.

Part III: Changing the School Work Environment: Practices and Programs

Part III examines specific areas of the work environment that are serving (or might serve) as the focus of change in schools. This section begins with the issue of how teachers are inducted into the profession. Chapter Nine, written by Schwab, examines a five-year preparation program designed to lessen the stress and "reality shock" often experienced by beginning teachers. Directly addressing the concerns expressed by Carter and Richardson, teachers need a variety of resources in mastering the difficult and complex task of learning to teach. To improve their skills, competence, and confidence, a fifth year of clinical internship is recommended in which teachers work closely with support networks.

Chapter Ten, written by Roper, Mahaffy, Barker, Brim, and McDowell, examines how teachers are inducted into teaching. The authors criticize the traditional "sink-or-swim" method and suggest an alternative—a collaborative method for teacher induction. Work environment problems experienced by new teachers include classroom management and student behavior, social and professional demands, and lifestyle changes—problems that may be even more pronounced in special settings such as rural areas. A collaborative approach on the part of universities, research centers, schools, and districts may provide teachers with the support they need. Drawing on case data, the authors propose guidelines for improving the work lives of beginning teachers.

Chapter Eleven, written by Freiberg and Knight, reviews the literature on career ladders and discusses specific initiatives. Failures of career ladders in states like Tennessee have been due, the authors maintain, to increased competition among teachers, teacher isolation, and standardization of teachers' work. Further, architects of career ladders have largely excluded teachers from the planning and implementation of such schemes. The challenge is to design reward systems that provide teachers with "professional autonomy along with higher teacher salaries and more collegial principal management styles." Data from a longitudinal study of a district's career ladder in the state of Texas support these contentions.

Chapter Twelve, written by Trachtman, examines the issue of teacher leadership. The reports of 75 teachers in leadership positions suggest that new avenues for growth and professional renewal are being pursued. New leadership positions provide not only financial benefits but accord a new sense of prestige and professional empowerment. "The gains teacher leaders describe spoke directly to [ameliorating] the issues of isolation and low self esteem."

Chapter Thirteen, written by Kerchner and Koppich, describes a new collective bargaining arrangement called an educational policy trust agreement. Drawing on three cases, the authors show how teachers and administrators are using trust agreements to experiment with new forms of shared governance.

Chapter Fourteen, written by Cooper, reviews different models of school-based change. The author argues that regulation and central control cannot easily work, since education cannot really be managed from above. However, Cooper suggests that inherent tensions lie in restructuring the authority relationships among central office administrators, building administrators, and teachers. Provocative issues are raised about the types of organizational structures that may emerge given an increasing interest in expanding teacher collaboration and participation in schools.

The chapters contained in this volume suggest that policy makers, legislators, citizens, and educators are reassessing their views of teachers, classrooms, and schools. Many would argue that such reassessment has been a long time coming. Teaching and the structure of schooling seems to have changed little since the age-graded, closed-door, teacher-dominated classroom was created in the late nineteenth century (Cuban, 1988). Experiments in the 1960s and 1970s with "open classrooms," corridor classrooms, mixed ability/age grading, and team teaching did not become permanent realities in most classrooms. It seemed that following such innovations, grading and tracking returned, teams broke apart, and, once again, the teacher became a lone operative behind the closed door of the classroom.

This book suggests a break in this tradition. First and foremost, teachers, classrooms, and schools have been placed front and center in the public eye to an unprecedented degree. The structure of schools as organizations and the work teachers do in classrooms have been examined and reexamined. Teachers and their representatives are speaking out and becoming active leaders of reform on local, state, and national levels (Futrell, 1988). Reform initiatives such as school-site management and career ladders have caused teachers and administrators to reassess their traditional and longstanding relationships. Some of this is cause for uneasiness and caution, but much is cause for optimism.

We argued at the beginning of this chapter that the United States has never really known how to treat its teachers. The chapters in this volume seem to suggest that we are achieving a greater clarity on this question—a clarity that is to a large degree being defined by teachers themselves. Perhaps Governor Thomas H. Kean of New Jersey expressed it best: "We can explore ways to empower teachers to do their job better. We can get teachers more involved in professional decisions within the schools. We can help teachers better to share their talents and knowledge with their colleagues" (Carnegie Forum, 1986, p. 26).

Endnote

1. For an interesting discussion of standards and centralization, see Bacharach (1988). His point is that in the first wave of reform, standardized policy was seen as the way to achieve higher standards.

References

Bacharach, S. B. (1988, November). Four themes of reform: An editorial essay. *Educational Administration Quarterly, 24* (4), 484–496.

Bacharach, S. B., and Conley, S. C. (1986). Education reform: A managerial agenda. *Phi Delta Kappan, 67* (9), 641–645.

Bacharach, S. B., and Conley, S. C. (1989). Uncertainty and decision making in teaching: Implications for managing line professionals. In T. J. Sergiovanni and J. H. Moore (Eds.), *Schooling for tomorrow: Directing reforms to issues that count.* Boston: Allyn and Bacon, pp. 311–329.

Blau, P. M., and Scott, W. R. (1963). *Formal organizations.* San Francisco: Chandler.

California Commission on the Teaching Profession. (1985). *Who will teach our children?* Sacramento: Commission on the Teaching Profession.

Carnegie Forum on Education and the Economy's Task Force on Teaching as a Profession. (1986). *A nation prepared: Teachers for the 21st century.* New York: Author.

Cohen, D. (1988). *Restructuring the education system: Agenda for the 1990's.* Washington, D.C.: National Governors Association.

Cooper, B. (1989). *Bottom up participation in schools.* Paper presented at the annual conference of the American Educational Research Association, San Francisco.

Cuban, L. (1988). Constancy and change in schools (1880s to the present). In P. Jackson (Ed.), *Contributing to educational change: Perspectives on research and practice.* Berkeley: McCutcheon, pp. 85–105.

Darling-Hammond, L. (1986). Teacher evaluation: A proposal. *The Elementary School Journal, 86* (4), 531–551.

Futrell, M. H. (1988, November). Teachers in reform: The opportunity for schools. *Educational Administration Quarterly, 24* (4), 374–380.

Hall, R. (1969). *Occupations and the social structure.* Englewood Cliffs, N.J.: Prentice-Hall.

The Holmes Group. (1986). *Tomorrow's teachers: A report of the Holmes Group.* East Lansing, MI: Author.

Honig, B. (1988). The key to reform: Sustaining and expanding upon initial success. *Educational Administration Quarterly, 24* (3), 257–271.

Kerchner, C. T., and Mitchell, D. (1986). Teaching reform and union reform. *Elementary School Journal, 86* (4), 449–470.

Kirst, M. (1988). Recent state education reform in the United States: Looking backward and forward. *Educational Administration Quarterly, 24* (3). Cited in Bacharach, 1988, pp. 319–328.

Lortie, D. (1977). The balance of control and autonomy in elementary school teaching. In D. A. Erickson (Ed.), *Educational Organization and Administration.* Berkeley, CA: McCutcheon.

Lortie, D. (1975). *Schoolteacher: A sociological study.* Chicago: University of Chicago Press.

National Association of Secondary School Principals/ National Education Association. (1988, August). *Ventures in good schooling: A cooperative model for a successful secondary school.* Reston, VA: NASSP, NEA.

National Commission on Excellence in Education. (1983, April). *A nation at risk: The imperative for educational reform.* Washington, DC: U.S. Government Printing Office.

National Governors' Association. (August, 1986). *Time for results: The Governors' 1991 report on education.* Washington,

DC: National Governors' Association Center for Policy Research and Analysis.

Shedd, J. B. (1988, November). Collective bargaining, school reform, and the management of school systems. *Educational Administration Quarterly, 24* (4), 405–415.

Waller, W. (1932). *The sociology of teaching.* Reprinted ed., 1965. New York: John Wiley.

PART I

Teachers' Work Cultures and Contexts

Chapter Two

Are initiatives that restructure roles and redistribute power compatible with the existing cultures of schools? In this chapter, Smylie maintains that school improvement efforts must be informed by an analysis of the concept and content of school organizational culture. The chapter makes two related arguments: (1) the contexts into which change is introduced are formed by the culture of the school, and (2) unless the cultures themselves are changed, school improvement based on structural and political approaches will surely fail. Even though cultural change is difficult, the author insists on the undertaking in order to provide belief systems that support the improvement of teaching and learning.

Organizational Cultures of Schools: Concept, Content, and Change

Mark A. Smylie
University of Illinois at Chicago
College of Education

Since the late 1970s and early 1980s, this nation has engaged in a frenzy of activity at the national, state, and local levels aimed at improving its public schools. A central focus of this activity has been on enhancing the quality and effectiveness of teachers. That focus is grounded in a belief that teachers are central to the function of schools. This belief is shrouded, however, in a cloak of ambivalence. Much of the blame for the conditions of our schools has been placed squarely on teachers' shoulders. Yet the emphasis of this reform movement on teachers also suggests that schools cannot get better without them. Teachers are viewed as both a source of our problems and our hope for their solution.

The course of the current reform movement may be charted not only by beliefs concerning the central role that teachers play in schools but also by changes in the perspectives that underlie initiatives designed to enhance teacher quality and effectiveness. As Cooper and Conley (this volume) make clear, the movement's earliest initiatives presumed that the problems associated with teaching originated and were manifest at the level of the individual teacher. Little regard was paid to the organizational contexts in which teachers work as individuals and as members of groups.

I wish to thank Robert Crowson, Mary Driscoll, Gary Griffin, and Kent Peterson for their ideas and comments on earlier drafts of this chapter. I also wish to thank Anna Lowe, Thomas Loesch, and Mary Zeltman for their assistance in identifying and reviewing relevant literature. These people share the credit for what is worthwhile here. I absolve them of all blame for what is not.

Only recently have these contexts been recognized as critical factors in teachers' work and in the improvement of practice (see Darling-Hammond and Berry, 1988; Elmore and McLaughlin, 1988; Lieberman, 1988).

This chapter, focusing on the organizational cultures of schools, makes two related arguments. First, the cultures of schools provide contexts for change and influence substantially whether that change will succeed or fail. Second, unless the cultures themselves are a focus of change, structural and political approaches to improve schools and teaching will surely fail. This analysis begins by exploring the concept and content of school organizational culture. It then reviews relevant findings from research on educational change that illustrate the relationships between school culture and improvement, and concludes by examining the issue of cultural change.

THE CONCEPT OF CULTURE

In recent years, organizational theorists have argued that many different perspectives guide the study of organizations and their behavior (see Bolman and Deal, 1984; Morgan, 1986). These perspectives are grounded in different disciplines and embody different assumptions and theories about social and organizational reality. Each view may be considered a lens that enables us to see and understand organizations in distinctive ways.

During the past several decades, structural and political perspectives have dominated the study of educational organizations and efforts to reform them (Deal and Peterson, 1987; Firestone and Corbett, 1987; House, 1981). The structural perspective focused attention on organizational goals and hierarchies, formal roles and responsibilities of and relationships among members at different levels of the organization, and formal strategies used to coordinate diverse efforts within the organization toward common objectives and to coordinate the work of the organization with its external environment (e.g., Blau and Scott, 1962; Perrow, 1972; Weber, 1947). The political perspective focused attention on individual and group self-interests, conflict, and power (e.g., Bacharach, 1981; Bacharach and Lawler, 1980; Cyert and March, 1963; Downs, 1967; Gamson, 1968; Hoyle, 1986).

Each of these perspectives provides valuable insight for understanding different dimensions of educational organizations and their behavior. However, when evoked independently or even collectively, each may be inadequate to explain them (Deal, 1986; Lieberman and Miller, 1986). In recent years, other views have gained greater attention and popularity. One of those views is that of organizational cultures (Bolman and Deal, 1984; House, 1981; Tichy, 1983).

According to Morgan (1986), culture is a relatively modern concept. Its application to the study of educational organizations can be traced to Waller's (1932) sociological analysis of teaching. More recently, increasing numbers of researchers have emphasized the importance of organizational culture in studies of school performance and change. The current literature has provided a window to look inside the structural and political dimensions of schools. However, the view we see through that window is murky and confusing.

The Problem of Definition

The literature has failed to generate a unitary concept of *school culture.* This failure may be attributable in part to different disciplinary perspectives from which it has been studied (Deal and Peterson, 1987). It is also attributable to the variety and vagueness of definitions across studies that make synthesis extremely difficult. The term has been employed loosely. Much like Justice Potter Stewart's "I know it when I see it" definition of obscenity (*Jacobellis* v. *Ohio,* 1964, p. 197), its varied use has communicated multiple and conflicting meanings.

Many studies have equated school culture with ethos and climate (e.g., Gottfredson and Gottfredson, 1987; Purkey and Smith, 1983; Rutter, Maughan, Mortimore, Ouston, and Smith, 1979) or ethic (e.g., Noddings, 1988). It has been subsumed in the concept of school as community (e.g., Bryk and Driscoll, 1988; Hallinger and Murphy, 1986; Lightfoot, 1983; Sizer, 1984). Some studies have characterized it as code, script, and bits of information (e.g., Erickson, 1987), saga, theater, and narrative (e.g., Clark, 1972), or frames of reference (Mitchell, Ortiz, and Mitchell, 1987). Others have viewed it in terms of behavioral regularities, symbols, and the symbolic value of shared experience and common activity (e.g., Bolman and Deal, 1984; Meyer and Rowan, 1977; Weinberg, 1967). Similar variation and vagueness characterize the history of efforts to define organizational culture outside the education literature (Morgan, 1986; Schein, 1988).

A thread that runs through most definitions is that school culture is rooted in knowledge, beliefs, assumptions, and values shared by its members (e.g., Deal, 1986; Grant, 1988; Kottkamp, 1984; Metz, 1986; Meyer, 1970; Rossman, Corbett, and Firestone,

1988; see also Williams, 1970; Wilson, 1971). Deal and Peterson (1987) focus on this theme in their effort to develop a comprehensive definition of school culture:

> Culture is the stable underlying social meanings that shape beliefs and behavior over time. . . . [It is] a historically rooted, socially transmitted set of deep patterns of thinking and ways of acting that give meaning to human exprience, that unconsciously dictate how experience is seen, assessed and acted on. . . . Culture is not something "out there." It is not concrete, touchable, easily reproduced and sold in quantity. It is deeply embedded in the thoughts, words, deeds, and routines of everyone [in an organization]. (pp. 5, 8, 12–13)

This definition goes farther than most others to identify and synthesize aspects of an organization that, according to Deal and Peterson (1987), define its culture. The problem with this definition is that it may be overly broad. It suggests that virtually everything about a school reflects its culture. It fails to distinguish between the culture itself, its reflections and manifestations, and what characteristics of a school may be attributable to situational contingencies or external influences.

The Essence of Culture

Schein (1988) argues that the term *culture* should be reserved for the deep pattern of assumptions and beliefs that are shared by members of an organization. These assumptions and beliefs are implicit and unconscious, and concern the nature of truth and reality related to human nature, human activity, human relationships, and relationships to the environment (see also Ryle, 1949; Williams, 1970; Wilson, 1971). Specifically, Schein (1988) defines culture as:

> A pattern of basic assumptions—invented, discovered, or developed by a given group as it learns to cope with its problems of external adaptation and internal integration—that has worked well enough to be considered valid and, therefore, to be taught to new members as the correct way to perceive, think, and feel in relation to those problems. (p. 9)

This conceptualization distinguishes deep patterns of assumptions and beliefs from (1) artifacts—the constructed physical and social environment, language, symbols, and patterns of behavior; and (2) values—espoused operating principles to guide the day-to-day behavior of individual members of an organization.

Artifacts and values may be grounded in varying degrees in the patterns of deeply held beliefs and assumptions concerning truth and reality. As such, they may be considered surface levels of the culture. Yet, what organizational participants say and do and what environments and symbols they construct do not always mirror those basic beliefs and assumptions. Artifacts, especially patterns of behavior, and espoused values may be influenced significantly by situational contingencies and pressures that arise from both inside and outside the organization. Artifacts and espoused values may be as much reflections of these contingencies and pressures as of the culture, and therefore should not be the primary basis for defining it.

Rossman and colleagues (1988) adopt a similar definition that distinguishes among deep and surface levels of culture. They argue that there are two types of beliefs and values that characterize culture—the sacred and the profane. These beliefs and values form the basis for thought and action. The sacred types, which mirror Schein's deep patterns of beliefs and assumptions, represent strongly held convictions or world views of what is and ought to be. They define "the realm of reality that gives life its meaning or purpose" (p. 11). These convictions are implicit, enduring, and relatively immutable. They are considered unquestionably true and supported by irrefutable evidence. The profane types, which reflect Schein's espoused values, are more explicit and transient. They are more susceptible to external influence, improved knowledge, and redefinition. They accommodate and reflect temporary adjustments to everyday life.

These definitions of culture make important distinctions between different levels of organizational culture and between culture and its manifestations. They accommodate the possibilities of external pressure and influence. At the bottom line, they suggest that if we are concerned about the role that culture plays in an organization's life, its behavior, and its functions, we must look past words and deeds and identify the basic beliefs and assumptions of its members.

The Functions of Culture

Schein (1988) argues that culture functions to solve two fundamental related problems of organizations. First, it promotes organizational adaptation to and survival in the external environment. Second, it integrates internal processes of an organization to enhance its capacity to adapt and survive (see also Thompson, 1967). As a system of beliefs, assumptions, and values, culture creates an organization's identity and establishes its boundaries in relationship to the external environment. It defines the organization's core mission and operational goals. It specifies the most efficacious means and strategies by which goals are to be achieved. These include organizational structure, tasks, division of labor, reward systems, and systems of governance. The culture specifies further the criteria by which the attainment of goals can be measured and the strategies that should be taken if goals are not met. The culture also functions as a lens through which the organization perceives, interprets, and constructs meaning of the external environment and the expectations, opportunities, and constraints the environment poses for the organization.

The ways that culture defines organizational identity, boundaries, mission, goals, means and strategies, and criteria for goal attainment create common directions and internal pressures for individual and group behavior, coordination, and compliance (see also March and Simon, 1958). It promotes group cohesion by creating a basis for the development of shared language, group boundaries and roles, individual status and responsibilities, rights and obligations, and peer relationships. Finally, the culture creates a basis for shared knowledge and ideology that gives common interpretive meaning to behaviors and events, and reduces the ambiguities, uncertainties, and anxieties associated with the unexplainable and uncontrollable (e.g., Deal and Peterson, 1987; Meyer and Rowan, 1977).

There are two important considerations in assessing the functions of organizational culture. The first concerns an organization's interaction with its external environment. As stated earlier, culture functions as a lens through which an organization perceives, interprets, and constructs meaning of the external environment. It may act as a buffer, an insulator, or a stabilizer against environmental pressure and serve the organization well by filtering out inaccurate information or conflicting and confounding pressures (Hansen, 1979; Thompson, 1967). On the other hand, culture may introduce organizational rigidity that thwarts innovation and adaptation to changing conditions, thereby compromising organizational effectiveness and survival (e.g., Hawley, 1975; Janis, 1972).

The second consideration relates to the existence of subcultures within an organization, an issue that will be addressed next. Differences among groups of organizational members with respect to their beliefs and assumptions and the intensity with which those different beliefs and assumptions are held may lead to intraorganizational divisiveness. This divisiveness may create fragmentation, compromise internal integration, and lead to organizational dysfunction. Cultural cohesion or sharedness thus becomes an integral factor in organizational effectiveness. On the other hand, intergroup comparison, competition, and conflict may build and maintain intragroup culture (Alderfer, 1977; Blake and Mouton, 1961). This more positive outcome may depend on the level of the culture at which intergroup differences exist. If those differences exist at the deepest levels of belief and value, the risks posed to organizational function may be more severe than if the differences exist at other levels of the culture.

THE CONTENT OF SCHOOL CULTURE

If the cultures of organizations are defined in their essence by systems of deeply held beliefs and assumptions, we must articulate what those beliefs and assumptions are in schools if we are to understand school culture. This task is complicated by a number of different factors.

Cultures as Local Phenomena

Most studies of school culture have viewed it primarily as local phenomena. This view stems from anthropological and phenomenological perspectives and indeed from early studies that emphasize the distinctiveness of individual school cultures (e.g., Waller, 1932; McPherson, 1972). It has been reinforced in more recent studies that have sought to identify specific beliefs and values, behavioral regularities, and symbolic activity that differentiate individual schools from one another and explain variations in performance or the implementation of innovations (e.g., Lightfoot, 1983; Metz, 1986; see also Fullan, 1982; Sarason, 1982).

That differences exist across the cultures of individual schools is not disputable. Such variation may be relative to founding leadership, the beliefs and assumptions held by subsequent leaders and other members of the school over time, the events and critical incidents that shape the school's history, and pressures from the school's external environment (see Schein, 1988). The content of a school culture, therefore, is dependent significantly on local context and history. According to the view of cultures as local phenomena, they cannot be understood outside the boundaries of individual schools.

The Issue of Sharedness

Most definitions of school cultures incorporate the notion of sharedness (e.g., Grant, 1988; Rutter et al., 1979). Some imply that the culture of a school is monotypic, that a school has but one culture and teachers, students, and administrators either share in that culture or they do not. Only a few studies suggest that sharedness is a relative concept. For example, Rossman and colleagues (1988) argue that school members may hold beliefs about the same subjects but those beliefs may be held at varying degrees of intensity (see also Schein, 1988).

In addition, the concept of subcultures has not been well articulated in the study of school cultures. Studies that have examined cultures of other organizations have shown that different groups or functional parts of an organization may hold different and conflictual beliefs and assumptions about similar subjects (e.g., Lawrence and Lorsch, 1967; Martin and Siehl, 1983; Turner, 1971; Van Maanen and Barley, 1985). Deal and Peterson (1987) argue that subcultures are an inevitable characteristic of schools. They suggest that school subcultures may exist among teachers, administrators, and students. Furthermore, they suggest that individuals belong to different cultures outside of schools. For example, teachers belong to cultures associated with the teaching profession, unions, home, and community. Students belong to cultures associated with home, peer groups, and community. In all, these studies suggest that the culture of a school and its content may consist of a mosaic of interrelated subcultures that are grounded both within and outside the school. It would be a mistake, therefore, to imply that where sharedness is lacking a school culture is weak or nonexistent. Instead, that culture must be defined in terms of the characteristics of and relationships among its subcultures. It must be understood as multicultural (Sosniak, 1989).

Cultural Commonalities

Because they are not completely closed systems and because they are nested in district, community, and professional contexts, school cultures may be affected by pressures and conforming influences of broader social and cultural environments (Homans, 1950; Meyer and Rowan, 1977; Rossman et al., 1988; Williams, 1970). There is evidence to suggest that school cultures may be influenced substantially by these environments during the early stages of their development (Schein, 1988; see also Van Maanen and Barley, 1985). Such influences raise the prospect that there are certain commonalities in the content of school cultures that transcend local context.

Very few studies have sought to identify common features of school cultures. Those that have typically focused on loosely articulated norms of the teaching profession (e.g., Feiman-Nemser and Floden, 1986; Hargreaves, 1984; Lortie, 1975; Rosenholtz, 1985, 1989; Sarason, 1982) or on structural and behavioral commonalities that may be presumed to represent surface levels of professional culture (Cohen, 1988; Cuban, 1984; Sarason, 1982; see also Goodlad, 1984; Miles, 1981). We know very little about the professional norms of teachers. We know much less about the norms that might be held locally or universally by parents, students, administrators, and other members of school cultures. Therefore, while the possibility of a common culture of schools exists, we have little understanding of what that culture might be.

A Generative Framework

In all, very little is known about the content of school culture. The view of culture as local phenomena suggests that no two school cultures are alike. Yet, the evidence on external influence suggests that a school's culture may reflect broader social and cultural contexts and that commonalities may exist across school cultures. Most likely, the content of a school's culture is a mixture of the local and the universal. It is the variation in this mixture that gives individual school cultures their unique identity (Rossman et al., 1988).

Although it is difficult to articulate the content of beliefs that teachers, administrators, students, and other members of school cultures hold within and across local settings, it is possible to suggest a framework of common subjects of beliefs that are likely to be held. For example, all members of a school are likely to hold beliefs about self and self in relation to others. They may hold beliefs about their own abilities, esteem, worth, and efficacy. They may hold assumptions about what they want to achieve, what it means to succeed and fail, and the sources that influence success and failure. They may hold beliefs about futures and how much control they have over them.

In addition, members of school cultures are likely to hold beliefs about one another. These beliefs concern justice and fairness, the rights of individuals and their obligations toward one another, and what one can expect in terms of another's ability, cooperation, behavior, and performance. These beliefs may also concern relative status and how persons of the same and different status should behave toward and interact with one another. Such beliefs may be held for others as individuals or as groups.

Individuals will likely hold beliefs about knowledge. These beliefs may concern the meaning and relative value placed on certain types and forms of knowledge. They may also concern the validity and reliability of knowledge and the legitimacy of different sources of that knowledge. They concern fundamentally what is worth knowing, by whom, and under what circumstances. They concern how one comes to know and how one uses knowledge.

Finally, members of a school culture are likely to hold beliefs about schooling. These beliefs include those related to the purposes of schooling and how those purposes are best achieved. They concern what is valuable about schooling and how it relates to broader social and cultural issues and contexts. They also concern the roles and responsibilities that individuals have in the process of schooling. These beliefs may be related to schooling in general and to the specific school of which one is a member.

This framework is not exhaustive. It should be considered generative. There are likely to be many other subjects for which beliefs are held. Nevertheless, this framework illustrates the complexity and richness of school culture. It provides one approach to mapping its characteristics and exploring its content.

SCHOOL CULTURE AND CHANGE

There is growing evidence that culture is a significant variable in school change. Culture forms a context into which change is introduced (Deal and Peterson, 1987; House, 1981). It influences adoption or rejection as well as implementation and continuation of change.

The Role of Culture in Change

Almost inevitably, planned change implicates existing culture. It challenges old meaning (Deal, 1985). It poses prospects of having to adopt new definitions of what is and what ought to be (Rossman et al., 1988).

The relationship between school culture and change hinges on the congruence between the content of the culture and the content of the change (Heckman, 1987). The beliefs, assumptions, and values that compose a school's culture articulate ways of thinking, acting, and interacting. These patterns determine in large part the responsiveness of teachers, administrators, and indeed students and parents to innovative ideas and practices (Deal, 1985; Goodlad, 1975; Heckman, 1987; Sarason, 1982, 1983).

Rossman and colleagues (1988) argue that innovations will be evaluated according to how well they mesh with a school's culture. Those that are consistent with or promote established patterns of belief are more likely to be accepted. Those that are incompatible will be resisted and abandoned (see also Heckman, 1987; Sarason, 1982). These relationships are illustrated in Waugh and Punch's (1987) review of research on teachers' receptivity to change at the implementation stage. This review concludes that receptivity depends fundamentally on the relationship between the innovation and teachers' beliefs about their work and the extent to which the innovation is more consistent with those beliefs than the present system. If the innovation is more consistent with their beliefs than the present system, teachers will be more receptive to change (see also Fullan, 1982).

Waugh and Punch's (1987) findings remind us that the culture of a school, as defined by beliefs, assumptions, and values, may not mirror the structural and social dimensions of the school that are presumed to reflect and support it. They suggest further that change may challenge an organization at different levels of its culture. Change may be more acceptable if it seeks to alter the surface levels (espoused values or profane norms and patterns of behavior) than if it seeks to alter more deeply imbedded beliefs (Rossman et al., 1988; Schein, 1988). If change seeks to alter surface levels of the culture to bring them more in line with its deepest levels, the change may be more readily accepted. Even if the surface-level changes sought are incompatible with the deep levels, some change may occur "at the margins" (Cuban, 1988). Where such incompatibility exists, the change achieved will most likely be short lived. This may explain why so many educational innovations fail to become implemented and incorporated into the life of a school and why they are abandoned when external impetus and support are withdrawn (Berman and McLaughlin, 1977).

The relationship between school culture and change is more complex than these relationships suggest. The existence of subcultures may lead to the acceptance of change by only certain groups within the school (Wallace, 1970). Unless these groups form a critical mass that can support the change over time, it is likely to be abandoned eventually. In addition, culture may explain partial or selective implementation or the mutual adaption of innovations (Berman, 1981; Corbett, Dawson, and Firestone, 1984; McLaughlin, 1976; McLaughlin and Marsh, 1978). The process of mutual adaption suggests that innovations not only alter but are altered by the organization in implementation. Mutual adaption is yet another way that culture may influence planned change.

Illustrative Findings

The literature on planned change is voluminous. Whereas a relatively small proportion focuses on school culture per se, a substantial number of studies have examined the role of beliefs, assumptions, and values in the change process (Fullan, 1982). As culture is defined in such terms, these studies are relevant to our discussion.

This section presents several findings from research that illustrate the relationships between elements of school culture and change. These findings focus specifically on beliefs, assumptions, and values held by teachers. The focus on teachers in the literature is important because their work constitutes the technical core of schools (Hawley and Rosenholtz, 1984). They are the implementors of most educational programs and policies and the final arbitors of what transpires in classrooms (Clark and Peterson, 1986; Fullan, 1982; Lipsky, 1980). Indeed, they are the focus of most of the current efforts to improve our schools.

These findings are presented with two qualifications. Although teachers are clearly essential to the change process, examining the relationships between their beliefs, assumptions, and values and change is not the same thing as examining the relationships between school culture and change. There are other members of a school's culture besides teachers. The importance of the principal in successful change is well established (e.g., Bossert, Dwyer, Rowan, and Lee, 1982; Fullan, 1982; McLaughlin and Marsh, 1978). Student and parent cooperation, while relatively unexplored, are important elements too (Deal, 1985; Doyle, 1986). By focusing on teachers, I do not presume to represent the culture of a school as a whole.

In addition, most studies fail to determine the levels at which teachers' beliefs, assumptions, and values are held. Therefore, it is very difficult to assess whether relationships described across studies illustrate the workings of deep or surface levels of the culture (see Rossman et al., 1988).

Nevertheless, there is a growing body of evidence that reveals relationships between teachers' beliefs and their receptiveness to and implementation of different types of innovations (Fullan, 1982; Waugh and Punch, 1987). One of the strongest and most replicated findings indicates that teachers' beliefs about their professional efficacy—their perceived instrumentality in contributing to students' learning and development—are significantly related to their participation in and implementation of planned change (Berman and McLaughlin, 1977; Dembo and Gibson, 1985; Fullan, 1982; Smylie, 1988; Ashton and Webb, 1986). Related to this finding is that implementation is related to teachers' beliefs regarding the degree to which an innovation is likely to increase their success with students (McLaughlin and Marsh, 1978; see also Bolster, 1983, Smylie, 1989b). These findings suggest that change is substantially influenced by teachers' beliefs about an innovation's relevance and value to what they believe should be achieved in their classrooms. They suggest further that change is influenced by teachers' beliefs about themselves and their instrumentality in the classroom.

Other findings suggest relationships between change and teachers' beliefs and concerns regarding classroom order (Doyle, 1986; Smylie, 1988; Willover and Landis, 1970). These findings suggest that teachers may be unreceptive to an innovation if it is believed to pose risks to the order they have established in their classrooms. This relationship is likely to be dependent on how teachers define order (Grace, 1978) and on their beliefs regarding their ability to achieve and maintain order so defined (Ashton and Webb, 1986).

Several recent studies have focused on the relationships between change and teachers' professional norms. For example, Darling-Hammond and Wise (1985) found that teacher resistance to standardized curricular reform and student assessment policy is grounded in their beliefs about the importance of professional autonomy in meeting the needs of children in their classrooms (see also Devaney and Sykes, 1988; Sarason, 1982). Wolcott (1977) found a similar relationship in his study of program planning and budgeting systems.

Other studies reveal that teachers' reactions toward recent career enhancement plans (e.g., teacher career ladders, merit pay, and evaluation) are influenced by the compatibility of these plans with their beliefs regarding professional autonomy, equality, and justice (e.g., Lieberman and Rosenholtz, 1987; Rosenholtz and Smylie, 1984; Smylie and Smart, 1990). Cohen and Murnane (1985) suggest that teacher support of such plans is dependent on their consistency with teachers' beliefs about how to improve teaching. Finally, in a recent study of the development and exercise of teacher leadership roles at the building level, Smylie and Denny (1990) argue that classroom teachers' support of and perceived benefits from these roles are related to their beliefs regarding professional status, help-giving and help-receiving behaviors among teachers, and the relevance and usefulness of teacher leaders' activity to their work with students in classrooms (see also Lieberman and Rosenholtz, 1987; Little, 1990).

This last finding raises another important issue. The content of change includes not only the innovation itself or the new ways of thinking and doing it seeks to bring about. It also involves the process by which implementation of that innovation is to be achieved. The literature suggests strongly that any successful change in schools depends on processes of teacher collaboration, mutual assistance, joint problem solving, and participation in decision making related to implementation (Fullan, 1982; Lieberman and Miller, 1986; Little, 1982, 1986; Rosenholtz, 1989). These processes may represent a form of change themselves, implicating teachers' and administrators' beliefs regarding professional relationships, interactions, and rights and obligations (Jones, 1983; Little, 1990; Smylie, 1989a). Attempts to promote these processes, as means of achieving programmatic change or change in the work environments of teachers, pose similar issues of compatibility with existent school culture.

Predicting Cultural Influence

Although the research reviewed above suggests important relationships between certain beliefs of teachers and specific types of planned change, there are several reasons why it is very difficult to predict cultural influence on change. The relationship between school culture and change hinges on the congruence between the content of the culture and the content of the change. We know very little about the content of school cultures in either their local or universal dimensions. Beliefs, assumptions, and values are likely to vary across schools by time and local context. There are likely to be subcultures that create cultural variation within schools. Variance is also likely to exist in the levels at which or the intensity with which members of school organizations hold their beliefs, assumptions, and values.

The conclusions that can be drawn about school culture and change are therefore limited. The evidence strongly suggests that culture plays a significant role in receptivity toward and implementation of change. It constitutes a preexisting context into which change is introduced. However, because little is known about the content of school culture (except perhaps that it is likely to vary within and across settings), we are unable to predict the nature and the extent of cultural influence with respect to individual schools or schools in general.

THE NEED FOR CULTURAL CHANGE

As I argued at the beginning of this chapter, current efforts to improve education have shifted toward restructuring the work environments of schools, redefining teachers' roles and responsibilities, and redistributing leadership and power within schools. These efforts seek to alter prevailing patterns of thinking, acting, and interacting in schools. They seek to alter established relationships among teachers and administrators.

The success of these new initiatives is likely to depend on their compatibility with the existing cultures of schools. Where they are compatible with prevailing systems of belief, assumption, and value, they may be accepted. Where they are not, they are likely to be rejected, if not sooner then later. However, if these initiatives, or any others, are believed to be essential for improving teaching and enhancing learning opportunities for children, we must confront possibilities of the need for cultural change. We cannot expect these initiatives to last long or make much difference unless there exist systems of belief that support them. Most analysts agree that cultural change is a long, difficult, and frustrating task (Deal and Peterson, 1987; Schein, 1988). It is, nevertheless, a task that must be engaged if we are to achieve meaningful change.

References

Alderfer, C. P. (1977). Group and intergroup relations. In J. R. Hackman and J. L. Suttle (Eds.), *Improving life at work*. Santa Monica, CA: Goodyear, pp. 227–296.

Ashton, P., and Webb, R. (1986). *Making a difference: Teachers' sense of efficacy and student achievement.* New York: Longman.

Bacharach, S. B. (Ed.) (1981). *Organizational behavior in schools and school districts.* New York: Praeger.

Bacharach, S. B. and Lawler, E. J. (1980). *Power and politics in organizations.* San Francisco: Jossey-Bass.

Berman, P. E. (1981). Toward an implementation paradigm. In R. Lehming and M. Kane (Eds.), *Improving schools: Using what we know.* Beverly Hills, CA: Sage, pp. 253–286.

Berman, P. E., and McLaughlin, M. W. (1977). *Federal programs supporting educational change, Vol. VII: Factors affecting implementation and continuation.* Santa Monica, CA: Rand.

Blake, R. R., and Mouton, J. S. (1961). Reactions to intergroup competition under win-lose conditions. *Management Science, 7* (4), 420–435.

Blau, P. M., and Scott, W. R. (1962). *Formal organizations: A comparative approach.* San Francisco: Chandler.

Bolman, L. G., & Deal, T. E. (1984). *Modern approaches to understanding and managing organizations.* San Francisco: Jossey-Bass.

Bolster, A. S., Jr. (1983). Toward a more effective model of research on teaching. *Harvard Educational Review, 53* (3), 294–308.

Bossert, S., Dwyer, D., Rowan, B., and Lee, G. (1982). The instructional management role of the principal. *Educational Administration Quarterly, 18* (3), 34–64.

Bryk, A. S., and Driscoll, M. E. (1988). *The school as community: Theoretical formulations, contextual influences, and consequences for students and teachers.* Chicago: University of Chicago, Benton Center for Research in Curriculum and Instruction.

Clark, B. (1972). The organizational saga in higher education. *Administrative Science Quarterly, 17* (2), 178–184.

Clark, C. M., and Peterson, P. L. (1986). Teachers' thought processes. In M. C. Wittrock (Ed.), *Handbook of research on teaching* (3rd ed.). New York: Macmillan, pp. 255–296.

Cohen, D. K. (1988). Teaching practice: Plus que ca change. . . . In P. W. Jackson (Ed.), *Contributing to educational change: Perspectives on research and practice.* Berkeley, CA: McCutchan, pp. 27–84.

Cohen, D. K., and Murnane, J. R. (1985). The merits of merit pay. *Public Interest, 80* (Summer), 3–30.

Corbett, H. D., Dawson, J. L., and Firestone, W. A. (1984). *School context and school change.* New York: Teachers College Press.

Cuban, L. (1984). *How teachers taught.* New York: Longman.

Cuban, L. (1988). Constancy and change in schools (1880s to the present). In P. W. Jackson (Ed.), *Contributing to educational change: Perspectives on research and practice.* Berkeley, CA: McCutchan, pp. 85–105.

Cyert, R. M., and March, J. G. (1963). *A behavioral theory of the firm.* Englewood Cliffs, NJ: Prentice-Hall.

Darling-Hammond, L., and Berry, B. (1988, March). *The evolution of teacher policy* (JRE-01). Santa Monica, CA: Rand.

Darling-Hammond, L., and Wise, A. E. (1985). Beyond standardization: State standards and school improvement. *Elementary School Journal, 85* (3), 315–336.

Deal, T. E. (1985). The symbolism of effective schools. *Elementary School Journal, 85* (5), 601–620.

Deal, T. E. (1986). Educational change: Revival tent, tinkertoys, jungle, or carnival? In A. Lieberman (Ed.), *Rethinking school improvement: Research, craft, and concept.* New York: Teachers College Press, pp. 115–128.

Deal, T. E., and Peterson, K. D. (1987, November). *Symbolic leadership and the school principal: Shaping school cultures in different contexts.* Nashville, TN: Peabody College, Vanderbilt University.

Dembo, M., and Gibson, S. (1985). Teachers' sense of efficacy: An important factor in school improvement. *Elementary School Journal, 86* (2), 173–184.

Devaney, K., and Sykes, G. (1988). Making the case for professionalism. In A. Lieberman (Ed.), *Building a professional culture in schools.* New York: Teachers College Press, pp. 3–22.

Downs, A. (1967). *Insider bureaucracy.* Boston: Little, Brown.

Doyle, W. (1986). Classroom organization and management. In M. Wittrock (Ed.), *Handbook of research on teaching* (3rd ed.). New York: Macmillan, pp. 392–431.

Elmore, R. F., & McLaughlin, M. W. (1988, February). *Steady work: Policy, practice, and the reform of American education* (R-3574-NIE/RC). Santa Monica, CA: Rand.

Erickson, F. (1987). Conceptions of school culture. *Educational Administration Quarterly, 23* (4), 11–29.

Feiman-Nemser, S., and Floden, R. E. (1986). The culture of teaching. In M. C. Wittrock (Ed.), *Handbook of research on teaching* (3rd ed.). New York: Macmillan, pp. 505–526.

Firestone, W. A., and Corbett, H. D. (1987). Planned organizational change. In N. Boyan (Ed.), *Handbook of research on educational administration.* New York: Longman, pp. 321–340.

Fullan, M. (1982). *The meaning of educational change.* New York: Teachers College Press.

Gamson, W. A. (1968). *Power and discontent.* Homewood, IL: Dorsey.

Goodlad, J. I. (1975). *The dynamics of educational change: Toward responsive schools.* New York: McGraw-Hill.

Goodlad, J. I. (1984). *A place called school.* New York: McGraw-Hill.

Gottfredson, G. D., and Gottfredson, D. C. (1987, July). *Using organizational development to improve school climate* (Report

No. 17). Baltimore: The Johns Hopkins University, Center for Research on Elementary and Middle Schools.

Grace, G. (1978). *Teachers, ideology, and control.* New York: Routledge & Kegan Paul.

Grant, G. (1988). *The world we created at Hamilton High.* Cambridge, MA: Harvard University Press.

Hallinger, P., and Murphy, J. F. (1986). The social context of effective schools. *American Journal of Education, 94* (3), 328–355.

Hansen, J. F. (1979). *Sociocultural perspectives on human learning.* Englewood Cliffs, NJ: Prentice-Hall.

Hargreaves, A. (1984). Experience counts, theory doesn't: How teachers talk about their work. *Sociology of Education, 57* (4), 244–254.

Hawley, W. D. (1975). Dealing with organizational rigidity in public schools: A theoretical perspective. In F. M. Wirt (Ed.), *The polity of the school: New research in educational politics.* Lexington, MA: Lexington Books, pp. 187–210.

Hawley, W. D., and Rosenholtz, S. J. (1984). Good schools: What research says about improving student achievement [Special issue]. *Peabody Journal of Education, 61* (4).

Heckman, P. (1987). Understanding school culture. In J. I. Goodlad (Ed.), *The ecology of school renewal: Eighty-sixth yearbook of the National Society for the Study of Education, Part I.* Chicago: University of Chicago Press, pp. 63–78.

Homans, G. (1950). *The human group.* New York: Harcourt Brace Jovanovich.

House, E. R. (1981). Three perspectives on educational innovation: Technological, political, and cultural. In R. Lehming and M. Kane (Eds.), *Improving schools: Using what we know.* Beverly Hills, CA: Sage, pp. 17–41.

Hoyle, E. (1986). *The politics of school management.* London: Hodder & Stoughton.

Jacobellis v. *Ohio.* (1964). 378 U.S. 184 (Stewart, J., concurring).

Janis, I. L. (1972). *Victims of groupthink.* Boston: Houghton Mifflin.

Jones, G. R. (1983). Transaction costs, property rights, and organizational culture: An exchange perspective. *Administrative Science Quarterly, 28* (3), 454–467.

Kottkamp, R. B. (1984). The principal as cultural leader. *Planning and Changing 15* (3), 152–160.

Lawrence, P. R., and Lorsch, J. W. (1967). *Organization and environment.* Boston: Harvard Graduate School of Business Administration.

Lieberman, A. (Ed.) (1988). *Building a professional culture in schools.* New York: Teachers College Press.

Lieberman, A., and Miller, L. (1986). School improvement: Themes and variations. In A. Lieberman (Ed.), *Rethinking school improvement: Research, craft, and concept.* New York: Teachers College Press, pp. 96–111.

Lieberman, A., and Rosenholtz, S. J. (1987). The road to school improvement: Barriers and bridges. In J. I. Goodlad (Ed.), *The ecology of school renewal: Eighty-sixth yearbook of the National Society for the Study of Education, Part I.* Chicago: University of Chicago Press, pp. 79–98.

Lightfoot, S. L. (1983). *The good high school.* New York: Basic Books.

Lipsky, M. (1980). *Street-level bureaucracy.* New York: Russell Sage Foundation.

Little, J. W. (1982). Norms of collegiality and experimentation: Workplace conditions of school success. *American Educational Research Journal, 19* (3), 325–340.

Little, J. W. (1986). Seductive images and organizational realities in professional development. In A. Lieberman (Ed.), *Rethinking school improvement: Research, craft, and concept.* New York: Teachers College Press, pp. 26–44.

Little J. W. (1990). The mentor phenomenon and the social organization of teaching. *Review of Research in Education, 16,* 297–351.

Lortie, D. C. (1975). *Schoolteacher.* Chicago: Unversity of Chicago Press.

McLaughlin, M. W. (1976). Implementation as mutual adaption: Change in classroom organization. *Teachers College Record, 77* (3), 339–351.

McLaughlin, M. W., and Marsh, D. (1978). Staff development and school change. *Teachers College Record, 80* (1), 69–94.

McPherson, G. (1972). *Small town teacher.* Cambridge, MA: Harvard University Press.

March, J. G., and Simon, H. A. (1958). *Organizations.* New York: Wiley.

Martin, J., and Siehl, C. (1983). Organizational culture and counter culture: An uneasy symbiosis. *Organizational Dynamics, 12* (2), 52–64.

Metz, M. H. (1986). *Different by design.* New York: Routledge & Kegan Paul.

Meyer, J. (1970). The charter: Conditions of diffuse socialization in schools. In W. R. Scott (Ed.), *Social processes and social structures.* New York: Henry Holt, pp. 564–578.

Meyer, J., and Rowan, B. (1977). Institutionalized organizations: Formal structure as myth and ceremony. *American Journal of Sociology, 83* (2), 340–363.

Miles, M. B. (1981). Mapping the common properties of schools. In R. Lehming and M. Kane (Eds.), *Improving schools: Using what we know.* Beverly Hills, CA: Sage, pp. 42–114.

Mitchell, D. E., Ortiz, F. I., and Mitchell, T. K. (1987). *Work orientation and job performance: The cultural basis of teaching rewards and incentives.* Albany: State University of New York Press.

Morgan, B. (1986). *Images of organizations.* Beverly Hills, CA: Sage.

Noddings, N. (1988). An ethic of caring and its implications for instructional arrangements. *American Journal of Education, 96* (2), 215–230.

Perrow, C. (1972). *Complex organizations: A critical essay.* Glenview, IL: Scott, Foresman.

Purkey, S. C., and Smith, M. S. (1983). Effective schools—A review. *Elementary School Journal, 83* (4), 427–452.

Rosenholtz, S. J. (1985). Political myths about education reform: Lessons from research on teaching. *Phi Delta Kappan, 66* (5), 349–355.

Rosenholtz, S. J. (1989). *Teachers' workplace: The social organization of schools.* New York: Longman.

Rosenholtz, S. J., and Smylie, M. A. (1984). Teacher compensation and career ladders. *Elementary School Journal, 85* (2), 149–166.

Rossman, G. B., Corbett, H. D., and Firestone, W. A. (1988). *Change and effectiveness in schools: A cultural perspective.* Albany: State University of New York Press.

Rutter, M., Maughan, B., Mortimore, P., Ouston, J., and Smith, A. (1979). *Fifteen thousand hours: Secondary schools and their effects on children.* Cambridge, MA: Harvard University Press.

Ryle, G. (1949). *The concept of mind.* New York: Hutchinson's University Library.

Sarason, S. B. (1982). *The culture of the school and the problem of change* (2nd ed.). Boston: Allyn and Bacon.

Sarason, S. B. (1983). *Schooling in America: Scapegoat and salvation.* New York: Free Press.

Schein, E. H. (1988). *Organizational culture and leadership.* San Francisco: Jossey-Bass.

Sizer, T. R. (1984). *Horace's compromise: The dilemma of the American high school.* Boston: Houghton Mifflin.

Smylie, M. A. (1988). The enhancement function of staff development: Organizational and psychological antecedents to individual teacher change. *American Educational Research Journal, 25* (1), 1–30.

Smylie, M. A. (1989a, March). *Teachers' collegial learning: Social and psychological dimensions of helping relationships.* Paper presented at the annual meeting of the American Educational Research Association, San Francisco.

Smylie, M. A. (1989b). Teachers' views of the effectiveness of sources of learning to teach. *Elementary School Journal, 89* (5), 543–558.

Smylie, M. A., and Denny, J. W. (1989, March). *Lead teachers: Ambiguities and tensions in organizational perspective.* Paper presented at the annual meeting of the American Educational Research Association, San Francisco.

Smylie, M. A., and Denny, J. W. (1990). Teacher leadership: Tensions and ambiguities in organizational perspective. *Educational Administration Quarterly, 26* (3), 235–259.

Smylie, M. A., and Smart, J. C. (1990). Teacher support for career enhancement initiatives: Program characteristics and effects on work. *Educational Evaluation and Policy Analysis, 12* (2), 139–155.

Sosniak, L. (1989). Personal communication, February 24.

Thompson, J. D. (1967). *Organizations in action.* New York: McGraw-Hill.

Tichy, N. M. (1983). *Managing strategic change: Technical, political, and cultural dynamics.* New York: Wiley.

Turner, B. A. (1971). *Exploring the industrial sub-culture.* New York: Macmillan.

Van Maanen, J. (1979). The self, the situation, and the rules of interpersonal relations. In W. Bennis and Others (Eds.), *Essays in interpersonal dynamics.* Homewood, IL: Dorsey.

Van Maanen, J., and Barley, S. R. (1985). Cultural organization: Fragments of a theory. In P. J. Frost, L. F. Moore, M. R. Louis, C. C. Lundberg, and J. Martin (Eds.), *Organizational culture.* Beverly Hills, CA: Sage, pp. 31–53.

Wallace, A. F. (1970). *Culture and personality* (2nd ed.). New York: Random House.

Waller, W. W. (1932). *The sociology of teaching.* New York: Wiley.

Waugh, R. F., and Punch, K. F. (1987). Teacher receptivity to systemwide change in the implementation stage. *Review of Educational Research, 57* (3), 237–254.

Weber, M. (1947). *The theory of social and economic organization* (T. Parsons, trans.). New York: Free Press.

Weinberg, J. (1967). *The English public schools.* New York: Atheron.

Williams, R. (1970). *American society: A sociological interpretation* (3rd ed.). New York: Knopf.

Willower, D. J., and Landis, C. A. (1970). Pupil control ideology and professional orientation of school faculty. *Journal of Secondary Education, 45* (3), 118–123.

Wilson, E. K. (1971). *Sociology: Rules, roles and relationships.* Homewood, IL: Dorsey.

Wolcott, H. F. (1977). *Teachers vs. technocrats.* Eugene: University of Oregon, Center for Educational Policy and Management.

Chapter Three

Redesign of the school work environment is necessary to help teachers engage in an ongoing inquiry about classroom problems. Rather than having a staff developer tell teachers what works in a specific context, teachers can establish reflective conversations about their own particular work setting. In this chapter, Carter presents the case of a junior high school English teacher who is an ineffective classroom manager. According to the author's analysis, the teacher's way of thinking prevents her from developing ways of handling disruptive behavior and engaging students in learning.

Creating a Teacher Work Environment for the Development of Classroom Knowledge

Kathy Carter
University of Arizona

Teaching, many have commented, is demanding. Doing the visible work of this profession (e.g., discussing assignments, grading papers, presenting content, interacting with numerous students, etc.) is, in itself, exhausting. Were this the only work of the job, substantial energies and adequate resources would need to be devoted to the support of these daily "doings" of teaching. But many teachers suggest that it is the *in*visible work—the mental framing of functional solutions to complex classroom problems—that makes teaching particularly taxing. In the midst of recent rhetoric directed toward improving the teacher work environment, we need to consider carefully the thought required in teaching. New conceptions of teaching call for shaping portions of the teacher work environment to account for the complex nature of the knowledge required in teaching.

This chapter initially discusses recent research on teachers' knowledge and how it is acquired. A case of a teacher having serious problems with classroom management is presented, which underscores the mental work required in accomplishing teaching tasks. In discussing the case, some recent proposals for improving the work environment will be described. When teaching is going awry, school-based solutions that focus only on changing teachers' actions fall severely short of the mark of improved teaching. Successful proposals focus on the knowledge teachers need and the

All names used in the case study in this chapter are pseudonyms to protect the anonymity of the teacher and her students.

possible design of a work environment that has potential to support the acquisition and development of that knowledge.

BACKGROUND

Until recently, research has adopted a technical "skills-based" approach to the improvement of teaching. Investigators generally have focused on the effects of training and feedback on skills rather than knowledge or cognition (see Gleissman, 1984; Waxman and Walberg, 1986). The underlying assumption of much of this work was that improving teaching implied a change in a teacher's observable behaviors.

The legacy left by this view can be seen in many of the staff development, mentoring, and teacher evaluation plans and practices that are a prominent part of the present teacher work environment. It can be argued that any of these plans carries with it a conception of a teacher and provides an implicit argument about how teaching improvement occurs. In the preponderance of these plans, the teacher is conceived as someone who needs to change, who needs to "do" something differently. Here, a "teacher-as-technician" view often prevails, a view which suggests that teaching is a matter of following some fairly straightforward guidelines derived from research-based principles of practice. A deficit model of teaching seems to dominate these plans, one which sees the teacher as needing to do teaching *better*, usually according to the dictates of some particular, and, for the moment, popular model of teaching. The task for the staff developer, mentor, or evaluator becomes that of conveying the "standard" for teachers to follow.

Attempts to convey standard practices and hold teachers accountable for following them are logical in a view of teaching that assumes teaching contexts are stable and skills can be used with similar success across settings. A classroom problem, then, is a problem in one's practice, and remediation is rightfully directed to training teachers in effective techniques.

Recent reviews of the literature in teacher education (e.g., Carter, 1990a) and school improvement (e.g., Conley, Schmidle, and Shedd, 1988) suggest that these long-held views of teaching are being reformulated. Current conceptions of teaching focus on the mental lives of teachers (Clark and Peterson, 1986), on teachers' knowledge structures (Leinhardt and Smith, 1985), interpretive capacities (Doyle, 1990), practical arguments

(Fenstermacher, 1986), and comprehension processes (Carter, in press). In this recast view, teaching "problems" are defined somewhat differently from previous formulations. Just how problems might be described and dealt with in the work environment in light of new frameworks will be an important focus of this chapter.

TEACHERS' KNOWLEDGE

The question of what teachers need to know in order to teach successfully is at the center of the educational enterprise. Only recently, however, have researchers begun to explore the knowledge that teachers need and the knowledge experienced and effective teachers act upon in teaching. Even in its infancy, this research is calling into question the more traditional view that teachers need to be "trained" to carry out specific techniques for teaching.

Teaching knowledge refers broadly to the knowledge teachers have of classroom situations and the practical dilemmas they face in carrying out purposeful action in these settings. The modern focus is on the complexities of interactive teaching and thinking-in-action. In this work, emphasis is placed on the complicated interpretations and decisions that professionals make under conditions of inherent uncertainty (Doyle, 1986) and on the practical thinking necessary to act appropriately in a particular situation. Some suggest that the knowledge required for practice under these circumstances is experiential (i.e., it evolves out of "reflection-in-action" [Schon, 1983]), and many are beginning to agree that it cannot be captured by a list of context-free competencies for teaching (e.g., Richardson, 1989; Richert, 1987).

For one thing, teaching knowledge is probably much more *personal and particularistic* than implied in a "teacher-as-technician" view (e.g., Clandinin and Connelly, 1986; Connelly and Clandinin, 1985; Elbaz, 1983, 1987; Lampert, 1985; Munby, 1986, 1989; Russell and Johnston, 1988; Russell, 1989). Teachers' personal biographies, their professional histories, and their classroom experiences all play a part in the way they practice their craft. Moreover, teaching knowledge is likely tied much more closely to a teacher's knowledge of her or his discipline (see Grossman, 1987; Gudmundsdottir, in press; Shulman, 1986, 1987; Wilson and Wineburg, 1988) than has been recognized in the past. Finally, a teacher's knowledge is at the core, one's own comprehension of *classroom events* and an understanding about how one acts on and reacts to students, scenes, and situations in these complex environments (see Carter and Doyle, 1987, 1989).

Classroom Knowledge

Is it possible to construct a work environment that helps teachers acquire and continue to develop the classroom knowledge necessary to navigate the complex settings in which they work? What would the environment look like?

In this chapter, it is argued that this focus might be achieved through creating a work environment where programs and processes are used to assist teachers *in acquiring and developing the knowledge they need to accomplish the major tasks of teaching.* The basic premise is that tasks organize situations for individuals and thus shape cognition and the development of knowledge (see Doyle, 1979, 1986). Tasks define what teachers must think about to get the work of teaching done. Tasks also serve to "situate" knowledge and learning to teach in the context of commonly occurring classroom events (e.g., Morine-Dershimer, 1989).

Doyle (1986) has argued that teachers' knowledge is organized around two major tasks: (1) the task of representing and enacting the curriculum, and (2) the task of solving the problem of order. His recent work (Doyle, 1990) suggests that teacher education might fruitfully direct its activities to understanding the nature of these tasks and to working with new teachers to reveal the thought, knowledge, and actions necessary to accomplish these tasks.

In the following section, a case of a teacher who was unsuccessful in her attempts to accomplish the second of these tasks (i.e., solving the problem of order) will be presented. The purpose of this case is to argue that a "cure" for this teacher's problems would not be forthcoming through staff development and evaluation programs that have been founded on a skills-based view. A close examination of the case points to some possibilities for improving the teacher work environment along the lines of more current conceptions of teaching.

A BRIEF PREFACE TO THE CASE

The case to be presented was originally developed as a part of a larger effort to understand how classrooms are managed. For a detailed summary of qualitative methods and analysis techniques used in the development of these cases, see Carter (in press). The teachers described in these cases were selected from a sample of 17 English teachers who participated in the Junior High Classroom Organization Study (JHCOS) conducted at the University of Texas R & D Center for Teacher Education. The data for each teacher consisted of 10 to 14 detailed narrative observations in each of two class periods. Observers in the original study were instructed to focus on classroom rules and procedures and on how activities were conducted. Observations were made throughout the year with a concentration on the first three weeks of school.

The case is presented in three sections. First, a general description of the structures and processes observed in Ms. Dove's classes is presented. This description allows the reader to move quickly into the daily life of the classroom teacher and her students, and provides an analysis of the typical activities, routines, and actions the teacher used to solve the problem of order in a particular context.

Next, the case presentation contains a description of the teacher's reaction patterns as she goes about carrying out the work of teaching amid the contingencies of everyday classroom life. Here, traditional and cognitive frameworks of teaching will be applied to the case in order to explore the effect of different perspectives on the shape of support structures in the work environment.

Finally, the cognitive framework will be further pursued by providing an analogical description of Ms. Dove's understandings as she acted to solve the problem of order in her classroom. In this section, a metaphor is used to communciate the teacher's way of comprehending the task of managing the classroom environment. The metaphor is, in other words, a means to model this teacher's way of thinking about classroom management. The purpose here is to uncover the way a particular teacher views the problem of classroom management, and to illustrate that her reactions and actions are keenly connected to her interpretations and understandings of classroom events.

This focus on a teacher's cognition and comprehension illustrates a modern conception of teaching and points to a possible redesign of the school work environment to afford teachers the opportunities to become more analytical about their work, to confront their own conceptions of teaching, and to engage others in conversations about how they comprehend the tasks of teaching and about how they formulate solution strategies to complex classroom problems.

THE CASE OF MS. DOVE: SOLVING THE PROBLEM OF ORDER

Background Information

Ratings on management success taken by observers during the collection of long-term narrative records suggested that Ms. Dove was not an effective manager. Comments made by observers suggest that Ms. Dove could be aptly described over the year as fragmented and frustrated in her attempts to accomplish order.

Observations were made in Ms. Dove's fourth-period and sixth-period classes, both which were designated as "low-ability" groups. Relatively few variations were noted in the teacher's classroom management strategies across classes, or, in fact, in the content covered and instruction delivered there. In both classes, the teacher arranged work primarily into oral reading, seatwork, and film/filmstrip viewing activities. Content topics (e.g., grammar, mythology, composition, literature) seemed to be loosely connected across and within class periods.

Processes and Structures in Ms. Dove's Classes

Getting Started. Ms. Dove began the school year in ways prescribed by much of the present literature on classroom management (see Emmer, Evertson, Sanford, Clements, and Worsham, 1981). She had both the school rules and her classroom rules posted, called them to the students' attention, provided a rationale for many of them, and secured selected information (on blue 3 × 5 index cards) on each member of her class. She spent considerable time making students aware of supplies they would need for her class, and described in detail appropriate headings and the format for written work in her class. In describing why students should take her rules seriously and come to class with appropriate materials and attitudes, Ms. Dove let students know that she believed "School is not just preparation for life—it is your life."

In addition to describing classroom rules and routines, Ms. Dove attempted to initiate academic activities early. On the first day of school she administered a diagnostic spelling test to students, and on the second day she asked students to write a 1½-page story "told from the point of view of an inanimate object." In both of her classes, Ms. Dove had an extremely difficult time establishing and maintaining these activities. Students were noticeably resistant to becoming involved and "sidestepped" involvement by attempting to negotiate work demands (e.g., "How long is it supposed to be?" "Can I skip lines to make the pages longer?" "How is the title supposed to be?" "Can't we use a pencil this time?") or by calling out unrelated statements that successfully distracted the teacher and students from the work at hand (e.g., "I lost my cap," "Tony is going to copy," "Man, I wish the bell would ring," "You want to hear a joke, teacher?").

In these early observations in both classes, problems of establishing order took on distinctive shapes. It was apparent that Ms. Dove's statements of displeasure to students and her methods for resolving order problems were not having the desired effect. Numerous instances of student testing of the teacher were recorded, and a number of impotent behavioral warnings and desists were witnessed. Problems noted in these first few days foreshadowed events of later sessions.

Format and Routines. On a typical day in Ms. Dove's classrooms, many of her students would enter the room, in the words of the observer, "extremely noisily" or "aggressively." Ms. Dove appeared to try desperately to minimize contact with individual students during this time. When the teacher *did* attempt to remind students to make their way to their seats or to pick up materials located at the front of the room, her statements often went unheard or unheeded.

During this opening time, the teacher's actions suggested she wanted to make a visible production out of checking roll in order to let students know she was occupied and unwilling to respond to their call-outs and often blatant misbehavior. She emphatically counted aloud numbers of students present and called roll in the midst of student movement. When students solicited her attention, she would often ignore their comments and persist with a public display of her handling of housekeeping matters. Occasionally, the teacher inserted reprimands like, "When you come in here, you should act like you are in church. You don't act up. You get quiet and sit down." And at times, the teacher would make statements directed to the whole class about upcoming work or necessary supplies. Importantly, the teacher often scattered these comments in the midst of student chatter and movement when she herself appeared unprepared to move into the curriculum with students. Generally, Ms. Dove did not get activities going for several minutes after her first attempts. As a result, openings to work time were often fragmented and difficult.

Work activities, regardless of their type, generally progressed no more smoothly than they began. A few students continuously tested the teacher, content was unfolded roughly, and instructional themes were often hard to follow. Narratives suggested that even early on, academic activities were extremely uncomfortable for both the teacher and many of her students.

Instances of inappropriate and disruptive behavior were recorded during all instructional activities and transition times. The teacher was clearly bothered by the students' noncooperation and often pulled away from both her intended course of action and behavioral interactions with students as problems escalated. Consequently, maintenance of the work system was often abandoned or only loosely held in place.

Although the blatant misbehavior of a few key visible students was regularly ignored by Ms. Dove, she interacted with these particular students almost exclusively in instructional matters. In both classes, these "visible" students were called on to read aloud, answer questions, and offer their opinions or thoughts much more often than comparatively quieter, more well-behaved students. As will be shown later, this heavily weighted attention to a few students affected the natural rhythms of the activity flow and the communication patterns between the teacher and her students.

Activities Established by Ms. Dove

Seatwork was the predominant work arrangement in both of Ms. Dove's classes. In her fourth-period class, seatwork accounted for 41 percent of the observed time, and in the sixth-period class, for 45 percent of the observed time. Other common activities were oral reading activities and film/filmstrip viewing activities, together accounting for between 25 and 30 percent of observed class time in both classes. Comparatively small percentages of time were spent in other activities, including lecture, small group, and oral drill and practice activities.

A brief summary of the three predominant activities in Ms. Dove's classes is presented here to provide necessary background for subsequent sections of this case study.

Oral Reading Activities. Ms. Dove had an extremely difficult time establishing and maintaining oral reading activities. Narrative records indicated that students had considerable difficulty reading aloud and following along in the text. Ms. Dove typically warned students that they might need her help because the reading would possibly be difficult. Along with this admission, she often offered a rationale for the reading selection.

Each observed reading activity was plagued by an uneven and interrupted course of action. Ms. Dove was rarely able to travel smoothly through the text with students. When she managed to get a student to read aloud (usually one of the more visible students), she had him or her read quite lengthy passages. The extraneous comments readers made often slowed the pace of the activity even more.

Student call-outs were common during reading activities, and the group apparently found it difficult to attend selectively to the text they were to follow. Ms. Dove regularly ignored these bothersome call-outs (usually generated by the same few visible students). She focused her attention mostly on correcting students' pronunciations as they attempted to read. It should be noted, however, that during each reading activity one or two students were asked to stand out in the hall as punishment for their actions.

Film/Filmstrip Viewing Activities. Film/filmstrip viewing activities generally followed the same tumultuous course as oral reading activities. Film/filmstrip activities also became increasingly more common as the year progressed.

Although students often expressed enthusiasm over the opportunity to see a film in Ms. Dove's classes, their glee appeared to be short-lived. High levels of off-task behavior characterized these activities and persisted largely from the beginning to the end of the activities.

Often at the conclusion of these filmstrips, the teacher asked (in a private contact) only a few very visible students (who had been inattentive and disruptive throughout the filmstrip) what they thought about the film. Critiques from other students were not solicited. This pattern of ignoring visible students' misbehavior and attending to them in nonbehavioral matters persisted across all activity types.

Seatwork. Seatwork activities suffered from serious production problems in both of the teacher's classes. Students rarely were actively engaged in the assigned work, and behavior patterns were similar to those observed in reading and film/filmstrip activities. Noticeable misbehavior (emanating from three or four continuously visible students) was ignored. Yet these same students were most often contacted and offered friendly help by the teacher. Narratives suggested that other students who solicited help from the teacher often suffered from, in the observer's words, "wilted hands," as their arms grew quite tired from trying to engage the teacher's help. Many, in, fact, appeared to give up.

In the observers' estimates, the time allotted by the teacher for students to complete seatwork assignments seemed excessive, and students often successfully negotiated to continue their work during the next class session. This usually meant that the teacher allowed students to finish up the previous day's work as she attempted to install a new activity. As a result, it was frequently difficult for the observers to locate beginnings and endings of work activities.

In summary, oral reading, film/filmstrip activities, and seatwork alike were characterized by problems of timing, flow, engagement, and production. The teacher's intended agenda was consistently interrupted, and the students' movement through the curriculum was, at best, irregular.

TEACHER REACTION PATTERNS

In the previous section the overall activity structures that Ms. Dove established to solve the problem of order in her classes were described. Attention now turns to an analysis of how this teacher reacted to specific events that occurred as she created and maintained these activities. In other words, the focus is on what Ms. Dove reacted to and talked about as she tried to hold her activity systems in place. As will be seen in the final section, knowledge of these reaction patterns is especially useful in constructing a comprehension model to account for the "solution strategies" Ms. Dove used in managing her classrooms.

Ms. Dove's Reaction Patterns

Analysis of classroom narratives suggested that Ms. Dove attended and/or reacted to:

1. A small number of highly visible students who were consistently inattentive, resistant to work, and often blatantly disruptive
2. A small set of stereotypical student behaviors, which she could label or categorize as "immature"
3. Extremely serious problems to order (e.g., student or group disorderly behaviors that had escalasted to a level she appeared to fear or feel ill-equipped to handle or control)
4. Student hints that her actions were ill-reasoned or unfair.

A description of these reaction patterns follows:

Highly Visible Students. Across both classes, Ms. Dove attended and reacted almost exclusively to a small number of highly visible students whose behavior was often problematic. Importantly, the focus of her attention to these students was rarely their behavior, regardless of how blatant or rude it became. Rather, her energies were spent in assuring their instructional participation (nominal as that participation might be), in responding to their negotiations about stated requirements, in reacting to their statements of displeasure or unhappiness, and in handling their requests for special favors.

Ms. Dove often bypassed volunteers in order to call on these disruptive students during oral reading and film/filmstrip viewing activities and allowed sleeping students to avoid participating in class while refusing to tolerate nonparticipation from visible students. During seatwork activities, these students were consistently given more assistance. In addition, the teacher focused her eye contact in the areas of the room occupied by visible students, displayed her warmth and sense of humor comparatively more often with them, and granted more often their special requests to play with puzzles, go to the restroom or library, or get assistance from their peers (typically other visible students).

In focusing so much attention on these students, little attention was paid to academic interactions with other students or to the content or the instructional activity itself. Moreover, Ms. Dove's narrow attention to these students probably made tracking classroom events, interpreting incidents, and predicting consequences of actions enormously difficult. By regularly calling attention to these students (who tended to use public occasions to embarrass the teacher or illustrate her ineffectiveness in establishing order), Ms. Dove lost much of her credibility as well as her ability to regulate the flow, pacing, and direction of the activity.

"Immature" Student Behaviors. Some specific student behaviors triggered reactions from Ms. Dove. Typically, she reacted to incidents that enabled her to lecture her students on mature behavior. When students became "excitable," did not "sit properly in their chairs," or chattered while she was talking, she reminded them that she was "unwilling to babysit," that they were "not at a maturity level for this class—Sit up straight, that is not good for your spine," or "This is not Orange Goose School."

Ms. Dove's expressed concern for the maturity level of students was often ignored or did not rest well with students. If any effect at all could be seen, it was short-lived.

Serious Threats to Order. In almost every class session, there were persistent problems to order. Ms. Dove's behavior suggests she felt ill-equipped to handle serious threats to order and lacked confidence that she could stop or control problem situations or behaviors. Analysis of narrative records revealed that a common reaction pattern for Ms. Dove during these troublesome times was obvious nonreaction. Often, she would ignore the most blatant misbehavior (including ethnic slurs, obscene remarks, and the like) for so long that students would attempt to take control of the class. Students would point out their peers' misbehavior to the teacher (or would even publicly call to her attention their own disruptive behavior, such as, "I'm going to hit this boy, Ms. Dove"), would try to get her to move on with the activity ("Come on, turn off the lights and let's see the film"), would try to quash other students' undesirable behavior ("Listen! Listen! She already said that; be smart like me!"), or would become so frustrated that they would simply shout "Shut up!" numerous times. Ms. Dove consistently avoided reprimanding misbehaving students. If frustrated by misbehavior, she would offer to let students help one another with their assignments (which had the effect of making it even more unlikely that students would get busy with their work). Ms. Dove also occasionally publicly asked students to help her in controlling visible students.

Ms. Dove's reaction patterns to serious disorder did little to help. Problems persisted with regularity throughout the observational period.

Hints Suggesting Ill-Reasoned or Unfair Teacher Actions. Ms. Dove was visibly bothered when students' actions suggested they felt requirements were not sensible or were unfair. In these instances, Ms. Dove often provided lengthy rationales and explanations. On several occasions, students' reactions indicated that Ms. Dove's explanations were not accepted and/or easy to follow. When students wanted to use a pencil rather than a pen, Ms. Dove explained, "A pen is permanent—you are almost adults now." When a student wanted to know why he had to work if he didn't get paid, Ms. Dove spent several minutes offering the whole class an explanation. When students were having difficulty with a pop quiz and were negotiating to get clues or answers from the teacher, she repeatedly pointed out that her test questions were valid because the same content had been covered in class. And when students were not following Ms. Dove's procedures for a written assignment, she provided a seemingly strange rationale for supplying an example for students (e.g., "I'll give you an example, since this class isn't quite as attentive as the others.").

Ms. Dove's reactions to student claims of unfairness or to their demands for the "whys" of their work were often sources of eventual embarrassment for her. Students seemed to find her rationales confusing and unsatisfying.

PERSPECTIVES ON SUPPORT STRUCTURES IN THE WORK ENVIRONMENT

It may be worthwhile at this point to explore common responses to this teacher's problems in dealing with the task of classroom management. Traditionally, this situation would cry out for a quick solution and would call for staff development aimed at Ms. Dove's skill development and for evaluative feedback directed to helping her change her classroom performance. Ms. Dove might be asked, for example, to adopt a particular "proven" model of classroom management (e.g., assertive discipline) or to pattern her behavior after that of a mentor or model teacher.

Examining this case from a cognitive perspective, however, suggests that these responses may not be useful in helping this teacher. Teachers must mentally jumble input from students and the environment, and must make sense of classroom scenes and situations that are not always straightforward. If we assume that Ms. Dove is responding to classroom situations based on *her personal understandings* of classroom events, then from her own perspective, *she is behaving sensibly* and would likely see little sense in shifting to another course of action in her classroom. Teachers form interpretations about what events in classrooms mean and manage those events according to their interpretations. A teacher's comprehension of classroom events, then, may serve as a filter for *any* intervention and may blunt even the best research-based advice offered by improvers. Perhaps, then, prior to planning an intervention to change the way a teacher works in the classroom setting, it is important to know what working theories a teacher holds about his or her teaching tasks.

This alternative approach would open up possibilities to capture the sense-making activities of teachers, and ultimately would lead to a redesign of the work environment to provide opportunities for teachers to reflect on the validity and utility of their own understandings. In the next section, a cognitive framework will be employed to explore Ms. Dove's working theories of classroom management.

ORGANIZING PRINCIPLES IN UNDERSTANDING CLASSROOMS

In this section, Ms. Dove's comprehension of classroom management is summarized in terms of an organizing metaphor and several principles consistent with that metaphor. By modeling Ms. Dove's understandings through the use of metaphor, it is possible to gain some insight into ways the work environment might be restructured to support teachers in developing functional solution strategies to their classroom problems.

The Metaphor: Gentle Persuader and Arbiter of Adult Conscience

Ms. Dove seemed to see the classroom as a place where students needed to learn some important lessons in adulthood (e.g., to be socially "polite," to understand the reasons adults—and specifically teachers—did things the way they did). If these lessons could be learned, then misbehavior would disappear and all students would accomplish their schoolwork. By lecturing students in the participation rites of adulthood and maturity (more specifically by suggesting they must be willing to listen to longer content presentations in school as they got older, must come prepared to class with appropriate materials, sit properly, and the like) and by ignoring blatant "immature" behaviors, Ms. Dove could hold on to a goal of helping students become responsible. (Although it is impossible to argue the point from the data, this way of thinking may have allowed Ms. Dove to disguise a very real fear resulting from a history of interacting with problem students.)

Most of Ms. Dove's management efforts consisted of softly persuading misbehaving students to participate nominally in the curriculum, as if the problem of order could be solved by "winning over" these students or getting them to practice desirable behaviors. Such actions in solving the problem of order reflect a conception of her role as gentle persuader and arbiter of adult conscience. If one were to take on these roles, calling attention to blatant incidences of public misbehavior would be less important than affording students adultlike opportunities to participate in the work. Moreover, incidents of extreme misbehavior would likely not be workable occasions for soft persuasive techniques. Rather, interactions during these occasions might take the shape of comparatively more didactic discussions in adult/child relationships. With a schema organized around persuasion, then, blatant misbehaviors may best be ignored. In a class of what Ms. Dove believed to be "immature" students, perhaps it was less risky to be *obviously* reasonable with students and to be *especially* considerate to those who were least mature in hopes that she might help them grow up.

At least five general principles would seem to be consistent with this teacher's conception of classroom management:

1. Classroom order is a consequence of helping selected students understand adulthood and adult responsibilities.
2. Less mature students need to be given special attention and afforded opportunities to participate in an effort to "win them over" to adult logic, behavior, and responsibility.
3. With careful persuasion, these students will become involved in schoolwork and will cease to behave inappropriately.
4. Student disruptions are caused by student immaturity and are best ignored.
5. Students will respond to the teacher's requests if the teacher is able to instill in them a sense of maturity and to supply for them a rationale for his or her actions.

This focus on a small number of individuals rather than on activities and student work accomplished within activities often meant that the teacher neglected the intended course of action in the classes. By attending to these students so regularly, content was commonly sacrificed. In fact, as the year progressed, the content became synonymous with what got read aloud in class or what got viewed in films. In addition, Ms. Dove was unable to protect activities and to keep work systems in place. Moreover, holding students accountable for work was problematic, especially since the students to whom Ms. Dove attended most often were extremely successful at renegotiating requirements. Finally, tracking antecedent events and predicting consequences of present events appeared to be impossible for Ms. Dove since she was consumed with moment-to-moment "management" of a few individuals rather than the management of activities or work systems.

We can see that Ms. Dove's way of comprehending the task of classroom management led to actions that negatively affected the quality of life in her classrooms. Indeed, this way of thinking provided little opportunity for Ms. Dove to construct a workable technology to deal with disruptive behavior. On those infrequent occasions when she attempted to reprimand students, for instance, she appeared to apply a weak technology against a strong opponent. Moreover, the case points to the difficulty of short-term solutions to long-term teaching problems. Once classroom histories have begun to shape and a teacher has begun to act and react based on dysfunctional understandings of classroom events, any "ready remedy" will likely take the unfortunate route of many preceding teaching innovations. Most importantly, the case of Ms. Dove strongly hints that any attempt to change a teacher's actions without understanding the practical arguments on which his or her actions are based will, in all likelihood, be futile (Richardson Koehler and Fenstermacher, 1988).

In summary, as Richardson (1989) suggests, if the present object of change remains teachers, and specifically, teachers' actions, teachers will be placed in a position to continue to appear as "recalcitrant" when they do not adhere to advice from agents who claim to be acting in their best interest. Or perhaps even worse, they will appear to be unable to follow even the simplest steps to improve their own teaching, for when they try them, the effect may well not be the intended one.

It may be, then, that the content and processes employed within the school environment to support teachers' development should themselves be the focus of change.

TOWARD A REDESIGN OF THE CONTENT AND PROCESSES EMPLOYED IN THE SCHOOL ENVIRONMENT TO SUPPORT TEACHERS

Change in Content

Perhaps, as Griffin (in press) has argued, it is time to attend to the voices of teachers who have complained consistently about the content and quality of inservice and evaluation programs, and more recently, about mentoring programs that are beginning to surface in school settings. In staff development, a longstanding, major criticism by practicing teachers is directed to the superficiality of solutions outsiders offer to classroom problems. The often whispered challenge, "I would like to see them try that in *my* classroom," is a point, long ignored, that may be at the heart of what the content should be in staff development programs. Rather than importing information from laboratory settings, and telling teachers "what worked" there, some have begun to suggest that perhaps staff development content should be grounded in the contexts where hoped-for improvements are to take place (e.g., Richardson Koehler and Fenstermacher, 1988). This would mean that staff development, in part, would enable teachers to engage in their own inquiry into the problems associated with their teaching tasks that present themselves in a particular school setting. (See Conley, Schmidle, and Shedd, 1988, for a fuller discussion of teachers' participation in school inquiry and decision making.) The results of this inquiry would frame the content that would be explored in inservice sessions.

Similarly, the content of mentor programs may well need to change to focus on cognitive aspects of teaching tasks and context-bound difficulties in accomplishing those tasks. Rather than communicating content about standards for teaching practices and suggesting ways that teachers might behave to meet those standards, mentor teachers and their counterparts would engage in a conversation that would allow both to become more analytical about their teaching tasks, to begin to reflect on teaching and what it means to teach in a particular environment, and to learn to articulate, justify, and critique their own ways of comprehending their teaching tasks (see Carter, 1988). The focus of the content conveyed in conversations, then, is not necessarily on new ways of doing things but rather on understanding how different ways of thinking about teaching might affect teachers' and students' actions in classrooms.

And perhaps as Peterson and Comeaux (1989) have argued, the content conveyed indirectly through teacher evaluation instruments must be reconstructed to reflect the range of knowledge teachers must possess and must employ to teach effectively. Is it possible to evaluate, in some very careful manner, the functional value of teachers' working theories of their teaching? Surely this would mean a radical revision of the processes used to evaluate teachers. Indeed, it may even suggest that there can be nothing "standardized" about teaching evaluations, for any evaluation is bound by the context where a teacher works and perhaps can only occur on a case-by-case basis.

Change in Processes

These shifts in content would carry with them a need to change present processes employed in the work environment to support teacher development. Staff development processes would be redirected to engage teachers in thinking through pedagogical puzzles, the pieces of which cannot be put together in a single inservice session or even across several sessions. Rather, staff development processes would be designed to provoke teachers' interests and elicit their thinking for extended periods of time. Staff development would resemble rigorous inquiry and would take the form of continued and careful study into the dilemmas teachers face and the solution strategies they use to deal with these dilemmas. The transportable bag of tricks, then, gets tucked away for good, and processes are used to allow professionals the time and trust to converse about their craft, to study the work of teaching seriously, and to engage others in continued conversation about how they cope successfully in the complex arena of the classroom.

Carter and Richardson (1989) have suggested the possibility of case study and writing as a form of staff development. Cases of teaching that address the different pedagogical problems germane to a particular school site might be used as the primary basis for staff development sessions. The study of these cases could be structured to bring together teachers, administrators, and university professors and to allow them to begin to build bridges from practice to research and from research to practice.

Carter and Richardson (1989) have also suggested that cases might be used as a tool to foster mentor/novice conversations about teaching. In a preliminary study, Carter (1990b) has documented the potential of using cases in such programs, as it illustrates cooperating teachers' success in developing cases of their student teachers' comprehension of the task of classroom management (modeled after cases like that of Ms. Dove) and in using the metaphors developed through these cases as a basis for conversations about their understandings of classroom teaching tasks. Case-bound simulations and videotapes of teaching may also be carefully developed as processes that would meet the goals for support in the teacher work environment outlined in this chapter (see Copeland, 1988).

CONCLUSION

Anyone who has taught or traveled often in the corridors and classrooms of schools knows that teaching asks much of teachers, and that most teachers try diligently, despite the often hurtful criticisms leveled against them, to ask much of themselves and their students.

This chapter suggests that it is possible to reconstruct the work environment in ways that offer the support teachers need to develop the knowledge and thought processes consonant with the dilemmas and demands of teaching. It argues that this revision will require new conceptions of what teaching means and what teaching knowledge is, as well as alternate understandings about what a supportive environment might be and how it might function.

Perhaps this is the time to realize that the mission to change teachers has been misdirected. What is needed is a change of mind within the profession—a change that reengages the thinking of educators about how to represent the range and depth of the knowledge that is necessary for teaching. Will we continue to accept the present rhetoric of change or will we change the rhetoric to more accurately reflect the real-life work world of teachers? The answer to this question is critical to the task of reconstructing the teacher work environment toward making education a more effective enterprise.

References

Carter, K. (1988). Using cases to frame mentor-novice conversations about teaching. *Theory into Practice, 27* (3), 214–222.

Carter, K. (1990a). Teachers' knowledge and learning to teach. In W. Houston (Ed.), *Handbook of research on teaching.* New York: Macmillan, pp. 291–310.

Carter, K. (1990b). Meaning and metaphor: Case knowledge in teaching. *Theory into Practice, 29* (2), 109–115.

Carter, K. (in press). Teacher comprehension of classroom processes. *Elementary School Journal.*

Carter, K., and Doyle, W. (1987). Teachers' knowledge structures and comprehension processes. In J. Calderhead (Ed.), *Exploring teachers' thinking.* London: Cassell, pp. 147–160.

Carter, K., and Doyle, W. (1989). Classroom research as a resource for the graduate preparation of teachers. In A. E. Woolfolk (Ed.), *Research perspectives on the graduate preparation of teachers.* Englewood Cliffs, NJ: Prentice-Hall, pp. 51–68.

Carter, K., and Richardson, V. (1989). A curriculum for an initial-year-of-teaching program. *Elementary School Journal, 89* (89), 405–420.

Clandinin, D. J., and Connelly, F. M. (1986). Rhythms in teaching: The narrative study of teachers' personal practical knowledge of classrooms. *Teaching and Teacher Education, 2* (4), 377–387.

Clark, C., and Peterson, P. (1986). Teachers' thought processes. In M. C. Wittrock (Ed.), *Handbook of research on teaching* (3rd ed.). New York: Macmillan, pp. 255–296.

Conley, S., Schmidle, T., and Shedd, J. (1988). Teacher participation in management. *Teachers' College Record, 90* (2), 259–280.

Connelly, F. M., and Clandinin, D. J. (1985). Personal practical knowledge and the modes of knowing: Relevance for teaching and learning. In E. Eisner (Ed.), *Learning and teaching the ways of knowing.* (84th yearbook of the National Society for the Study of Education). Chicago: University of Chicago Press.

Copeland, W. (1988). *Developing cognitive abilities for classroom management.* Paper presented at the annual meeting of the American Educational Research Association, New Orleans.

Doyle, W. (1979). Making managerial decisions in classrooms. In D. L. Duke (Ed.), *Classroom management* (78th Yearbook of the National Society for the Study of Education, Part 2). Chicago: University of Chicago Press.

Doyle, W. (1986). Classroom organization and management. In M. C. Wittrock (Ed.), *Handbook of research on teaching* (3rd ed.). New York: Macmillan, pp. 392–431.

Doyle, W. (1990). Themes in teacher education research. In R. Houston (Ed.), *Handbook of research in teacher education.* New York: Macmillan, pp. 3–24.

Elbaz, F. (1983). *Teacher thinking: A study of practical knowledge.* New York: Nichols.

Elbaz, F. (1987). Teachers' knowledge of teaching: Strategies for reflection. In J. Smyth (Ed.), *Educating teachers: Changing the nature of pedagogical knowledge.* London: Falmer, pp. 45–53.

Emmer, E., Evertson, E., Sanford, J., Clements, B., & Worsham, M. (1981). *Organizing and managing the junior high school classroom.* (R&D Rep. No. 6160). Austin: Research and Development Center for Teacher Education, University of Texas.

Fenstermacher, G. (1986). Philosophy of research on teaching: Three aspects. In M. C. Wittrock (Ed.), *Handbook of research on teaching* (3rd ed.). New York: Macmillan, pp. 37–49.

Gliessman, D. (1984). Changing teacher performance. In L. G. Katz and J. D. Raths (Eds.), *Advances in teacher education, 3* (1), 11–18.

Griffin, G. (in press). The future of teachers and teachings: Imperatives and possibilities. *Peabody Journal of Education.*

Grossman, P. (1987). *A tale of two teachers: The role of subject matter orientation in teaching.* Paper presented at the annual meeting of the American Educational Research Association, Washington, D.C.

Gudmundsdottir, S. (in press). Pedagogical models of subject matter. In J. Brophy (Ed.), *Advances in research on teaching.* Greenwich: JAI Press.

Lampert, M. (1985). How do teachers manage to teach? Perspectives on problems in practice. *Harvard Educational Review,* 178–184.

Leinhardt, G., and Smith, D. (1985). Expertise in mathematics instruction: Subject matter knowledge. *Journal of Educational Psychology, 77* (13), 247–271.

Morine-Dershimer, G. (1989). *Peer teaching: "Model" lessons vs. "free style" lessons.* Paper presented at the annual meeting of the American Educational Research Association, San Francisco.

Munby, H. (1986). Metaphor in the thinking of teachers: An exploratory study. *Journal of Curriculum Studies, 18* (2), 197–209.

Munby, H. (1989). *Reflection-in-action and reflection-on-action.* Paper presented a the annual meeting of the American Educational Research Association, San Francisco.

Peterson, P., and Comeaux, M. (1989). Assessing the teacher as reflective professional: New perspectives on teacher evaluation. In A. Woolfolk (Ed.), *Research perspectives on the graduate preparation of teachers.* Englewood Cliffs, NJ: Prentice-Hall.

Richardson, V. (1988). The evolution of reflective teaching and teacher education. In R. Clift, W. R. Houston, and M. Pugach (Eds.), *Encouraging reflective practice: An examination of issues and exemplars.* New York: Teachers College Press.

Richardson, V. (1989). *Practice and the improvement of research on teaching.* Division K Invited Address for the annual meeting of the American Educational Research Association, San Francisco.

Richardson Koehler, V., and Fenstermacher, G. (1988). The use of practical arguments in staff development. *Resources in Education.* ERIC Document Reproduction No. SP030047.

Richert, A. (1987). *The voices within: Knowledge and experience in teacher education.* Paper presented at the annual conference of the American Educational Research Association Special Interest Group for Women and Education, Portland, Oregon.

Russell, T., and Johnston, P. (1988). *Teachers' learning from experiences of teaching: Analysis based on metaphor and reflection.* Paper presented at the annual meeting of the American Educational Research Association, New Orleans.

Russell, T. (1989). *The roles of research knowledge and knowing-in-action in teachers' development of professional knowledge.* Paper presented at the annual meeting of the American Educational Research Association, San Francisco.

Schon, D. (1983). *The reflective practitioner: How professionals think in action.* New York: Basic Books.

Shulman, L. (1986). Those who understand: Knowledge growth in teaching. *Educational Researcher, 15* (2), 4–14.

Shulman, L. (1987). Knowledge and teaching: Foundations of the new reform. *Harvard Educational Review, 57* (1), 1–21.

Waxman, H. C., & Walberg, H. J. (1986). Effects of early field experiences. In J. D. Raths and L. G. Katz (Eds.), *Advances in teacher education* (Vol. 2). Norwood, NJ: Ablex, pp. 165–184.

Wilson, S., and Wineburg, S. (1988). Peering at history from different lenses: The role of disciplinary perspectives in the teaching of American History. *Teachers College Record, 89* (4), 525–539.

Chapter Four

Studies of "teacher change" often focus on teachers' responses to externally imposed innovations, and pessimistically conclude either that teachers are resistant to change or that they are pawns of the organization with little autonomy to change. Studies of "teacher learning" conclude that teachers do *change continually in response to classroom experiences, but the direction and extent of this change depends on a teacher's personal characteristics. The first body of research is too distant from teachers and their work, whereas the second comes so close that it presents an idiosyncratic view of the teacher. As a way out of this dilemma, Richardson proposes that teachers, both collectively and individually, can take control of the "justifications" for their classroom decisions. Teachers can develop their own discourse on practice, which does not refer to either external control or individual preferences as the basis for change.*

How and Why Teachers Change

Virginia Richardson
University of Arizona
College of Education

McLaughlin (1987) recently suggested that the notion that teachers are resistant to change is no longer viable in the educational change literature; however, this view does persist in some literatures. In an investigation of the history of change in schools, for example, Cuban (1988) stated that "widespread resistance to change by teachers and administrators has marked the history of public schooling" (p. 86). And in a recent article summarizing what they had learned in attempting to change teachers' reading instructional practices, Duffy and Roehler (1986) stated, "Getting teachers to change is difficult. They particularly resist complex, conceptual, longitudinal changes as opposed to change in management routines, or temporary changes. . . . Teacher educators and researchers interested in making substantive change in curricular and instructional practice need to understand this resistance" (p. 55).

Are teachers resistant? Do they ever change? If so, how and why? This chapter addresses the issue of teacher change. In order to do so, I will draw on two literatures that traditionally have not been examined together: the teacher change research, most of which is encompassed within the program implementation literature, and the teacher learning literature. Learning, of course, implies change, but the assumptions inherent in the teacher change and the learning to teach literatures are quite different. I will also refer to a teacher change research project being conducted at the University of Arizona, which is based on an amalgam of the change and learning to teach research.[1] This review leads to a different way of thinking about teacher change—one that places at the heart of the issue of recalcitrance the political question of whose changes teachers are resisting or implementing, and at the core of teacher learning, the educative function of experience.

TEACHER CHANGE

Much of the literature on teacher change relates to the question of why innovations are not implemented as their developers anticipated. McLaughlin (1987) presents a history of this literature, and suggests that the initial disappointment with the seeming lack of success of various implementation experiments led to the diagnosis of teachers being resistant to change. Lortie's (1975) investigation of the sociology of the teaching occupation and Jackson's (1968) study of classroom life provided one level of explanation for this recalcitrance.

Based on a large-scale survey of teachers and in-depth interviews, Lortie (1975) concluded that a number of norms drive the teaching occupation. These norms of individualism, presentism, and immediacy relate to his conclusion that teachers are less rational and analytic than other types of college graduates. Jackson (1968) suggested that teachers are conceptually simplistic and intuitive, and do not use scientific or objective measures in assessing student growth. Thus, a change deemed by others on rational grounds as good for teachers may not fit individual teachers' intuitive and nontechnical sense of what they should be doing. In this view, the experts are educational scholars and administrators who have been trained in scientific thought. (See Berlak and Berlak, 1981, and Feiman-Nemser and Floden, 1986, for a critique of this view of teacher thinking.)

A second wave of explanation for the lack of implementation of new programs was somewhat more sympathetic to teachers. No longer were teachers simply resistant because of the nonscientific, nonrational norms of the teaching occupation. The new approaches to explaining why teachers did not willingly adopt the practices developed by experts suggested one or both of two factors. One factor is organizational, the other is personal. March and Simon (1958), for example, suggested that individual behavior and decision to change within an organization is influenced by (1) an individual's beliefs, attitudes, goals, and knowledge acquired from experience in relation to the change; and (2) cues from the organizational environment. This view of change is similar to Hargreaves's (1984) two types of change strategies: working with an individual teacher's consciousness or structural redefinition that adjusts teachers' working conditions, and cultural interruption.

A number of scholars lean toward the structure of the organization as accounting, in large part, for teachers' engagement, commitment, and willingness to change or learn. Little's (1987) work, for example, has focused on school conditions such as norms of collegiality and experimentation that propel a faculty toward an improvement orientation. Rosenholtz, Bassler, and Hoover-Dempsey (1986) investigated school organization features as they relate to teachers' stated commitment and their willingness to learn. They found a number of school-level features such as teacher collegiality, instructional coordination, and other factors found in the school effectiveness literature as affecting teachers' perceptions of their skill acquisition. Hatton (1987) wrote that the radical attempt by Grant and Sleeter (1985) to change teachers' cultural responses can only come about through structural change.

On the other hand, other scholars focus on teachers' beliefs, knowledge, attitudes, and perceptions as either inhibiting or promoting their adoption of new practices. Doyle and Ponder (1977) suggested that teachers, as a group, are oriented toward the concrete and practical, and thus are more or less receptive toward change on the basis of three "ethics": practicality (Does it allow for classroom contingencies?), situational (Does it fit my classroom situation?), and cost. Waugh and Punch (1987) concluded that the Doyle and Ponder ethics, plus beliefs about how the system would look, accounted for 60 percent of the variance in their sample teachers' receptivity toward change in the system (see also Sparks, 1983). Tobin (1987) concluded from a number of studies on the implementation of practices designed to promote mathematics understanding that teacher beliefs about how students learn and what they ought to learn had the greatest impact on what they did in the classroom and whether or not they changed. And Guskey (1988) concluded from his study of teacher change that highly efficacious teachers were more likely to implement a new mastery learning program than those who were less efficacious.

Scholars who look to both the organization and the individual to explain the factors that affect the implementation of change do so in one of two ways. The first is to determine which aspects of personal characteristics and organizational structure account for individual teacher change. This approach is exemplified by Smylie (1988), who investigated the individual characteristics and school factors of teachers who volunteered for an inservice program designed to improve management skills. He measured a number of factors and concluded that personal teaching efficacy was an important factor contributing to changes in behavior in the classroom, as were teachers' certainty about practice, the concentration of low-achieving students in the classroom, and interactions teachers have with their colleagues about instruction.

The second approach ties organizational with personal attributes theoretically through concepts such as the incentive system. This requires a sense of what motivates teachers in combination with structural conditions that meet those needs. Most of the work in this area suggests that teachers are motivated by student performance and engagement rather than salary incentives and other external rewards (Stern and Keislar, 1977). Bryk's (1988) work suggests the importance of school organization in shaping the perceptions of personal encounters among faculty members, and thus psychic rewards. Mitchell, Ortiz, and Mitchell (1987) concluded that incentives for teachers are "deeply imbedded in school and classroom cultural values" (p. 15), and relate to student achievement and cooperation. And McLaughlin and Yee (1988) found that the quality of a teacher's experience far outweighed the potential for promotion as an incentive. According to Talbert (quoted in Hechinger, 1988), this aspect of teachers' motivations explains why teachers of high-achieving students are more easily rewarded by their teaching than those who work with low-achieving students and turn more often to their organizations for rewards. This literature suggests a more complex role for school structure and organization—one that supports teachers in their pursuit of effective teaching rather than simply holding out the carrots of merit pay and promotion.

The change literature has, therefore, moved from the sense of surprise and condemnation that teachers are resistant to change, to an examination of the structure of the organization and personal attributes of teachers that affect whether or not they implement new programs. It is important, however, to note that *change*, in this literature, is defined as teachers doing something that others are suggesting they do. Thus, change, as defined by the system, becomes a good in itself, and recalcitrance is bad. Even the recent work that is more sensitive to teachers' norms and beliefs fails to question the reforms themselves (see Donmoyer, 1987). Further, the constant changes that teachers make when meeting the changing needs of the students in the classroom or trying out ideas that they hear from other teachers do not count as changes in these conceptions.

Two scholars have examined the nature of the change being proposed in terms of the probability that teachers will adopt it. Cuban (1984, 1986, 1988) suggested two types of change: first order and second order. First-order changes, those designed to improve schools without fundamentally changing their organization, functions, or the nature of the student and teacher roles, are quite easy to affect. However, second-order changes seem much more difficult to implement. These are changes, such as voucher education, that fundamentally alter the nature of schooling. Cohen (1987, 1988) has also looked at a particular genre of second-order change to determine why it has not permeated our classrooms. The change described by Cohen is toward a philosophy or way of thinking that treats learning as an active process in which knowledge is constructed in the classroom. Although this view has been promoted for some time, Cohen suggests that it has not been implemented on a large scale because it would require a fundamental change in the view of the role of teachers.

However, the implementors and change agents are seldom asking for the fundamental changes that Cuban and Cohen describe. Many times, the change may be a new curriculum or a new management-by-data system for Chapter I students (Huberman and Miles, 1984). The important aspect that drives the discourse in this literature is that someone outside the classroom decides what changes teachers will make.

It is not surprising, then, that the organization would be turned to as a major barrier in the implementation of imposed change. The organization is external to the individual teacher, as is the promoter(s) of the particular change. Focusing on the organization takes the blame off the individual teacher, but suggests that the teacher is a pawn in the system with little power to make autonomous decisions. *Autonomy*, in fact, is not a term that is commonly used in this literature. If we want teachers to implement a practice, we can hardly suggest that an important element in this type of change is teacher autonomy. It is to another literature that we must turn to begin to understand the importance to the change process of teacher autonomy.

TEACHER LEARNING

In both the change and teacher learning literature, there are fundamental questions about what teachers do and how they do it, why teachers do what they do, and why teachers begin to do something differently. The learning to teach literature is not constrained, however, by a focus on a particular practice, nor on a locus of power located outside the classroom. Thus, the way these questions are investigated is quite different in these two literatures.

It is also the case that the teacher learning literature is not entirely about learning. In addition, it is about how teachers think; what propels their actions or why they think, believe, and teach as they do; and differences between expert and novice teachers in how they think and teach. Nonetheless, this literature does for us what Cuban (1988) concluded is necessary in understanding teacher change: answering the questions of how teachers teach and why they teach as they do. Since the purpose of this chapter is not to synthesize the learning to teach literature, a task that has been accomplished by others (Borko, 1989; Calderhead, 1988; Carter, 1990; Feiman-Nemser, 1983), but to draw on it for purposes of understanding teacher change, the next sections will simply mention several important aspects of the literature.

The current work on teacher learning assumes that teachers learn to teach when they begin teaching (Feiman-Nemser and Buchmann, 1986; Richardson-Koehler, 1985; Russell, 1988). Preservice education provides a grounding in notions such as lessons, planning, special student populations, and subject-matter instruction, and provides for an internlike situation in a classroom. However, the learning to teach process begins when the teacher is responsible for a classroom. Thus, most of the teacher learning work investigates student, beginning, and expert teachers. However, as described next, the learning about teaching process begins well before students enter their preservice programs.

WHAT TEACHERS DO AND WHY

Much of the initial work on teacher learning focused on differences between teachers at different stages of their careers. These studies, as do most of the current research on teacher learning, investigate the mental life of teachers—knowledge, cognitive processes, beliefs, and perceptions. Carter, Cushing, Sabers, Brown, and Berliner (1988), for example, found that the ways in which expert teachers perceive and process visual classroom information differ from those of novice and postulant (those with subject-matter expertise but no pedagogical training) teachers.

These studies have provided us with useful information about how experts think and what they do. They also suggest (but do not test since the studies work with different sets of teachers) that there is a developmental or learning process involved in the acquisition of these processes. However, they do not provide us with information about the learning process nor about conditions that would enhance or detract from the development of expert traits. Interestingly enough, they also have not examined experienced nonexperts—a group that could possibly provide us with a clue as to individual or organizational aspects that inhibit the development of expert cognitive processes.

These questions have been investigated in another type of study that follows a group of teachers through preservice education into the beginning years of teaching. In such a series of studies, Tabachnick and Zeichner (1984; Zeichner and Tabachnick, 1985) concluded that the maintenance of perspectives learned in teacher education into the first year of teaching depended on both the nature of the individual teacher and the context in which that teacher was teaching. Shulman and colleagues (Shulman, 1987; Grossman, 1987; Marks, 1987) investigated expert and experienced teachers to develop a way of thinking about pedagogical content knowledge. They also looked at preservice and beginning teachers, longitudinally, as they began to learn the process of transforming their content knowledge into activities and tasks that would enable their students to learn the content. Feiman-Nemser and colleagues at Michigan State University also followed preservice students through their programs and into their student teaching classrooms. Ball and Feiman-Nemser (1988) chose to focus on what the student teachers did not learn in preservice programs or from their cooperating teachers in terms of pedagogical thinking. And longitudinal studies of preservice student teachers and novice teachers by Borko and colleagues (Borko and Livingston, in press; Borko, Lalik, and Tomchin, 1987) provided information concerning the effect on students' learning to teach on content area knowledge as it interacted with personality factors and the expectations of the school.

These studies have been extremely helpful in developing an understanding of the cognitive demands on teachers, but they have not shed much light on processes of learning how to respond to them nor on why some teachers learn to perform them expertly. They do not seem satisfactorily to get to the soul of teaching—at a type of understanding that would allow us to think more creatively and authentically about teacher change. It is to another body of work that we must turn to develop this understanding—one that relies on case study techniques and thus emphasizes the idiosyncratic and personal nature of teaching.

This literature investigates the nature of teachers' practical knowledge (Elbaz, 1983), situational knowledge (Leinhardt, 1988), images (Calderhead, 1988), knowledge-in-action (Schön, 1982) practice-generated theories (Jordell, 1987), and practical arguments (Fenstermacher, 1986), and how such knowledge develops in individual teachers. For all of these investigators, this type of knowledge is different than formal theoretical (or research) knowledge, and interacts with the particular context and classroom situation in which the knowledge is transformed into action (or in Schön's formulation, interacts with the action). These studies employ case study methodology, the case being a teacher.

Two related aspects of the teacher's life emerge as being important in the development of this knowledge: experience and the teacher as a person. In the past, these two aspects have been investigated as norms—shared beliefs of the nature of teaching on the part of the teaching occupation (Lortie, 1975; Doyle and Ponder, 1977). These more recent studies help their readers understand how the norms could have developed.

THE ROLE OF EXPERIENCE

Teaching experience may not be the only teacher, but it is essential to the learning to teach process. As Clandinin and Connelly (1986) formulate the process: "Practical knowledge is gained through experience with the cyclic nature of schooling and classroom life. The experience is known in terms of a narrative which is reconstructed on the basis of additional experience" (p. 380). For Schön (1982), experience in like situations allows the practitioner to interact with a particular situation and bring forth knowledge-in-action. Teachers, too, are quite aware of the role of experience; in fact, in their minds, experience may be the only teacher. It is such a strong theme in teachers' responses to the question "Where did you learn to do that?" that their responses have acquired the label of a norm of the teaching profession (Lortie, 1975). Richardson-Koehler (1988) found that student teachers in her sample picked up this understanding within five or six weeks of commencing student teaching. Nonetheless, it is clear that practical knowledge, and perhaps even Shulman's concept of pedagogical content knowledge cannot develop fully without experience.

Leinhardt (1988), drawing on her classroom observations and interviews with mathematics teachers, presents a case of how a teacher could have come to understand the nature of third-grade mathematics and teach it the way she did. Looking at the history of exposure to subtraction in math, starting with the teacher's own third-grade education, moving to the way in which this content was portrayed in preservice education, in the curriculum in her first year of teaching and in her twentieth year, the structure of the math portrayed in her present lessons becomes quite understandable in terms of her personal biography.

Russell and Johnston (1988) describe case studies of four beginning teachers as they begin to see practice differently on the basis of their experiences during their first year. They suggested that this seeing is "played out *in the actions of teaching* [their italics] and is not necessarily thought out" (p. 16). A study of preservice teacher education led Russell (1988) to conclude that experience in classroom teaching should probably precede the teaching of pedagogical and learning theory. Thus, while Feiman-Nemser and Buchmann (1986) caution us that experience may not be the best teacher, for many teachers, isolated as they are in the classroom, it is the only teacher; although as Schön (1982), Shulman (1987), and others have pointed out, experience is only educative with reflection. This suggests that the improvement of the teacher learning process requires augmenting the experience process, rather than attempting to replace it with another process.

THE ROLE OF THE PERSON

Bryk (1988) describes good teaching as an "intensely personal activity" (p. 275). Experience as a learner and teacher, of course, is a piece of the person, and perhaps the most important element. However, there are other aspects related to who the teacher is and, perhaps more importantly, her perceptions and beliefs about herself as as learner and teacher. The personal nature of teaching has been amply demonstrated in a number of case studies. Clandinin (1986) and Clandinin and Connelly (1986) suggest how teachers' personal narratives, or constructions of their personal biographies, interact with particular situations to help teachers acquire a practical knowledge "that is embodied, experiential and reconstructed out of the narratives of their classroom lives" (p. 383). In a case study of a high school mathematics teacher, Marks (1987) found a strong relationship between the teacher's definition of problem solving, his perceptions of himself as a problem solver and his need for classroom control, and the way he taught his algebra classes. Richardson-Koehler and Fenstermacher (1988) indicated how a sixth-grade math teacher's beliefs about how children learn to read as well as his classroom practices were strongly tied to his views of himself as a reader and how he learned to read. And Hollingsworth (1989) concluded from a longitudinal study of 14 elementary and secondary preservice teachers throughout their fifth-year teacher education program that prior beliefs about teaching and learning strongly affected their patterns of intellectual change.

The prevalence of these two influences, experience and personal biography, in teachers' perceptions of how they learned to teach has caused some concern. As mentioned earlier, Feiman-Nemser and Buchmann (1986) suggest that experience is not the best teacher. And Buchmann (1986) feels that the view of teaching as an extension of the individual person, particularly in the minds of teachers, is detrimental to the improvement of teaching. She feels that teachers ought to be able to provide justifications based on a commonly understood professional language and set of standards. However, this case literature is quite convincing in elucidating the powerful and inevitable relationship between experience and personal biography, and what and how one learns to teach. Such an understanding is essential to those interested in the change process.

The relationship, however, between this understanding of teacher learning and the type of change addressed in the change literature is quite oblique. As a function, in part, of the methodology of case study, this teacher learning literature leads to an idiosyncratic view of the teacher. That is, the teacher teaches as he or she is. This could suggest that in order to work with the teacher toward improvement, we need a type of individualistic, psychoanalytic approach to teacher education, such as Combs (1965) developed decades ago, rather than the organizational change approach suggested in the teacher change literature. Researchers in this case study genre also have difficulty dealing with the normative elements of teaching. A narrative case study either remains neutral about the value or quality of the observed teaching and views of teaching, thus presenting a relativistic view, or injects judgment into the narrative without adequate bases provided for those judgments.

The question for those interested in change, then, is whether it is possible to bring together the ways of thinking exemplified in the change and learning to teach literatures in planning for improvement. The next section will address this question, with examples drawn from a three-year study of the use of research in the teaching of reading comprehension that attempted to use both literatures in developing and examining the results of a particular change process.

THE READING INSTRUCTION STUDY

This study was designed to respond to the question in an OERI grant announcement: Why don't teachers use the current research on reading? We restructured the question to address the following five:

1. What does current research say about the teaching of reading comprehension in grades 4, 5, and 6?
2. What types of practices are teachers using in teaching reading comprehension, and are these "research-based"?
3. What affects whether or not teachers are using research-based practices?
4. Does a staff development program based on the notions of practical arguments (Fenstermacher, 1986) affect teachers' beliefs and reading comprehension instruction practices?
5. Do these changes affect student learning? (Anders and Richardson, 1988).

Of interest to the issue of teacher change and learning are questions 3 and 4.[2] For question 3, we focused on individual teacher beliefs and on school-level cultural and organizational factors. Ethnographic belief interviews were conducted with teachers in six schools, with questions focusing on beliefs about reading comprehension, students, learning to read, and teaching reading (Richardson-Koehler and Hamilton, 1988). School-level data were collected using principal interviews, a structured survey of all instructional personnel in all six schools concerning school organizational conditions given to all instructional personnel in the six schools, and continual collection of ethnographic observations.

To respond to question 4, the staff development program was conducted in two schools at two levels: the individual and the school. The approach is designed to elicit teachers' value, empirical, and situational premises (Fenstermacher, 1986), and discuss them in relation to research on the teaching and learning of reading comprehension. This process is designed to help change the truth value of teachers' premises.

At the individual level, reading instruction was videotaped in each classroom and observed by the teacher and the two co-principal investigators. The teacher was asked to describe what was going on and to provide rationale for an action.[3] In this way, practical arguments surfaced and were discussed in relation to other premises about reading instruction based on current research. The session ended with the teachers agreeing to think about and try different practices in the classroom. There were followups with individual teachers during the course of the staff development program. All sessions were taped, and notes were maintained on each contact with the teachers.

At the school level, all grades 4, 5, and 6 teachers in each school met regularly as a group. The goal of this element of the staff development process was to deal with the school-level organizational issues described in the change literature, and to introduce a process that would permit teachers to continue to discuss practices and their justifications among themselves. The purpose of the sessions was to develop an environment for the construction of a shared meaning around the topics of reading comprehension. The group identified and addressed issues of common interest, relevant theoretical approaches and understandings of the reading process were discussed, and the staff developers and teachers presented reading comprehension instructional practices through description, modeling, or videotapes. The following are some preliminary observations on this change process.

Teacher Change

Contrary to the many observations concerning teacher recalcitrance, the teachers in our study changed practices all the time. Most changes that we observed would fit into Cuban's (1988) notion of first-order change (changing the number and composition of reading groups, trying a new activity, creating several learning centers for students who have completed their work, using fewer worksheets, emphasizing writing activities more than in the previous year, etc.). One teacher was undergoing a more fundamental or second-order change. She was adopting the whole language philosophy, which was slowly affecting what she was doing in the classroom. Some of the changes we observed are system-impelled, such as when a new basal reader is selected by the school district. But most of the changes, including the whole language change, were individual teacher decisions.

Changes that were adopted and tried out in the classroom were often dropped if they didn't "work" for that teacher. "Working" for the teachers in our study meant that the activities matched the teacher's beliefs about what classroom reading is, engaged the students, permitted the amount of control over students felt necessary by the teacher, and helped him or her respond to system-level demands such as high test scores. The original theoretical rationale for an adopted activity was seldom referred to in the practical argument sessions. For example, the rationale for insisting that the students read the comprehension check questions before reading the passage consistently was expressed as getting the right answers and doing better on the test, rather than theoretical rationale derived from schema theory and current research literature about reading as a cognitive process. This change in the teaching of reading comprehension, therefore, has received widespread acceptance among the teachers we worked with (although several of the teachers feel that this is "cheating") because of the teachers' belief that it will help students do better on the standardized tests.

Perceptions of Self and Teaching

The strong relationships among the individual teacher's perceptions of how he or she learned to read, how students learn to read, what reading is, and the actions taken by the teacher in the classroom became quite clear in the interviews, observations, and individual and group sessions. One teacher, for example, seemed to equate classroom reading with reading out loud, and effective reading with the ability to read out loud with feeling. We talked with her about the benefits of silent reading, but she was clearly skeptical. Several weeks later, she was asked about how she reads silently. "Just like I read out loud! I read and hear every word." In her perception, then, reading out loud was the same as, and, in fact, preparation for reading silently. She was asked to focus, during the week, on how she read silently. At the next meeting she announced her discovery that she read silently quite differently than she had thought. She "skipped words" and sometimes "peeked ahead."

The idiosyncratic or individual explanation for teachers' practices helped us account for what and why these teachers were teaching as they were. At times there were contradictions between their premises and practices (some of which were caught by the teachers in the course of watching the videotapes and explaining the practices). However, the fundamental core of the teachers' explanations of these practices related to their perceptions of personal experiences such as a particular teacher in whose classroom they had been and their own or their children's learning to read processes.

Organizational Issues

For many of the teachers, the nature of the discourse at the group level was quite different than that at the individual level. At the group level, the teachers focused on systematic barriers or mandates that caused them to institute practices over which they had no control, and of which they may (although not always) have disapproved. Although the nature of the manifestations of the barriers varied in the two schools, the practices did not. For example, basals were used in both schools, and their use was justified in one school on the basis of a supposed school board policy that 80 percent of reading instruction had to be in the basals; and in the other school, on the basis that there were no other books to use. Further, in the first school, the teachers agreed that school board members could walk into their classrooms at any time. The quick nodding of heads in agreement indicated that this was an idea that had been discussed among the faculty (referred to as a school-level myth by Richardson, Casanova, Placier, and Guilfoyle, 1989). Other school-level justifications concerned the nature of poor-achieving or poor-behaving students' families, and that parents and the public demand to see many "objective" measures of students' performance.

At the individual level, the teachers appeared more willing to talk about their practices and justifications. These justifications ranged from the view of teaching as an extension of self ("I just felt like doing that . . . it was my mood that day") to elaborate, coherent theories of the learning to read process. Although barriers were mentioned during the individual sessions, they were not emphasized. It appears that the shared language for justifying or explaining[4] a practice at the school level resolved around barriers and mandates, even though the individual teacher may have held strong personal justifications for the given practice.

There were, however, differences between the two schools. In one school, a relatively inexperienced faculty indicated a high sense of efficacy on the survey, and strong, socially collegial relationships. The barriers/mandates justifications for instructional practices dominated the conversations; and discussions of individual reading comprehension practices and their accompanying personal justifications were seldom brought up or pursued by others if they were. The other school, with a more experienced faculty, was noncollegial, and its teachers evidenced a low sense of efficacy. During the staff development sessions, they moved quite quickly beyond the barriers/mandates to discussions about classroom practice and, to a certain degree, their justifications for these practices. It would appear, in our preliminary analysis, that the norms of social collegiality inhibited the faculty in the first school, and the lack of any collegiality norms at all in the second school allowed the group to push ahead into group discussions of practices and the premises on which they are based. Of course, of interest to us in this study is the way in which the teachers in both schools used this staff development to affect changes in their classroom practices. This question must await further study.

TEACHERS AND CHANGE

This analysis of the change and learning literature and the preliminary observations from our research indicate that teacher resistance to change is not a problem at all. Teachers change practices all the time. Getting teachers to do what someone else wants them to may be a problem, and very often there is good reason for resistance to this type of change. Externally mandated or proposed practices often do not make sense within a particular context. Further, even when implemented by teachers, practices are often adopted in classrooms for reasons quite different from the theoretical rationale that drove their development. For example, the notion of objective and continual testing for purposes of diagnosis of student progress, for many teachers, has been found useful as a control mechanism. As one teacher pointed out, "Kids won't work as hard [on a task] if you don't grade it." Thus, this mandated research-based practice has been appropriated for purposes related to the need for control over students' efforts, and thus is quite distorted in practice from the original conception.

The problem, then, is not one of change or nonchange. It centers on the degree to which teachers can take control of the justifications for their classroom actions, and that these explanations or justifications go beyond those related to an extension of person. In our study, the school-level culture in both schools that provided justifications for action based on external forces allowed the teachers to ignore questions related to their own beliefs, understandings, and practices. Thus, as long as the district imposed the use of basals and their workbooks, for example, the teachers did not have to face up to their internal conflict between the sense that basals provide an easy way to plan for reading and maintain control over students, and the feeling that the basals do not really teach reading.

Taking control of one's justifications involves reflection on practices and an ability to articulate them to others in a meaningful way. If the misimplementation of practices such as we have seen with comprehension questions is to be avoided, the institution of a new practice in a classroom requires that a teacher reflect on the practice and that the content of the reflection relate to the practice's original theoretical framework. The implementation becomes an experience that, with reflection, adds to the practical knowledge about the teaching learning process.

Thus, experiences are truly educative only if accompanied by reflection.

Without reflection, practices will be accepted or rejected primarily on the basis of whether they meet the personality needs of the teacher and/or other more ecologically created concerns such as classroom management (see Doyle, 1986) and content coverage. Teachers thus become trapped by their own inability to take control of the justifications for practices, and instead resort to explanations based on external pressures. Empowerment of teachers should allow them to take control of their justifications. However, empowerment without reflection and the development of means to express their justifications will trap teachers into becoming victims of their personal biographies and systemic political demands and ecological conditions. This type of reflection requires languages and ways of thinking that go beyond teaching as an extension of personality, and permits consideration of subject matter in relation to student learning.

The challenge to the school and school system is enormous. Many mandates have attempted to impose classroom practices that focus in theory on content and learning. Without an understanding and acceptance of the theoretical concerns that drive the mandates, however, teachers may misapply or ignore them. How, then, may a school free its teachers of justifications that relate to external mandates, and support them in developing languages and ways of thinking about practice justification?

Our work suggests that attention must be paid to both the group of teachers at the school level and to the individual teacher. The development of analytic justifications is greatly aided by the creation of environments that allow for conversations around the justifications, empirical premises, and the formal theories that drive the development of new practices. This may be accomplished at the group level. It is also possible at the group level to explore the mythlike external justifications of practices that provide barriers to the development and exploration of personal justifications. However, reflection is an individual act. No one may reflect for someone else, since the teacher's particular set of experiences and personal biography play an important role in reflection. The organization should develop mechanisms for teachers to spend time reflecting on their practices and developing analytic justifications for how, what, and why they teach. This may be accomplished only by providing teachers with a sense of autonomy that permits them to take responsibility for and control of their justifications. It also suggests that accountability in schools should revolve around the exploration of teachers' justifications for their practices. This approach to staff development and accountability will take a long time to establish, since we must also consider the beliefs and justifications of the administrators. The belief, for example, that the way to improve teaching is to mandate and standardize practices will have to change. But what seems clear from this analysis of teacher change and learning is that change is not worthwhile unless it is thoughtful, and that thoughtful change is a long and sometimes painful process.

Endnotes

1. The Reading Instruction study is being funded by the OERI, Department of Education. Principal Investigators are Virginia Richardson and Patricia Anders. The chapter does not necessarily reflect the position taken by OERI on this topic.
2. The results of inquiry on the first two questions are available in a set of papers prepared by members of the project (Mitchell, Clarridge, Gallego, Lloyd, and Tidwell, 1988; Lloyd, Tidwell, Anders, Batchelder, Bos, and Bradley, 1988). These papers are available by writing to the author.
3. It is not assumed, as in the decision-making research, that the rationale really indicates what teachers were thinking at the time of the action (see Richardson-Koehler and Fenstermacher, 1988).
4. Buchmann (1986) describes *explanations* as the motivation for doing something and *justification* as a statement that allows others to consider the wisdom of a given action. Zeichner and Liston (1985) define *explanation/hypothetical discourse* as "attempts to identify causal relationships operating in the educational setting" (p. 163), and *justificatory discourse* as "concerned with the questions of why do this, in this way, with these particular students" (p. 163).

References

Anders, P., and Richardson, V. (1988). *A study of teachers' researched-based instruction of reading comprehension: Introduction to the symposium.* Paper presented at the annual meeting of the American Educational Research Association, New Orleans.

Ball, D. L., and Feiman-Nemser, S. (1988). Using textbooks and teachers' guides: A dilemma for beginning teachers and teacher educators. *Curriculum Inquiry, 18,* 401–424.

Berlak, A., and Berlak, H. (1981). *Dilemmas of schooling.* New York: Methuen.

Borko, H. (1989). Research on learning to teach: Implications for graduate teacher preparation. In A. Woolfolk (Ed.), *Research perspectives on the graduate preparation of teachers.* Englewood Cliffs, NJ: Prentice-Hall.

Borko, H., Lalik, R., and Tomchin, E. (1987). Student teachers' understandings of successful teaching. *Teaching and Teacher Education, 3,* 77–90.

Borko, H., and Livingston, C. (in press). Cognition and improvisation: Differences in mathematics instruction by expert and novice teachers. *American Education Research Journal.*

Bryk, A. (1988). Musings on the moral life of schools. *American Journal of Education, 96,* 256–290.

Buchmann, M. (1986). Role over person: Morality and authenticity in teaching. *Teachers College Record, 87,* 529–544.

Calderhead, J. (1988). The development of knowledge structures in learning to teach. In J. Calderhead (Ed.), *Teachers' professional learning.* Philadelphia: Falmer, pp. 51–64.

Carter, K. (1990). Teachers' knowledge and learning to teach. In R. Houston (Ed.), *Handbook of research on teacher education.* New York: Macmillan, pp. 291–310.

Carter, K., Cushing, K., Sabers, D., Brown, P., and Berliner, D. (1988). Expert-novice differences in perceiving and processing visual classroom information. *Journal of Teacher Education, 38,* 25–31.

Clandinin, D. J. (1986). *Classroom practice: Teacher images in action.* Philadelphia: Falmer.

Clandinin, D. J., and Connelly, F. M. (1986). Rhythms in teaching: The narrative study of teachers' personal practical knowledge of classrooms. *Teaching and Teacher Education, 2,* 377–387.

Cohen, D. K. (1987). Educational technology, policy, and practice. *Educational Evaluation and Policy Analysis, 9,* 153–170.

Cohen, D. K. (1988). Teaching practice, plus que ca change . . . In P. Jackson (Ed.), *Contributing to educational change: Perspectives on research and practice.* Berkeley: McCutcheon, pp. 27–84.

Combs, A. W. (1965). *The professional education of teachers: A perceptual view of teacher preparation.* Boston: Allyn and Bacon.

Cuban, L. (1984). *How teachers taught: Constancy and change in American classrooms: 1890–1980.* New York: Longman.

Cuban, L. (1986). *Teachers and machines.* New York: Teachers College Press.

Cuban, L. (1988). Constancy and change in schools (1880s to the present). In P. Jackson (Ed.), *Contributing to educational change: Perspectives on research and practice.* Berkeley: McCutcheon, pp. 85–106.

Donmoyer,R. (1987). Why case studies? Reflections on Hord's and Hall's three images. *Curriculum Inquiry, 17,* 91–102.

Doyle, W. (1983). Adademic work. *Review of Educational Research, 53,* 159–199.

Doyle,W. (1986). Classroom organization and management. In M. Wittrock (Ed.), *Handbook of research on teaching* (3rd ed.). New York: Macmillan, pp. 392–431.

Doyle, W., and Ponder, G. A. (1977). The practicality ethic in teacher decision making. *Interchange, 8,* 1–12.

Duffy, G., and Roehler, L. (1986). Constraints on teacher change. *Journal of Teacher Education, 36,* 55–58.

Elbaz, F. (1983). *Teacher thinking: A study of practical knowledge.* New York: Nichols.

Feiman-Nemser, S. (1983). Learning to teach. In L. Shulman and G. Sykes (Eds.), *Handbook of teaching and policy.* New York: Longman, pp. 6–170.

Feiman-Nemser, S., and Buchmann, M. (1986). Pitfalls of experience in teacher preparation. In J. Raths and L. Katz (Eds.), *Advances in teacher education* (Vol. 2). Norwood, NJ: Ablex, pp. 61–73.

Feiman-Nemser, S., and Floden, R. E. (1986). The cultures of teaching. In M. Wittrock (Ed.), *Handbook of research on teaching.* New York: Macmillan, pp. 505–526.

Fenstermacher, G. D. (1986). Philosophy of research on teaching: Three aspects. In M. Wittrock (Ed.), *Handbook of research on teaching* (3rd ed.). New York: Macmillan, pp. 37–49.

Grant, C., and Sleeter, C. (1985). Who determines teacher work: The teacher, the organization or both? *Teaching and Teacher Education, 1,* 209–220.

Grossman, P. L. (1987). *A tale of two teachers: The role of subject matter orientation in teaching.* Paper presented at the American Educational Research Association Conference, Washington, DC.

Guskey, T. R. (1988). Implementation of instructional innovation. *Teaching and Teacher Education, 4,* 63–69.

Hargreaves, A. (1984). Experience counts, theory doesn't: How teachers talk about their work. *Sociology of Education, 57,* 244–254.

Hatton, E. (1987). Determinants of teacher work: Some causal complications. *Teaching and Teacher Education, 3,* 55–60.

Hechinger, P. (1988). Does school structure matter? *Educational Researcher, 17,* 10–13.

Hollingsworth, S. (1989). Prior beliefs and cognitive change in learning to teach. *American Educational Research Journal, 26,* 160–190.

Huberman, A. M., and Miles, M. (1984). *Innovation up close.* New York: Plenum.

Jackson, P. (1968). *Life in classrooms.* New York: Holt, Rinehart & Winston.

Jordell, K. O. (1987). Structural and personal influences in the socialization of beginning teachers. *Teaching and Teacher Education, 3,* 165–177.

Leinhardt, G. (1988). Situated knowledge and expertise in teaching. In J. Calderhead (Ed.), *Teachers' professional knowledge.* Philadelphia: Falmer.

Little, J. (1987). Teachers as colleagues. In V. Richardson-Koehler (Ed.), *Educators' handbook: A research perspective.* New York: Longman, pp. 491–518.

Lloyd, C., Tidwell, D., Anders, P., Batchelder, A., Bos, C., and Bradley, J. (1988). *Research-based comprehension.* Paper presented at the annual meeting of the American Educational Research Association, New Orleans.

Lortie, D. (1975). *Schoolteacher.* Chicago: University of Chicago Press.

March, J., and Simon, H. (1958). *Organizations.* New York: Wiley.

Marks, R. (1987). *Problem solving with a small 'p': A teacher's view.* Paper presented at the annual meeting of the American Educational Research Association, Washington, DC.

McLaughlin, M. (1987). Learning from experience: Lessons from policy implementation. *Educational Evaluation and Policy Analysis, 9,* 171–178.

McLaughlin, M., and Yee, S. M. (1988). School as a place to have a career. In A. Lieberman (Ed.), *Building a professional culture in schools.* New York: Teachers College Press, pp. 23–44.

Mitchell, D. E., Ortiz, F. I., and Mitchell, T. (1987). *Work orientation and job performance: The cultural basis of teaching rewards and incentives.* Albany: State University of New York Press.

Mitchell, J., Clarridge, P., Gallego, M., Lloyd, C., and Tidwell, D. (1988). *Teachers' comprehension instruction practices.* Paper presented at the annual meeting of the American Educational Research Association, New Orleans.

Richardson, V., Casanova, U., Placier, P., and Guilfoyle, K. (1989). *School children at-risk.* Philadelphia: Falmer.

Richardson-Koehler, V. (1985). Research on preservice teacher education. *Journal of Teacher Education, 36* (1), 23–30.

Richardson-Koehler, V. (1988). Barriers to the effective supervision of student teaching: A field study. *Journal of Teacher Education, 8* (2), 28–36.

Richardson-Koehler, V., and Fenstermacher, G. (1988). *The use of practical arguments in staff development.* Paper presented at the annual meeting of the American Association of Colleges of Teacher Education, New Orleans. ERIC Documentation Locator Number: SP 030047.

Richardson-Koehler, V., and Hamilton, M. L. (1988). *Teachers' theories of reading.* Paper presented at the annual meeting of the American Educational Research Association, New Orleans.

Rosenholtz, S., Bassler, O., and Hoover-Dempsey, K. (1986). Organizational conditions of teacher learning. *Teaching and Teacher Education, 2,* 91–104.

Russell, T. (1988). From pre-service teacher education to first year of teaching: A study of theory and practice. In J. Calderhead (Ed.), *Teachers' Professional Learning.* Philadelphia: Falmer, pp. 13–34.

Russell, T., and Johnston, P. (1988). *Teachers learning from experiences of teaching: Analyses based on metaphor and reflection.* Paper presented at the annual meeting of the American Education Research Association, New Orleans.

Schön, D. (1982). *The reflective practitioner.* New York: Basic Books.

Shulman, L. (1987). Knowledge in teaching: Foundations of the new reform. *Harvard Educational Review, 57,* 1–22.

Smylie, M. A. (1988). The enhancement function of staff development: Organizational and psychological antecedents to individual teacher change. *American Educational Research Journal, 25,* 1–30.

Sparks, G. M. (1983). *Inservice education: Training activities, teacher attitude, and behavior change.* Unpublished doctoral dissertation, Stanford University.

Stern, C., and Keislar, E. (1977). Teacher attitudes and attitude change: A research review. *Journal of Research and Development in Education, 10,* 63–76.

Tabachnick, R., and Zeichner, K. (1984). The impact of the student teaching experience on the development of teacher perspectives. *Journal of Teacher Education, 35,* 28–42.

Tobin, K. (1987). Forces which shape the implemented curriculum in high school science and mathematics. *Teaching and Teacher Education, 3,* 287–298.

Waugh, R., and Punch, K. (1987). Teacher receptivity to system wide change. *British Educational Research Journal, 11,* 113–121.

Zeichner, K., and Liston, D. (1985). Varieties of discourse in supervisory conferences. *Teaching and Teacher Education, 1* (2), 155–174.

Zeichner, K., and Tabachnick, B. R. (1985). The development of teacher perspectives: Social strategies and institutional control in the socialization of beginning teachers. *Journal of Education for Teachers, 11,* 1–25.

PART II

Teachers and the School Organization

Chapter Five

The teaching profession has been highly criticized, leading to the tightening of certification standards, prescriptive instructional models, and staff accountability through increased monitoring of outcomes (e.g., through the use of standardized tests). More recent efforts have shifted the focus of control from external accountability to internal "empowerment." This shift—from blaming teachers to empowering them—creates the expectation that forms of empowerment somehow are miracle cures for what ails our nation's schools. In this context, it is important to take a more systematic look at some of the important organizational conditions that affect what is at the heart of empowerment—the influence that teachers have over their work lives.

This chapter analyzes the organizational factors that contribute to various patterns of influence in schools. It is argued that influence is central to understanding how schools operate. And if changing patterns of influence are to be an important tool of school reform and improvement, then it is necessary to have a better understanding of the local organizational conditions that affect influence. The relationships among teacher influence and the school processes of goal consensus, communication, and principal leadership are explored.

Influence in Schools and the Factors That Affect It

Bruce L. Wilson
Research for Better Schools, Inc.

THE CONCEPT OF INFLUENCE

Contemporary social life is dominated by organizations (Scott, 1981). Understanding how they function is important, for it is in organizations that complex society "gets things done" (Parsons, 1960, p. 41). A sociological knowledge of how organizations operate is not complete without considering members' influence. As Tannenbaum (1962) points out, influence is an essential and universal aspect of organization, one to which every member must accommodate. Formal organizations offer the means by which individual actions take on some ordered form. It is through the processes of control (or influence) that idiosyncratic behaviors of individuals are constrained and the plans of the organization can be carried out. These control mechanisms become the means by which motivation and direction of individual members are ordered. When members agree about influence in organizations, it becomes easier to reach a shared belief system to guide the work of the organization.

Influence is defined as the ability to induce others to behave in ways that they ordinarily would not (Dahl, 1957; Emerson, 1962). It is used synonymously with the term *power* or *control*. Such a conception of

The preparation of this chapter was supported by funds from the U.S. Department of Education, Office of Educational Research & Improvement (OERI). The opinions expressed do not necessarily reflect the position or policy of OERI, and no official endorsement should be inferred.

influence derives from the social relationships between or among individuals or groups (Nyberg, 1981; Scott, 1981; Hickson, Hinings, Lee, Schneck, and Pennings, 1971). Not an attribute or characteristic of an individual, influence is something that some individuals or groups hold over another in a given social relation (Burbules, 1986). The importance of influence in organizations rests with the fact that organizations are the settings in which most social relations are acted out. This relational aspect of influence focuses not only on the formally constituted authority structures that are based on the hierarchical chain of command but also on informal sources such as charisma, expertise, or friendship (Bacharach and Aiken, 1976).

The importance of influence in understanding organizations is as true of schools as it is of any other organization. Yet, almost no systematic empirical attention has focused on influence in schools (Common, 1983; Nyberg, 1981). When it is examined, it is usually viewed through the formal authority structures (top-down perspective), producing an overestimation of the influence of administrators relative to teachers and other subordinates. Such an approach oversimplifies the nature of power relationships, since subordinates do often wield considerable influence vis-à-vis their superiors (Mechanic, 1962; Schlechty, 1976; Burbules, 1986).

A perspective that considers bottom-up influence hints at the power of teachers to influence organizational behavior. Indeed, as the reform effort in education evolves, increasing focus has been placed on the role of teachers as influential actors (Maeroff, 1988). Indirectly, these reform efforts have begun to highlight the role of subordinate influence on improvement efforts. For example, Conley, Schmidle, and Shedd (1988) suggest that while the first wave of reform did not involve teachers and put much of the blame for failure on poor training (hence the focus on teacher competency tests and restructuring of teacher education programs), a second wave has involved teachers by calling for them to have a "real voice in decision making" (National Governors' Association, 1986). Implicit in this argument is the recognition that a key tool for effective school-based change is the alteration of influence patterns in schools. As Elmore (1987) points out, the central issue in the construction of a normative order in schools is the determination of who has the influence to define what good teaching is and who controls the knowledge base for the delivery of instruction.

Influence has been described as a relational concept. That is, to know how much influence teachers have in a school, it must be understood in relation to some other role group. In our research we were interested in learning more about the influence of teachers vis-à-vis the principal. Therefore we asked teachers to report how much influence they, as a group, had in relation to how much influence their principal had. Furthermore, the focus of our concept was not on the amount of influence but rather on the degree of agreement about the level of influence.

Specifying the decision areas of interest over which this influence is exerted also is important. The sociological literature typically focuses on influence over strategic decisions that affect the basic destiny of the organization (Hage, 1980). However, in schools considerable interest lies in understanding who controls the day-to-day decisions governing how or what children are taught. This is generally an area over which teachers have considerable influence and has been labeled by Lortie (1969) as the "teacher zone of influence." Our research probed five items regarding the relative influence of teachers and the principal over classroom instruction. The items included:

- Selecting required texts or other materials
- Establishing objectives for each course
- Determining daily plans or activities
- Determining concepts taught on a particular day
- Identifying types of educational innovations to be adopted

A second decision area focused on larger schoolwide issues. These decisions are expected to fall in the "principal zone of influence" (Lortie, 1969). Five items were used to assess this area of decision:

- Determining the allocation of teaching materials, supplies, or other resources
- Determining the school's schedule (including teacher prep periods)
- Adding or dropping courses
- Making specific faculty grade-level or course assignments
- Determining the use of school space including classrooms, offices, or other areas

Our research treated these zones as conceptually distinct while recognizing that more recent literature on teacher participation (e.g., Conley et al., 1988) argues that the distinction may be artificial. This distinction was made since strong empirical evidence exists that support big differences between teachers' and principals' zones of influence (Wilson, Firestone, and Herriott, 1985).

It is important to note that the schools in our sample reported wide variation in their response to our measures of influence. That is, while in some schools there was little or no disagreement about how influence was distributed, in others there was a great deal of disagreement. Schools fell all along the continuum from low to high agreement about teacher influence vis-à-vis the principal.

In sum, understanding the role of influence in a school is critical to understanding clearly how and why a school operates the way it does. Since a neglected area of inquiry has been the variation of perceived influence by lower-level participants, this chapter addresses that poorly explored area by documenting the variability of perceived influence by teachers and by addressing some of the organizational process variables affecting that variation. Specifically, three organizational processes are hypothesized as having an impact on the variability of perceived influence: organizational goals, communication patterns, and leadership.

These hypothesized relationships were empirically assessed by administering the School Assessment Survey (SAS) to a sample of 10,559 teachers from 382 public schools from around the nation. The SAS instrument is a multidimensional questionnaire that applies teachers' perceptions to measures of key organizational characteristics of a school (Wilson, 1985). The focus of this instrument has been made to make use of teachers as informants about the school as an organization (Seidler, 1974). Since the primary objective of this chapter is to discuss conceptually the important organizational components of schools and how those are related to influence, most of the technical details concerning measurement and analysis have been eliminated. Readers interested in those issues are referred to Wilson (1988).

THE IMPACT OF SCHOOL CONDITIONS ON TEACHER INFLUENCE

Goals

The prevailing definitions of acceptable and appropriate behavior in an organization help to shape patterns of influence. The more these definitions are widely known and adhered to in the organization, the greater will be the agreement about the distribution of influence. An important indicator of the core expectations for behavior is the set of goals for an organization. An organization with greater consensus about goals is more likely to have higher agreement concerning influence patterns. As Mechanic (1962, p. 264) hypothesized, "Influence patterns in organizations are likely to be modeled by . . . the nature of organizational goals." Schools struggle with the larger number of goals placed on them by the local community and larger society. Yet, some schools are better able to create a purpose and direction by building consensus around a small core of goals (see Chapter Two of this text). It is suggested, then, that a direct relationship exists between school goals and influence: the greater the consensus about the goals of a school as perceived by teachers, the higher the agreement about the influence of teachers vis-à-vis the principal.

In pursuing the concept of goals, we were interested in learning more about the priority teachers gave to different areas of student development. Teachers were asked to indicate their preferences among the following areas:

- Appreciating and striving for excellence (in school work or other areas)
- Critical and original thinking
- Basic skills (reading and math)
- Respect for authority (discipline, character building, etc.)
- Vocational understanding and skills
- Understanding others (cultural pluralism, getting along with peers, etc.)
- Self-esteem (self-concept)

We found that a relationship existed between school goals and influence; specifically, the greater the consensus about the goals of a school as perceived by teachers, the higher the agreement about the influence of teachers vis-à-vis the principal on school decisions. That is, if teachers have a clear sense of direction about the purpose of the school, they are likely to agree about their influence on school decisions. It makes sense that if teachers do not share a sense of the schools' general goals and purposes for student learning, it will be more difficult to exercise collective influence over those purposes. Recent effective schools' research has highlighted the importance of clear goals as a tool for improving productivity (Wilson and Corcoran, 1988). We are suggesting that shared goals also may be important in providing teachers with a sense of influence over school decisions, particularly those decisions that affect the instructional practices that teachers are pursuing in classrooms with students.

Communication

The pattern of communication in an organization is another organizational process that may have an impact on influence. Communication in organizations is the process by which information is exchanged and meaning is transmitted. It is one of the most frequently discussed processes in the organizational literature (Price, 1972), since an effective communication system can provide organizational members with the information necessary to do their work effectively (Hall, 1982).

Schools are generally viewed as isolating environments for teachers, where staff members have precious little opportunity to discuss their work, work relationships, or learn from one another (Dreeben, 1973). However, researchers recognize the need for teachers and administrators to share ideas about the work of instruction. For example, Little (1982) documents the positive relationship between collegiality and school success. She found that successful schools were more likely to value norms of collegiality and continuous improvement. The more successful schools had staff who reported a greater range of professional interaction. Consequently, it is argued that by increasing the level of discourse in a school, influence patterns ought to be clarified. More specifically, the greater the communication between the teachers and the principal in a school, the more agreement there will be about the influence of teachers vis-à-vis the principal.

In our research we were interested in assessing the extent to which information about instructional issues is shared between teachers and school administrators. Teachers reported how frequently they talked to school administrators regarding such topics as:

- Lessons or curriculum units that work well or poorly
- Motivating or controlling specific children
- Improving discipline generally
- Defining or enforcing student performance, grading, or promotion standards
- Maintaining or improving positive relations with parents
- Obtaining materials or resources needed for classroom instruction

Schools with ample opportunities for teachers to exchange ideas with their principal concerning instructional issues reported greater agreement concerning their influence over work-related issues. It seems intuitive (but often overlooked) that when teachers lack opportunities to discuss important instructional issues with their principal, a climate of uncertainty is more likely to prevail regarding who has control. This may be counterproductive to the teaching and learning process, with teachers frequently second-guessing their roles and responsibilities and potential conflict developing with the principal.

With all the attention being placed on alterable conditions that help predict school success, there has been surprisingly little attention paid to the role of adult interaction. Yet, ample evidence exists in the larger sociological literature indicating the importance of strong communication patterns (Price, 1972). Not only is enhanced communication related to student performance (Little, 1982) but our research indicated it contributed to a coherence about influence over instructional matters—an important precondition before the task of teaching and learning can be accomplished.

Leadership

Leadership is the third organizational process hypothesized as being related to influence in schools. The effect of leadership on organizational productivity has received wide attention in the business literature (Peters and Waterman, 1982). It has also caught the attention of the education community and has been linked to school effectiveness (Edmonds, 1979; Greenfield, 1987). What is often not clear, however, is the nature of that leadership. One key element of leadership is the support that principals offer teachers (Gross and Herriott, 1965; McPherson, 1979). This support can range from buffering of outside interference, to enhancing resources for instruction, to building teachers' sense of importance as professionals, and to offering advice that will help them perform better.

Although it is acknowledged that the direct impact of supportive behavior by the principal on student performance may be minimal, principals can do a great deal to facilitate teachers' work (Firestone and Wilson, 1988), with the potential positive by-product being greater consensus about influence patterns. Thus, it is argued that the greater the perceived facilitative leadership of the principal, the greater the agreement about the influence of teachers vis-à-vis the principal.

We were interested in obtaining teachers' perceptions of how often the principal supported the professional behavior of the teaching staff. The teachers reported on the principal's behavior in such areas as:

- Treats teachers as professional workers
- Takes a strong interest in the professional development of teachers
- Gives teachers the feeling that their work is an "important" activity
- Has constructive suggestions to offer teachers in dealing with their major problems
- Gives teachers the feeling that they can make significant contributions to improving the classroom performance of their students
- Makes meetings a valuable professional activity

The evidence from our research indicated that more supportive principals helped create environments with more agreement about the pattern of influence in schools. That is, in settings where teachers reported their principals worked more closely with them to establish a professional environment in which to conduct their work, the teachers also reported more consensus about who had control over important issues related to the instructional program. On the other side of the coin, schools with principals who did not exhibit what teachers perceived as facilitative, supportive behavior were more likely to have environments where there was little agreement about influence. If allowed to continue, this could contribute to a negative teaching and learning environment.

Perhaps the most studied and widely discussed variable in the school effectiveness literature is principal leadership (Burdin, 1988). Much of that research describes the positive relationship between strong leadership and high student performance. Yet, as practicing educators know, the link is more complex than is portrayed by much of the research. Important intervening variables must be in place before student performance can be improved. Our research highlighted an important intervening variable—influence. In schools where there were supportive principals, there was greater consensus about influence. This, in turn, has the potential to help create an environment that encourages higher levels of learning.

Tenure and Size

Social reality is always more complex than the simple theoretical argument outlined above regarding influence in schools and how goals, communication, and leadership affect it. To understand fully the dynamics of organizational behavior in schools, it is also essential to consider some structural features of schools. For example, it is well known that large secondary schools function differently than small elementary schools (Wilson, Firestone, and Herriott, in press). Two structural features of schools are discussed and analyzed in this chapter: organizational tenure and organizational size. By considering the effects of size and tenure as important structural features, we may expand further our understanding of how influence operates in schools.

For prevailing definitions of acceptable and appropriate behavior to shape influence patterns, organizational members must have some tenure within the organization. Appropriate and acceptable behavior has little meaning if all the members are new to an organization. Likewise, it might be expected that influence patterns may differ when all the members are long-term employees or when a mix of new and long-term members exists. Thus, tenure may alter the effects of organizational processes on variation of influence. This argument suggests that after controlling for differences in the tenure of teachers in schools, the relationship between goal consensus, vertical communication, and facilitative leadership with agreement about influence may change.

The other important structural feature of schools that may distort the relationship between organizational processes and influence is size. Schools vary widely in size, with some as small as 4 or 5 teachers and others with more than 100. Increasing size invites complexity, which is often dealt with through specialization of roles or differentiation of assignments (Wilson and Herriott, 1989). This complexity may make it difficult to create a structure of shared definitions about patterns of influence. Thus, it is argued that after one controls for differences in the size of schools, the relationship between goal consensus, vertical communication, and facilitative leadership with agreement about influence may be altered. In our research, tenure was assessed by having teachers report the number of years they had been working in the school, and size was operationalized as the number of teachers employed in the school.

Our investigation of the relationships between influence and the organizational processes of goals, communication, and leadership when controlling for the effect of tenure led us to conclude that it did not change the relationships in any way. That is, the length of tenure in the school had little bearing on an explanation of differences in influence patterns. Rather than attributing important substantive meaning to this finding, we suggested that it may have been because the schools in our research sample employed veteran teachers. With the average tenure in each school being more than eight years and with 95 percent of the schools having average tenure of three or more years, variation was immaterial since almost all the schools were at the high end of a continuum of experience.

On the other hand, school size played an important role in reducing the relationship between the three organizational process variables and influence in schools. This finding suggests that consensus about influence is more difficult to affect through channels of communication, supportive leadership, or clearly articulated goals in larger schools. However, the interpretation of the impact of size is difficult to untangle. Although it is true that larger schools have less goal consensus, less communication between teachers and administrators, and lower facilitative leadership (Wilson et al., 1985), it remains unclear whether size is a proxy for something more important. For example, elementary schools are smaller than secondary schools. Perhaps the elementary/secondary distinction is more important. Certainly, enough caution has been offered about adopting changes for schools from one level based on research at another level (Rowan, Bossert, and Dwyer, 1983). That issue is too complex to unravel in this chapter. Nevertheless, the evidence suggests that structural variables have an impact on influence patterns in schools and more thought needs to be given to other structural variables that may affect influence patterns.

DISCUSSION

The argument of this chapter has been that influence is central to understanding how schools operate as organizations. Influence patterns are important because through those patterns, the work of schools is defined and some core norms of appropriate behavior are set. This argument becomes even more important as increasing attention is paid to teacher empowerment as a means of improving our nation's schools. However, before efforts are made to alter influence structures in schools, it is essential to have a better understanding of what influence is and what organizational factors have an impact on that influence. This chapter is a preliminary first step in that direction.

Influence is the ability to have others behave in ways they ordinarily would not. It is found in the social relationships between two or more individuals and is not the attribute just of the individual. Influence of subordinates on superordinates is as important if not more important than the reverse. This chapter summarized findings from recent research (Wilson, 1988) investigating the influence of teachers vis-à-vis their principal over instruction and school policy decisions.

Rather than discussing the amount of influence in schools, this chapter focused on the degree of consensus about where influence resides. Is there agreement or disagreement about the relative distribution of influence between teachers and the school principal? Consensus about influence is important because it is through agreement about influence that certain expectations for appropriate behavior are defined. As Corbett and Rossman (1988) point out, it is through a shared belief system that schools can improve. By learning more about the factors that have an impact on the variation in influence, schools may be in a better position to alter influence patterns and thus modify the understandings about the belief system that guides staff behavior in a school.

We are now entering a new wave of reform in U.S. education. As noted in our introductory comments, the focus of the latest wave may be shifting policy initiatives away from external control mechanisms (e.g., preservice training, certification standards, monitoring of outcomes) to working conditions for teachers already employed by the nation's schools. Central to many of these recent discussions of how to improve our schools has been the acknowledged need to restructure the basic ways that professionals operate in schools. Restructuring is changing the four Rs of organizational behavior: rules, roles, relationships, and results (Corbett, 1989).

Rules are defined as the universal norms in a school; that is, the expectations for behavior that apply across all the roles in a school. They would include both formal policy (e.g., curriculum guides, budgetary procedures, class schedules) and more informal understandings of the way things are done in a school. This category also includes the behavioral expectations that result from an articulated vision in a school. *Roles* refer to the specific rules of behavior and expectations that apply to particular positions in the schools (e.g., students, teachers). These expectations define the responsibilities of individual role occupants and the ways in which it is acceptable for role occupants to act. *Relationships* concern the distribution of authority and influence among individual role occupants and groups. Finally, *results* are the products of the particular patterns of rules, roles, and relationships that occur in a school.

The influence that teachers have over issues that affect their work is thus central to constructive change in schools. In other words, restructuring will be successful to the degree that acceptable patterns of influence are established that enable teachers to accomplish their work. This chapter has discussed some of the factors that have an effect on influence. Specifically, in schools with greater consensus on goals, more agreement existed about the influence of teachers vis-à-vis the principal. Where teachers reported more communication between them and the principal, teachers agreed more about influence. Finally, those schools where teachers reported more supportive leadership on the part of the principal were associated with greater agreement about teacher influence vis-à-vis the principal.

Influence patterns play an important role in defining appropriate norms of behavior for professional staff in schools. Much of the recent discussion on the most promising avenues for reforming schools focuses on the need to give teachers more influence as a critical feature of school-based change (e.g., The Holmes Group, 1986). Regardless of whether the locus of that influence is student-teacher (McNeil, 1988) or teacher-administrator (Elmore, 1987), the attention has been on the amount (i.e., the lack of teacher influence) and not on the variation of influence. Implicit in much of the discussion, then, is the notion that variation is either minimal or inconsequential. This chapter argues otherwise. Furthermore, it argues that important structural arrangements and organizational processes in schools help explain the variation in influence.

Efforts to improve schools would be enhanced by a better understanding of the factors that create divergence in patterns of influence and consequently introduce noise in the effort to establish an agreed upon set of professional behaviors. This chapter begins that dialogue by suggesting that goal consensus, vertical communication, and facilitative leadership contribute to building consensus about influence. In turn, agreement about patterns of influence offers improved prospects for a shared belief system that will constructively guide the professional behavior of teachers.

References

Bacharach, S. B., and Aiken, M. (1976). Structural and process constraints on influence in organizations: A level-specific analysis. *Administrative Science Quarterly, 21* (4), 623–641.

Burbules, N. C. (1986). A theory of power in education. *Educational Theory, 36* (2), 95–114.

Burdin, J. L. (Ed.) (1988). *School leadership: A contemporary reader.* Beverly Hills, CA: Sage.

Common, D. L. (1983). Power: The missing concept in the dominant model of school change. *Theory into Practice, 22* (3), 203–210.

Conley, S. C., Schmidle, T., and Shedd, J. B. (1988). Teacher participation in the management of school systems. *Teachers College Record, 90* (2), 259–280.

Corbett, H. D. (1989). *Empowerment and restructuring.* Philadelphia: Research for Better Schools.

Corbett, H. D., and Rossman, G. B. (1988). *How teachers empower superordinates: Running good schools.* Paper presented at the annual meeting of the American Educational Research Association, New Orleans.

Dahl, R. A. (1957). The concept of power. *Behavioral Science, 2* (3), 201–215.

Dreeben, R. (1973). The school as a workplace. In R. M. W. Travers (Ed.), *Second handbook of research on teaching.* Chicago: Rand McNally.

Edmonds, R. (1979). Effective schools for the urban poor. *Educational Leadership, 37* (1), 15–24.

Elmore, R. F. (1987). Reform and the culture of authority in schools. *Educational Administration Quarterly, 23* (4), 60–78.

Emerson R. E. (1962). Power-dependence relations. *American Sociological Review, 27* (1), 31–41.

Firestone, W. A., and Wilson, B. L. (1988). *Administrative behavior, school SES, and student achievement: A preliminary investigation.* Philadelphia: Research for Better Schools.

Greenfield, W. (Ed.) (1987). *Instructional leadership: Concepts, issues, and controversies.* Boston: Allyn and Bacon.

Gross, N., and Herriott, R. E. (1965). *Staff leadership in public schools.* New York: Wiley.

Hage, J. (1980). *Theories of organization: Form, process and transformation.* New York: Wiley.

Hall, R. (1982). *Organizations: Structure and process* (3rd ed.). Englewood Cliffs, NJ: Prentice-Hall.

Hickson, D. J., Hinings, C. R., Lee, C. A., Schneck, R. E., and Pennings, J. M. (1971). A strategic contingencies' theory of intraorganizational power. *Administrative Science Quarterly, 16* (2), 216–229.

The Holmes Group (1986). *Tomorrow's teachers.* East Lansing, MI: Author.

Little, J. W. (1982). Norms of collegiality and experimentation:

Workplace conditions of school success. *American Educational Research Journal, 19* (3), 325–340.

Lortie, D. C. (1969). The balance of control and autonomy in elementary school teaching. In A. Etzioni (Ed.), *The semi-professions and their organization.* New York: Free Press.

Maeroff, G. I. (1988). *The empowerment of teachers: Overcoming the crisis of confidence.* New York: Teachers College Press.

McNeil, L. M. (1988). *Contradictions of control: School structure and school knowledge.* New York: Routledge.

McPherson, G. H. (1979). What principals should know about teachers. In D. A. Erickson and T. R. Relker (Eds.), *The principal in metropolitan schools.* Berkeley, CA: McCutchan.

Mechanic, D. (1962). Sources of power of lower participants in complex organizations. *Administrative Science Quarterly, 7* (3), 349–364.

National Governors' Association (1986). *Time for results: The governor's 1991 report on education.* Washington, DC: Author.

Nyberg, D. (1981). A concept of power for education. *Teachers College Record, 82* (4), 535–552.

Parsons, T. (1960). *Structure and process in modern societies.* Glencoe, IL: Free Press.

Peters, T. J., and Waterman, R. H. (1982). *In search of excellence: Lessons from America's best-run companies.* New York: Harper & Row.

Price, J. L. (1972). *Handbook of organizational measurement.* Lexington, MA: D. C. Heath.

Rowan, B., Bossert, S. T., and Dwyer, D. C. (1983). Research on effective schools: A cautionary note. *Educational Researcher, 12* (4), 24–31.

Schlechty, P. C. (1976). *Teaching and social behavior: Toward an organizational theory of instruction.* Boston: Allyn and Bacon.

Scott, W. R. (1981). *Organizations: Rational, natural and open systems.* Englewood Cliffs, NJ: Prentice-Hall.

Seidler, J. (1974). On using informants: A technique for collecting quantitative data and controlling measurement error in organization analysis. *American Sociological Review, 39* (6), 816–831.

Tannenbaum, A. S. (1962). Control in organizations: Individual adjustment and organizational performance. *Administrative Science Quarterly, 7* (2), 236–257.

Wilson, B. L. (1985). The school assessment survey. *Educational Leadership, 42* (6), 50–53.

Wilson, B. L. (1988). *The effect of organizational factors on variation of influence in schools.* Paper presented at the annual meeting of the American Educational Research Association, New Orleans.

Wilson, B. L., and Corcoran, T. B. (1988). *Successful secondary schools: Visions of excellence in American public education.* London: Falmer Press.

Wilson, B. L., Firestone, W. A., and Herriott, R. E. (1985). *The school assessment survey: A technical manual.* Philadelphia: Research for Better Schools.

Wilson, B. L., Firestone, W. A., and Herriott, R. E. (in press). Explaining differences between elementary and secondary schools: Individual, organizational and institutional perspectives. In P. W. Thurston and P. Zodhiates (Eds.), *Advances in Educational Administration* (Volume 2). Greenwich, CT: JAI Press.

Wilson, B. L., and Herriott, R. E. (1989). *Formal subunits within American public schools: Their structure, power and consequences.* Philadelphia: Research for Better Schools.

Chapter Six

Participative decision making may be less central to principal/teacher interaction than presumed by the literature. Though reform proposals call for increased teacher involvement, operant constraints on principals and teachers alike pose practical limitations. Accordingly, teacher involvement in school decisions may be the exception rather than the rule. In this chapter, Glasman and Hajnik observe limited teacher participation in schoolwide issues. Data from a study of 13 principals suggest that principals more frequently announce decisions to teachers than solicit input or delegate decisions. Furthermore, only selected teachers (termed repeaters) may be regularly involved in decision making. "Participation" typically involves a small group of teachers, focuses on certain types of issues, has boundaries decided by the principal, and varies according to school size and the nature of the student population.

Participative Decision Making in Schools: Do Principals Facilitate Teacher Participation?

Naftaly S. Glasman
University of California,
Santa Barbara

Suzanne R. Hajnik
Orcutt Union School
District,
California

A central thrust of the second wave of reform has been to facilitate teacher involvement in school-site decisions (Cooper and Conley, this volume). In this context, the participatory model of shared decision making consists of attributes of organizational culture such as common meanings and a core value base (e.g., Smylie, this volume; Bolman and Deal, 1984; Mitchell, Ortiz, and Mitchell, 1987). This model assumes that decisions are outcomes of consensus among those who participate in the decision-making process (Wilson, this volume). The model also assumes that influence stemming from professional expertise enhances communication and status equalization among participants (e.g., Estler, 1988). The decisions themselves are assumed to be goal optimizing and the emphasis seems to be on human processes (e.g., Bolman and Deal, 1984).

Bridges (1967), for example, describes four modes of participative decision making in schools, all of which involve both a problem that a principal faces and a decision that a principal makes. In the first mode, which Bridges labels *announcing*, the principal takes a course of action and reports it to teachers. In another, the *testing* mode, the principal makes a tentative decision, presents it to teachers for their reactions, and makes the final decision. A third possibility is the *soliciting* mode. The principal solicits suggestions about possible courses of action and then selects a solution. The fourth mode is *delegating*. Here, the principal provides teachers with the opportunity to work on the problem and to make a decision about it. The teachers' decision determines the course of action taken.

One problem with the participatory model is that it has not been typically conceptualized in easily measurable terms. Only ambiguous results have been produced from attempts to measure the association between modes of participative decision making among principals and school outcomes (e.g., Conway, 1984), regardless of the school indicators chosen. Modes of participative decision making were also examined in relationship to staff morale and satisfaction (e.g., Hoy and Miskel, 1987). Morale and satisfaction were, in turn, viewed as determinants of staff motivation and consequently of school productivity (e.g., Mitchell et al., 1987). Participatory models may not be as realistic as some would expect because of such barriers as standard operating procedures in the schools and unequal time distribution between principals and teachers (e.g., Firestone, 1977).

With these and other current views of the principalship in mind, our aim in this chapter is to summarize a study of participative decision making in elementary schools. In this study we wanted to observe and inquire about participative decision making, specifically focusing on how principals elicit decision participation from teachers.

STUDY DESIGN

We investigated connections between the conceptual world of participative decision making and the real world of principal/teacher interactions. By documenting the nature of principals' everyday contacts with teachers, we hoped to describe accurately how participation decisions were actually made in the school. Our central research question was: What can be learned about teacher participation in schoolwide decision making by observing and recording the attributes of principals' interactions with teachers? We had five secondary research questions in mind:

1. What is the scope of the interaction between teachers and principals?
2. Do teachers (actors) share equally in the decision-making process?
3. What issues are the focus of joint decision making?
4. What are the parameters of the joint decision making and who decides on these parameters?

5. What are the variations among schools with respect to joint decision making?

In addition to observing and documenting principal/teacher interactions, we were also interested in principals' perceptions about these interactions. Accordingly, we added the following two research questions: What can be learned from postobservation interviews with principals about their perception of their use of teacher participation in schoolwide decision making and its relationship to their teachers' job satisfaction and morale? and How do principals' responses to interview questions compare with their actually observed interactions with teachers?

All aspects of this study were designed to test the assumption that participative decision-making practices are an integral part of present-day principal/teacher interactions. With the subtle, loosely coupled nature of schoolwide decision making (e.g., Weick, 1976), our research was conceived to include numerous aspects of principals' interactions with teachers. We felt that only by carefully observing and recording *all* situations of principal/teacher interaction could the components of decision making be detected and categorized. No attempt at decision-making analysis or categorization was made during the *actual* observations. In this way, bits and pieces of a decision-making puzzle and its situational context could be pieced together and analyzed *en toto*. Often teacher participation in schoolwide decision making could not be deciphered until that point.

Answers to the research questions of this study are thus based on firsthand observations of principals' interactions with teachers. A second aim of the study, however, was to delve into personal perceptions and ideals concerning decision making among principals. This aim was achieved with the aid of a structured interview, conducted near the end of the two-day observation period. The same four questions were asked of every principal during an interview, which averaged about 25 minutes in duration.

The first question was "How do you see yourself using participative decision-making practices with teachers on schoolwide issues?" It was hoped that a principal's response would reveal two things: (1) Was the principal aware of the attributres of participative decision making as expressed in the literature? and (2) Had this principal attempted to apply any of these concepts to his or her everyday work with teachers?

Second, principals were asked if they saw themselves interacting most frequently with a select group of teachers. The aim here was to test the proposition that teachers in a school can be categorized according to their decisional involvement. Third, in asking principals how they process a teacher's idea when initially presented to them, we were trying to map the extent to which a principal's sense of mission carries over into teachers' decisional involvement. Finally, by asking how all of this affects teachers' morale, we wanted to determine how principals view the outcomes of these decisions.

We compared the responses to these four questions to the findings of our observations during the two-day visit. The purpose of this was to connect the conceptual world of participative decision making to the real world of principal/teacher interaction.

Two forms of pilot work were conducted to determine the exact nature, sample size and makeup, and duration of the observations. A series of three unstructured interviews were conducted with three principals all working in the same district in California. The focus of each question was on the principal's initial processing of information from teachers. All three of these principals admitted to a very selective use of participative decision making, an art felt to be practiced and refined.

To determine the size and makeup of the sample and the duration of each observation period, two one-day observations were undertaken with four principals serving in two other districts. After these initial observations, it was determined that a sample size of 12 to 14 principals each followed in a two-day observation period would be optimal. The time, duration, setting, and substance of each work activity was to be recorded in the log with the structured interview held near the end of the second day.

Time restraints required the observer to do all observations during the summer months. Four central and southern California school districts were chosen with long-established year-round systems, where it was business as usual during the months of June, July, and August of 1986. The sample of 13 principals included 11 who were coping with large minority populations of students and their attendant needs for bilingual instruction.[1] One principal served in a small unified central district, whereas the last principal served in another central district with a considerably higher socioeconomic class of students.

During each two-day visit, the observer sat in the principal's office as inconspicuously as possible to record all work activity, then shadowed the principal on- and sometimes off-site to record all activities engaged in outside the office.[2]

A well-rounded sample was selected, with individuals varying according to race, sex, years of experience, and school setting.[3] All 13 principals observed were open, cooperative, and proud of their work, often filling the observer in on the background of each work situation. For purposes of confidentiality, each principal was identified by a single letter, A through M.[4]

The hundreds of topics of principal/teacher interactions observed fell into one of 14 topic categories: student affairs, curriculum planning, evaluation, scheduling, testing, personnel administration, student programs and assemblies, social pleasantries, materials and supplies, the physical plant, personal matters, information requests, personal planning, and public relations programs and events.[5]

Teachers with repeated contacts with the principal during the two days were compared with the remaining teachers on the staff to yield differences in decisional status among teachers. Schoolwide topics discussed between principals and teachers were defined by their relevance to individuals and school programs beyond the individual teacher's own classroom.[6]

FINDINGS AND DISCUSSION

We summarize our findings in five brief sections: (1) the scope of the practice of participative decision making, (2) the actors involved, (3) the issues with which the practice deals, (4) the parameters of the interaction, and (5) the variation among schools. When appropriate, we provide possible interpretations of what we found. At times we also relate the findings to earlier studies.

Scope of the Interaction

Our study found a limited practice of participative decision making on schoolwide issues among these principals. Table 1 depicts data about principal work time in contact with teachers (Hajnik, 1988). Even though principals averaged 22 percent of all their work time in contact with teachers, a majority of these contacts centered on matters of concern to the individual teacher only (e.g., a personal matter concerning the teacher, a concern associated with a specific student in the teacher's class). As can be seen from Table 1, these principals were found to spend *an average of 9 percent of their total work time interacting with teachers regarding schoolwide issues.* As can also be seen in the table, though comprising only 16 percent of the total number of interactions, schoolwide topic discussions averaged *40 percent* of all principals' *work time* in contact with teachers.

Of 777 topics of principal/teacher interaction observed over the 26-day period, 98 topics, or 13 percent of the total, were found to concern a broader population than the individual teacher and

Table 1 Principal Work Time in Contact with Teachers

	Work Time in Teacher Contact	Instances Re: Schoolwide Issues	Total Teacher Contact Time Re: Schoolwide Issues	Total Principal Work Time in Teacher Contact Re: Schoolwide Issues
Variation among Principals	10%–39%	7%–25%	19%–65%	3%–16%
Mean	22%	16%	40%	9%

his or her own students. Again, it must be emphasized that in close to 90 percent of all occasions of interaction, these principals and teachers spoke of matters of individual concern to the teacher.

Of the four modes of participative decision making outlined by Bridges (1977) (announcing, testing, soliciting, delegating) and discussed earlier, these 26 days of observation revealed an inverse relationship between a mode's placement along this continuum of participation and the frequency of its use by principals. In over 50 percent of these cases these principals most often simply "announced" their schoolwide decisions to teachers during faculty meetings or small group discussions. The "testing" of a principal's decisions for teacher reaction was the second most frequently employed method of participation, in almost 20 percent of the cases, again at faculty meetings where the principal did most of the talking.

"Soliciting" was a method of participation occasionally used by these principals, in less than 10 percent of the cases, and several broad generalizations can be made regarding its use. Soliciting, or meeting with a teacher to suggest some possible courses of action, was done informally, either one-on-one or in small groups holding casual conversations in the teachers' room. It was observed most often among more experienced principals, women principals, or among principals of smaller schools.

During the 26 days of observation, no instance of a principal "delegating" a schoolwide decision to an individual teacher or to a group of teachers was observed. Principals' actions and interview responses revealed outright delegation to be a very rare consideration, and one undertaken only in areas having a direct impact on the teachers' work with students. Never was a desire expressed to narrow teachers' zone of indifference in schoolwide areas.

Barnard (1938) stated that an administrator's key responsibilities often fall within subordinates' "zone of indifference" where administrative decisions do not appear to be questioned by teachers. However, decisions made outside this zone must be based on clear, forthright communication. Our research shows that these ideas are as valid for today's principals as they were for Barnard's executives in 1938. The data show that teachers in the 13 schools were initiating schoolwide topics as often as were principals (Hajnik, 1988). However, once such decisions are opened up to include some teachers, these teachers' zone of indifference become narrowed, and administrative compromise and bargaining skills become more necessary.

These principals were most often found to be resisting this phenomenon (e.g., including teachers in the making of decisions with schoolwide implications) by both design and circumstance. The ideal of holding regular discussions between the principal and teachers about schoolwide issues often did not materialize. Principals had to deal with pressing and immediate needs. Formal ideals of equitable staff relations, often expressed by these principals in their interview responses, did not always conform to the operative everyday goals, which reflected the actual tasks performed by the principals in their offices and the teachers in their classrooms.

Observations of these principals' contacts with teachers revealed a traditional orientation to the nature of their respective roles in the school. The topic of most interaction in 11 of the 13 schools was student affairs. Problems and successes with individual students are still the subjects of most concern when principals and teachers get together. However, the data from this study reveal that principals and teachers spend most of their time apart. Some observers (e.g., Hanson, 1979) may view the relatively infrequent interaction observed here as a sign of mutual trust and interlocking spheres of influence between the two role incumbents.

Actors

Another purpose of our study was to detect evidence to support the contention that teachers do not share equally in the decision process. To glean such evidence, the data were scrutinized to find teachers who interacted with the principal at least twice during the two-day observation period. The substance of these teachers' repeated interactions was then analyzed to detect schoolwide issues.

There is a definite predominance of these teachers' involvement in the 98 schoolwide topics observed. Of all schoolwide issues, a full 64 percent were discussed with teachers seen as repeaters during the two-day observation period. This heavy incidence of certain teachers' schoolwide involvement is shown at 11 of the 13 schools visited.

Specialist teachers were seen as repeaters on almost 30 percent of all occasions of principal/teacher schoolwide contact. These individuals included bilingual, resource, counselor, and speech teachers. Since most of these teachers served a population of children from throughout the school, one might surmise that they would adopt a more global perspective of the school, giving them a more common ground for interactions with the principal. These teachers were also free or in the office more often during certain periods of the day.

The research focus is often brought to the issue of time. The availability of certain teachers to the principal and their involvement with a wider population of students create more possibilities for interaction. Teachers with administrative aspirations and teachers experiencing difficulties in the classroom were also more likely to be seen repeatedly.

During the postobservation interviews, 8 of the 13 principals spoke about interacting with certain teachers as a "natural thing." One principal worded his response in no uncertain terms. He said, "To be philosophical, an effective principal forms an alliance with the top 25 percent of your teachers. These alliances are formed one-on-one. The whole group would blow up in your face." Another principal put it very succinctly: "The Prima Donnas—powerful teachers, excellent teachers—can be stepping on each other to get to the top. If you can tap that power, it's a great locomotive for education."

Since these strong teachers often assume a leadership role among a faculty, it is essential for a principal either to develop a harmonious, like-minded working relationship with them or to quell their expression of schoolwide opinions through transfer or a change in their behavior. Many principals said they do not wish to transfer or change the behavior of certain strong, vociferous teachers on their staffs. In fact, as their comments reveal, some principals view these teachers as among their best. Many principals admitted to seeking such teachers' input on a range of schoolwide topics requiring decision making.

Such decisional involvement of key teachers usually takes place on the principal's terms and turf. If there is a common thread running through this involvement of a select group of teachers in schoolwide decision making, it is a sharing of goals and common ideas as to what makes a good school. As one principal remarked, "Some teachers are naturally more comfortable around the boss." Their seemingly inconsequential, friendly exchanges of pleasantries and interaction might lay the groundwork for more frequent one-on-one interaction on schoolwide issues. Johnston and Venable (1986) found that elementary teachers respond more to such a personal relationship of consideration with the principal than to the joint involvement in decision making. Thus, pleasantries and personal interest play an important role in generating trust and influence between the principal and certain teachers.

Issues

The data of this study yielded a strong relationship between a schoolwide issue's relevance to direct classroom instruction and the amount of principal/teacher participative decision making witnessed regarding that issue. Of the 11 categories of topics found to include schoolwide issues, curriculum planning accounted for 30 percent of these interactions. Curriculum planning also required 34 percent of all principal/teacher contact time regarding schoolwide issues. This is evidence of teachers' primary orientation to the instructional program and the student. Of all schoolwide topics, the planning of overall curriculum for the school has the most direct bearing on the affairs of the classroom and the individual teacher.

Personal planning and personnel administration topics came next in frequency and accounted for an average of 19 percent and 17 percent of all schoolwide interaction time, usually in the context of formal staff meetings. Details of orientation, inservice training, teacher responsibilities and duties, and school rules were all ironed out at these meetings. It must be noted again that even though all staff meetings observed focused on schoolwide matters such as these, and teachers were encouraged to speak up, the principal actually did most of the talking.

Another commonly discussed schoolwide category was special student programs and assemblies. There was a good deal of participative decision making going on between the principals and teachers of four of the schools as to the exact nature of these programs. Once again, teachers were most extensively involved in an area of direct and immediate benefit to their students. Indeed, 25 percent of all teacher-initiated topics concerned the affairs of students. No other category came close to this percentage, materials and supplies at 13 percent being a far distant second.

Overall, student affairs and rules was the next most commonly initiated schoolwide topic among teachers, but not among principals. Curriculum planning was the most often initiated schoolwide topic among both groups. This situation indicates a general tacit agreement among principals and teachers that these two areas require a good deal of give-and-take participative decision-making interaction.

Three topics were rarely initiated by principals or teachers on a schoolwide basis: personnel evaluation policies, schoolwide concerns for materials and supplies, and schoolwide general information exchange. It is significant that all three of these topics were very popular on an individual basis of concern for principals and teachers.

Many principals stated unequivocably during the interview that their involvement of teachers in schoolwide issues was dependent on the situation and its relevance to the teacher's classroom situation. The data verified the reality of this contingency approach many times. The most frequently discussed schoolwide topics were curriculum planning, personnel planning, and special student programs. The traditional concerns of management, such as personnel evaluation, budget, the physical plant, and public relations, were rarely discussed with teachers on a schoolwide basis. All principals said they consult teachers at least occasionally, but as one principal said, "The tough decisions are mine."

The absence of testing from the list of schoolwide topics is a bit of a surprise. The only explanation for this that can be offered is that all teachers observed seemed to take individual, district, and state testing requirements for granted, as a necessary fact of life in the schools, just as they accepted formal evaluation procedures. This is a prime example of two topics proven in this research situation to be well within teachers' zone of indifference.

Thus, in choosing to become involved, or conversely in being invited to participate in only certain types of matters, teachers' participation in schoolwide issues was observed as being restricted to those issues most closely associated with the teachers' role in the classroom and the affairs of students. Principals, on the other hand, were often using the precepts of participative decision making as a mechanism to establish a social credit line or as a reciprocal arrangement of social exchange within the school (e.g., Gouldner, 1960; Blau, 1964). This is the "buy-in" mechanism so often spoken of by these prinipals.

When used skillfully, participative decision making can thus be of mutual benefit to principals and teachers in specific areas of mutual concern. Participative decision making can be used effectively to increase the authority and power of both principals and teachers in a few very specific areas (e.g., Dornbush and Scott, 1975; Pfeffer, 1981).

Parameters

We found the involvement of certain teachers in schoolwide decision making to be a very selective process that is outlined by the principal. We also found teacher involvement to be the exception rather than the rule. By broadening the scope of the data to include all work activities engaged in by each principal, it can be revealed that these principals were actually making the majority of schoolwide decisions alone, without teacher input. This finding in itself is extremely significant to any study purporting to focus on participative decision making.

Each principal was observed to have a particular style or slant toward school improvement, with many commonalities across the sample. Participative decision making was often seen by these principals as a very effective teacher "buy-in" mechanism for the principal's chosen school focus. The term *buy-in* was used rather consistently throughout the sample as a perceived benefit of participative decision making.

During the interview, each principal was asked the following question: "When an idea is initially presented to you by a teacher, how do you process the idea according to your own agenda for the school?" Five mitigating factors were mentioned with some consistency throughout the sample. Cost was a primary consideration for many. If there was insufficient funding available to carry out an idea, these principals would veto it. Time was a critical factor for many. The teacher, not the principal, must be willing to put in the additional hours to make an idea work. Another factor often mentioned was the track record of the individual teacher suggesting something. Many principals spoke of the importance of determining whether the teacher was speaking for his or her own needs or for the needs and wants of many teachers on the staff. Five principals mentioned one last important consideration in supporting a teacher's idea, "Does the idea agree with my own agenda for the school?"

Although some minced words more than others, all 13 principals openly admitted that they do process, filter, or channel ideas from teachers according to their own personal agenda. Most would encourage a teacher to try a new idea only if it passed many of the principal's preconceived requirements for a "good idea." Many specific examples were recorded in the log to illustrate the complexities of the initial processing of teachers' ideas according to each principal's own mindset for the school. Both positive and negative examples were recorded to emphasize the point that, for a variety of reasons, principals do not always choose to play the "good guy" in sponsoring a teacher's idea or carrying out a teacher's schoolwide suggestions.

One principal summed up the viewpoint of many of his sample peers concerning the parameters of participative decision making by stating, "The broader the base of the decision, the more positive the effect on morale. The more specific the issue, the more potential there is for frustration. You have to know when to take something back." Another principal explained her feeling on the moderate effects of participation: "There is an interesting balance here. A staff wants to be, yet they don't want to be, involved. They don't make decisions as much as they offer suggestions on ways to improve and make their job easier. I probably make the decisions. Their part is that they share in looking at the problem and making suggestions. I choose one of those and run with it. The simple fact that we sat down together and they had input before I ran with it is a definite factor in their morale."

These 13 principals were all observed to be making very conscious decisions regarding when and where to make themselves available to teachers. This in itself may be an effective technique for channeling the timing and amount of teachers' participative decision making. Only when direct relevance of a situation coincided with teachers' expertise in the affairs of the classroom or students was there much participative decision making solicited. A great deal of give-and-take discussion in this area indicates teacher participation in decision-making territories known to be of primary concern to them. Perhaps these correlations are the best indicators found here of healthy teacher morale.

Variation among Schools

We found two factors that may affect principal/teacher interaction on schoolwide issues: school size and the nature of the student population. Some conjecture as to the effects of school size and the nature of a school's student population may be made after examination of these data. First, the size of the school was found to have a discernible effect on the amount of a principal's work time spent in contact with teachers regarding schoolwide issues. The principals of the two smallest schools (both women) spent 16 percent and 13 percent of their work time in this fashion, well above the average of 9 percent. In contrast, three of the four principals in the largest schools spent much less than 9 percent of their total work time in contact with teachers regarding schoolwide issues.

As a possible explanation for this phenomenon, a principal of a small school may know the capabilities and personalities of his or her fewer teachers much better than the principal of a large school, who may be in charge of 40 or more teachers and who may be relying on an assistant principal to handle staff relations. The familiarity found within a small staff may breed a willingness to listen to more teachers' ideas concerning the school program. The principal of a small school is also simply more available and accessible to teachers. All of these factors do combine to produce a noticeable difference in the overall climate of large versus small schools.

When asked what effects participative decision making might have on teacher morale, five male principals serving in larger schools felt its practice had only a slight impact on their teachers' morales. They mentioned other more important factors such as district policies, personal evaluation philosophies, and the physical condition of the plant.

Such gradations in attitude among principals were also detected when the socioeconomic status of a school's student population was examined more closely as an intervening variable. The largest schools in the sample also served far more low-income students than the smaller schools. The highest incidence of principal-initiated evaluation topics, as well as the lowest regard for participative decision making as a factor in teacher morale, occurred in these schools. These principals regarded the improvement of student achievement, as reflected by test scores through higher-quality instruction, as a major thrust of their principalship. The intentions of two of these principals were in sharp contrast with those of the principal who served in the most affluent neighborhood of the sample.

This principal, one of the highest initiators of special student programs and pleasantries, had a model school with very high test scores and many gifted students. He stated several times that he did not need to worry about the quality of instruction at his school. He rated almost all his teachers as outstanding and initiated an evaluation topic only on one occasion. Thus, the nature of a school's student clientele, rather than the relative skill of its teachers, may have the most effect on the incidence of principal-initiated evaluation topics and the effects of teacher participation on morale.

Thus, two closely related variables found to influence the nature of principal/teacher contact and the role of the principal were the size of the school and the socioeconomic status of the school's student population. The principals of the smaller schools spent more time interacting with teachers than the principals of the larger schools. The larger schools of this sample were also serving more students of a low socioeconomic status than the smaller schools.

The enormous expenditure of resources and time required to educate and serve disadvantaged students in a large school employing a large staff was found to have a significant impact on the nature of principal/teacher interaction and the principal's role as evaluator. The pressure to improve student achievement in the face of overwhelming odds showed up most in two principals of large inner-city schools, each initiating fewer schoolwide topics with teachers and many more evaluation topics than the other principals in the sample.

In the face of these observations, it can be postulated that the socioeconomic status of a school's student population may be the most powerful variable influencing the nature of a principal's interactions with teachers and consequently also teacher participation in schoolwide decision making. Energies may become so focused on the enhancement of student achievement and the improvement of low test scores that most interactions with teachers on schoolwide and evaluation issues are colored by this socioeconomic factor.

CONCLUSION

The research described in this chapter uses evidence about what principals do within a context of participative decision making and also about what principals say about what they do. The research used evidence gathered from observations of 13 principals during only two days. Clearly, two days in the context of an entire school year represent only a small fragment of the character and culture of a principal's work life over time. The evidence gathered from interviews with the principals provided an augmentation of this small fragment. The study does not claim to have captured all but only some of what exists in participative decision-making practices in elementary schools. Nor does it aspire to prescribe a best method for such practices.

Nonetheless, this is compelling research because it captures phenomena associated with participative decision making as they occur. It does so without any preconceived notions as to what might have happened earlier or what might happen later in relationship to a given participatory phenomenon. The volume of the evidence is large. It includes over 300 pages of notes logged during two days of continuous observations of 13 principals' interactions with teachers.

The findings show participative decision making to be less central to the principals' interactions with teachers than some of the literature would lead us to expect. While normative standards of labor relations in the schools of the 1980s (e.g., McDonnell and Pascal, 1988) might dictate considerable teacher involvement in schoolwide decision making (e.g., Education Commission of the States, 1986; National Education Association, 1986; National Governors' Association, 1986), there are numerous operative constraints on principals and teachers alike toward such involvement. In-depth interviews of these principals found them to be acutely aware of many oft-cited benefits of participative decision management, yet ever ready to rationalize its practical limitations.

Participative decision making was typically viewed by these principals in relation to organizational goal achievement. Most of them felt participative decision making to be most useful and effective when employed as a mechanism to achieve greater joint decision making between teachers and principals.

The study has generated findings that may be summarized by the following key general points regarding participative decision making as observed in these schools:

1. Its practice is very limited with regard to schoolwide issues.
2. It may involve only a small group of teachers.
3. It may focus on only certain types of issues.
4. Its parameters may be decided by principals.
5. Variation in it may be a function of the size of the school and the nature of the school's student population.

Clearly, at this point, the findings can be viewed as tentative only. More extensive observations and interviews in the field can reveal much more than we have found about labor relations practices in the schools. If associations are found between such practices and outcomes of schools, then participative decision making can be conceptualized as a significant determinant of school productivity. Until such time, the least we could do would be to weed out counterproductive practices that may be wasting those precious resources of time and energy needed to properly educate young children.

Endnotes

1. These individuals included 8 serving in one central district, whereas 3 were in one large metropolitan southern district.
2. Over a period of 26 days of continuous observations, the observer was excluded on only 3 sensitive occasions.
3. In this way, if modal performance was discovered, the effects of these variables could be discounted. If significant variations were found, effects of these variables could be analyzed.
4. Nine of the principals were male. Their mean age was 51 years old, and their mean experience in education was 21 years, with 8 years being the mean experience as a school principal. Of the 13 principals, 11 served schools with an Hispanic majority of students, as is typical in many large southern and central California districts. The average school size was 609 students, with an average of 24 teachers serving on the faculty. Comparable demographic data on elementary school principals reflect similar means, attesting to a certain representativeness of this sample.

5. These same topics were treated according to those initiated by the principal and those initiated by the teacher to yield information regarding which topics are of most concern to each group.
6. Principals' work time devoted to interactions with teachers on these schoolwide issues was analyzed according to the percentage of total principal work time spent in teacher contact, the percentage of total interaction topics observed found to include schoolwide topics, the percentage of total principal/ teacher contact time regarding schoolwide issues, and the percentage of a principal's total work time actually spent in teacher contact regarding these schoolwide issues.

   The initiator of schoolwide topics was tracked along with the setting, time of day, and number of teachers per instance of contact. The data were also divided according to the relative formality or informality of the occasion and the duration of each teacher contact.

   Interview responses were analyzed along a continuum of participative decision-making components. These schoolwide topic interaction analyses and the descriptions pertinent to their surrounding circumstances have been pulled from over 300 pages of work activity notes in the log.

References

Barnard, C. (1938). *The functions of the executive.* Cambridge, MA: Harvard University Press.

Blau, P. M. (1964). *Exchange and power in social life.* New York: Wiley.

Bolman, L. G., and Deal, T. E. (1984). *Modern approaches to understanding and managing organizations.* San Francisco: Jossey-Bass.

Bridges, E. M. (1967). A model for shared decision making in the school principalship. *Education Administration Quarterly, 3* (1), 49–61.

Conway, J. A. (1984). The myth, mystery, and mastery of participative decision making in education. *Educational Administration Quarterly, 20* (3), 11–40.

Dornbush, S. M., and Scott, R. (1975). *Evaluation and the exercise of authority.* San Francisco: Jossey-Bass.

Education Commission of the States. (1986, July). *What next? More leverage for teachers?* Denver: Educational Commission of the States.

Estler, S. E. (1988). Decision making. In N. J. Boyan, (Ed.), *Handbook of research on educational administration.* New York: Longman, pp. 305–319.

Firestone, W. A. (1977). Participation and influence in the planning of educational change. *Journal of Applied Behavioral Science, 13* (2), 167–187.

Gouldner, A. W. (1960). The norm of reciprocity: A preliminary statement. *American Sociological Review, 25* (2), 161–178.

Hajnik, S. R. (1988). *Principal/teacher interaction: Participative decision making in practice.* Unpublished Ph.D. dissertation, University of California, Santa Barbara.

Hanson, E. M. (1979). *Educational administration and organizational behavior.* Boston: Allyn and Bacon.

Hoy, W., and Miskel, C. (1987). *Educational administration: Theory, research, and practice.* New York: Random House.

Johnston, G., and Venable, B. P. (1986). A study of teacher loyalty to the principal: Rule administration and hierarchical influence of the principal. *Educational Administration Quarterly, 12* (4), 4–27.

McDonnell, L. M., and Pascal, A. (1988). *Teacher unions and educational reform.* Santa Monica, CA: Rand.

Mitchell, D. E., Ortiz, F. I., and Mitchell, T. K. (1987). *Work orientation and job performance.* Albany: State University of New York Press.

National Education Association. (1986). *Ventures in good schooling: A cooperative model for a successful secondary school.* Reston, VA: National Association of Secondary School Principals/National Educational Association.

National Governors' Association. (1986). *Time for results: The governors' 1991 report on education.* Washington, DC: Center for Policy Analysis, National Governors' Association.

Noblit, G. W. (1986, Summer). The legacy of education in the social sciences: The case of organizational theory. *Issues in Education, 4* (1), 42–51.

Pfeffer, J. (1981). *Power in organizations.* Cambridge, MA: Pitman.

Weick, J. (1976). Educational organizations as loosely coupled systems. *Administrative Science Quarterly, 21* (4), 1–19.

Chapter Seven

In a natural extension of Chapter 6, participatory decision making is viewed as central to school-site management efforts. Conley and Bacharach suggest, however, that school-site management will not automatically guarantee a paradigmatic shift in school management. Schools, as they are currently managed, frequently conform to bureaucratic modes of management. Architects of school-site management will depart from this model only if they assume that teachers are professionals. The success of school-site management will greatly depend on the degree to which administrators allow teachers to make decisions and experiment in their classroom practices, without necessarily fearing the consequences of failure. School-site management must primarily foster the creation of a participatory and organic community of professionals.

From School-Site Management to Participatory School-Site Management

Sharon C. Conley
University of Arizona

Samuel B. Bacharach
Cornell University

In this second wave of school reform, the concept of school-site management has caught the attention of researchers, policy makers, and practitioners. In 1987 task forces of the National Governors' Association called for developing "school-site management" that respects the professional judgment of teachers (National Governors' Association, 1987). Similarly, the Carnegie Task Force (1986) called on local school districts to find ways of "giving teachers a greater voice in [school] decisions" (p. 57). A National Education Association report maintained that "site-based decision-making programs offer opportunities for local associations." In this context, these reports strongly emphasized the value of teachers participating in an expanded agenda of decision making at the school site (Glasman, this volume; Guthrie, 1986; Mertens and Yarger, 1988).

School-site management, however, will not guarantee that the same bureaucratic strategies for managing teachers will not emerge in the second wave of reform. For school-site management to succeed, it must be developed with the specific goal of creating a professional work environment for teachers. Without this goal, school-site management may become just another bureaucratic mode of control in the guise of reform. Indeed, school-site management alone does not guarantee administrative decentralization. Although it may be a response to the overcentralization of

This chapter is a revised version of an article that appeared in *Phi Delta Kappan*, March 1990. Adapted with permission.

reform, school-site management cannot reverse this trend without a participative managerial strategy. Even today, many schools that fit the criteria commonly ascribed to school-site management (e.g., decentralization of resources) are managed by one person: the principal (Glasman and Hajnik, this volume). Thus, the issue is not simply how to achieve school-site management but how to achieve collegial and collective management at the school level.

The recent support of school-site management by politicians, policy makers, administrators, and teachers indicates that they may not all view school-site management identically. Or is school-site management simply an umbrella of such size as to be operationally irrelevant? The purpose of this chapter is twofold: first, to examine the notion of school-site management as a thematic concern for school-based control and, second, to incorporate the strategic questions that must be asked to assure that school-based control will also mean schoolwide participation.

SCHOOL-SITE MANAGEMENT: A NEW PARADIGM OR A NEW METAPHOR?

School-site management, as popularly discussed, does not represent a paradigmatic shift in the management of schools and school districts. At best, it is a subtle variation on an old theme. Indeed, it can be more appropriately labeled a newly popularized metaphor than a new phenomenon. Clearly, the current concern with school-site management developed largely in response to the centralized spirit of the first wave of reform. Implicit in this concern was the notion of avoiding centralization.

It is important, however, to draw a distinction between *de facto* (actual) and *de jure* (by law) school-site management. Although there are some parameters in which schools are restricted in their decision making (such as budgetary decisions), for the most part, the managerial decisions currently being made in school districts are already being made at the school level. School administrators are accountable to districts, and districts, in turn, are accountable to states; the argument is that within the broad context of accountability, management does occur *de facto* at the school level. Therefore, in current discussions of school-site management, a *de facto* truth is being codified into a *de jure* truth, and we are attempting to structure something that occurs informally into something that occurs formally.

Unfortunately, this informal structuring of schooling all too often operates according to bureaucratic modes of management (Darling-Hammond, 1986). In this context, we should avoid defining the key issue of school-site management as the decentralization of decisions about resources, since schools with such a system may also have a site administrator who centralizes decisions (i.e., operates bureaucratically). Thus, the central issue in school-site management is not simply decentralization of resources but management through the participation of the school system's professional staff. Indeed, Caldwell (1987) suggests that while early school-site management was narrowly perceived in terms of budgetary and other resource concerns, it has increasingly become focused on the creation of team management and staff involvement in decision making.

Such a conception of school-site management has three critical components. First, successful school-site management consists of the delineation of a strategic plan for the decentralization of resources that is consistent throughout the district and is participatively developed by staff. Second, school-site management implies a school decision-making structure where teachers identify the "line" problems and the resources that are necessary to solve these problems. Third, the middle echelon of the school (e.g., the assistant principal and department heads) becomes the advocates, boundary spanners, and negotiators with principals on behalf of teachers. The principals, then, make the decisions regarding how resources are best allocated within organizational constraints and also act as advocates for additional resources on behalf of the entire school.[1]

These three components are based on the assumption that the central issue in school-site management is the creation of a participatory environment for the management of professionals. However, an important distinction must be drawn between two modes of participation: (1) traditional collective bargaining and (2) participatory decision making. Under traditional collective bargaining, administrators and school boards negotiate with teachers as peers. Traditional collective bargaining, although capable of resolving broad strategic issues (e.g., teacher salaries or class size), is not flexible enough for resolving daily management decisions. For daily school governance, participatory decision making retains the basic relationships among administrators and teachers but incorporates a process of advice and consent. The creation of a participatory structure, however, is dependent on management's view of teachers as professionals. It is to this issue that we turn in the next section.

SCHOOL-SITE MANAGEMENT AND PROFESSIONAL TEACHERS

In implementing school-site management, administrators must recognize that they are managing professionals, and that organizational success thus depends on cooperation and exchange of information with these professionals. Therefore, the first obstacle to a successful school-site management program is not structural but cognitive. The success of a school-site management program will first and foremost depend on how administrators view teachers.[2]

In this regard, administrators' managerial strategies are based on their beliefs regarding the control of uncertainty. That is, given that an organization's success depends on its ability to cope with and process uncertainty (March and Simon, 1958; Perrow, 1961; Thompson, 1967), administrators must determine the extent to which their subordinates control this process. This is particularly true in organizations (such as schools) where primary "line" employees are professionals, that is, individuals who are trained to cope with uncertainty (Hall, 1969). All too often, however, the strategy of leaving professionals in control of uncertainty is diametrically opposed to the administrator's desire for centralized control and coordination. Therefore, it may be posited that only when administrators hold the belief that their subordinates are "line" professionals who can successfully deal with the critical uncertainty the organization must manage, will administrators be willing to establish a participatory managerial strategy.

Specifically, in schools, the degree to which administrators create a participatory structure will be affected by the administrators' perceived dependence on teachers (Bacharach, Bamberger, and Conley, 1988). That is, only if administrators believe that the knowledge, the work, and the decisions made in contact with the students are under the control of teachers (and administrators thus depend on teachers for that knowledge) will they adhere to a participatory managerial philosophy. A participatory managerial philosophy is embedded, then, not in benevolence nor in effects to co-opt the subordinate professionals, but in the following three beliefs concerning teachers and their work:

1. *The primary control of pedagogical knowledge should be left to teachers.* Does the administrator believe that pedagogical knowledge is delineated for teachers, or does the administrator view pedagogical knowledge as something created by teachers as professionals? One recent study found that, more than other pro-

fessionals, teachers rely on written materials and data they develop themselves to carry out their work activities (Shedd and Malonowski, 1985). Research on reflective teaching also suggests that teachers continuously refine and adapt their pedagogical knowledge over time and that this is the essence of professional activity (Carter and Doyle, 1987; Fenstermacher, 1987).

Contrary to these notions, however, administrators often believe that they can best delineate the pedagogical knowledge teachers use (Bacharach and Conley, 1989). When they hold such beliefs about their ability to delineate pedagogical knowledge, administrators implement bureaucratic school-site managerial strategies designed to specify and control the knowledge teachers use in executing their primary function.[3] However, when administrators believe that teachers are the primary holders of critical pedagogical knowledge, they implement professional school-site managerial strategies that reinforce the allocation of pedagogical control to teachers.

2. *Teaching activities are nonroutine.* Do administrators believe teaching tasks are routine and uniform or nonroutine and variable? Studies consistently suggest that teaching activities are variable since the needs of clients (students) vary and are constantly changing (Doyle, 1986; Shedd and Malanowski, 1985).

Administrators who believe that the relationships between teachers and students lack variation will tend to bureaucratically manage and standardize teachers' work at the school site. On the other hand, administrators who view teaching activities as demanding variation will implement professional school-site managerial strategies, creating conditions for innovations, experimentation, and countering standardizing tendencies.

3. *The teacher's primary work activity is decision making.* Do administrators believe that teachers are professional decision makers, or do they believe that teachers primarily carry out the decisions of others? Studies of classroom management and decision making suggest overwhelmingly that teaching is fundamentally a process of making decisions in situations that are highly unpredictable and interactive in nature (Jackson, 1968; Lortie, 1975; Mosston, 1972; Doyle, 1986). Some observers suggest that teachers constantly make choices between dichotomous alternatives (Metz, 1978); others cast teachers as dilemma managers who fashion innovative solutions to problems stemming from conflicting objectives (Lampert, 1985). These various perspectives on teaching are consistent in that they cast teachers as professional decision makers and problem solvers.

The first wave of reform demonstrated that administrators, at times, view teachers not as decision makers but as bureaucrats or "paper pushers" (Conley, 1988). Administrators who hold this belief bureaucratically delineate steps and procedures for teachers to use in carrying out their work. If, however, school-site administrators cognitively define the work of teaching as decision making, they are more likely to specify goals or outcomes for teachers rather than delineate detailed procedures. In this case, administrators recognize that the success of school-site management depends on teachers' abilities to cope with uncertainty and make appropriate decisions. Thus, when teachers are viewed as professionals who must deal flexibly with problems, school-site administrators will allow teachers to deal flexibly with classroom situations. Success of school-site management, then, will depend on the degree to which administrators allow teachers to take calculated risks without necessarily fearing the consequences of failure.

ORGANIC AND MECHANISTIC SYSTEMS OF SCHOOL-SITE MANAGEMENT

In discussions of school-site management, a distinction should be drawn between an organic, or participatory, managerial philosophy and a mechanistic, or bureaucratic, managerial philosophy (Burns and Stalker, 1961). In organizations such as schools, there is an inherent tension between the professional ethos (which maintains that the management of uncertainty should be left to the autonomous discretion of professionals) and bureaucratic values (which maintains that administrators control uncertainty through the specification of rules and use of clear lines of authority). The tension between these two models is constantly negotiated between teachers and administrators and sometimes resolved in favor of professionals and other times resolved in favor of administrators (Bacharach et al., 1988).

In school-site management, the participatory or organic model simply suggests that what is true for the school is true for the classroom. According to the participatory model, the arguments that justify increased autonomy in decision making at the school level are exactly those arguments that justify the enhanced professional autonomy of teachers. Just as the administrative decisions of the district will be improved if they consider those involved in the schools' decision-making processes, the administrative decisions of schools will be improved if they include those who work in classrooms. However, since schools are, at best, fragile political coalitions (Pfeffer and Salancik, 1983), each decision must be considered strategically, examining its implications for all the key parties. Therefore, we must examine the strategic questions that must be weighed before implementing a participatory structure for school-site management.

STRATEGIC CONSIDERATIONS FOR TEACHER PARTICIPATION IN DECISION MAKING

Successful school-site management implies a structure of participative management that considers teachers as professionals. If districts implement school-site management but site administrators adhere to a bureaucratic mode of management, schools will not develop into the flexible and innovative organizations that are clearly intended in the reform reports. It is only through the participation of all professional colleagues that school-site management will truly be successful. Without such participation, the power to make decisions may well be decentralized to the school level, but the information that legitimizes these decisions will be limited and thus result in school-site management being no more successful than any other system of centralized control.

This notion of a participatory and organic community of professionals is linked to the earlier discussion of how administrators view teachers. If administrators view teachers as professionals who exercise primary control over pedagogical knowledge, deal with a high degree of uncertainty, and make numerous decisions in their work, administrators will feel that they need to utilize fully teacher input in schoolwide decisions. That is, teachers' input will be seen as something administrators cannot afford to do without. In this sense, administrators will feel that they require the information teachers possess to make effective managerial decisions.

It is important to point out that several forms of participatory decision making have traditionally existed in schools and have been an effective means of changing the influence structure of school organizations (Corcoran, 1987). These traditional forms include, among others, teacher committees, departmental structures, and team teaching. However, traditional structures such as committees have been criticized for limiting the input of teachers to formulating basic policy decisions (Conley, Schmidle, and Shedd, 1988). We might view newer participatory structures implicit in school-site management as structures that do not constitute totally new approaches but address the weaknesses of previous approaches.

In structuring new forms of participation, four strategic questions appear critical: In which decisions will professional teachers become involved? Who will make what decisions in school-site management? What are the basic tasks of teachers and administrators within the context of decentralized decision making? What is the role of teacher organizations in school-site management?

1. *In which decisions will professional teachers become involved?* Although it is (relatively) easy to obtain general agreement among various actors in school systems (e.g., teachers, their representatives, and administrators) that teachers, as professionals, should be more involved in making decisions, we need to specify those decision areas in which teachers will become involved.

One method of addressing this question is to examine those areas in which teachers report that they desire increased participation. Research on teachers' working conditions (Bacharach, Bauer, and Shedd, 1986; Shedd, 1987; Mohrman, Cooke, and Mohrman, 1978) suggests that teachers clearly want the most influence over *operational classroom decisions* that include such decisions as what to teach, how to teach, and the selection of textbooks. Teachers are least desirous of influence on *strategic organizational decisions* that are clearly outside the classroom realm, such as staff hiring and budget decisions. However, the decisions in which teachers feel most deprived (as measured by the difference between how much influence teachers would like to have versus how much influence they actually have) are those that address the *strategic-operational interface*, or the interaction between the school and the classroom (Shedd, 1987). Put another way, strategic-operational interface decisions regulate the perimeters of teachers' classroom activities and "constrain" teachers' decision making (Conley et al., 1988). These include decisions about how children are assigned to classes, how teachers are assigned to classes, and how students are disciplined and promoted. Indeed, Shedd (1987) suggests that district administrators most often set specific policies in these areas. This raises the question of whether, in the context of school-site management, districts may creatively devolve some of these strategic-operational decisions to the school level.

2. *Who will make what decisions in school-site management?* Besides delineating specific decision areas in which teachers might become involved, a second consideration is how much influence teachers have with respect to decisions affecting other parties in the school (e.g., students and administrators). One way to con-

ceptualize this is to develop a two-dimensional matrix with groups of actors on one dimension (e.g., students, teachers, teacher representatives, local administrators, central office administrators, and the school board) and types of decisions on the other—operational classroom decisions (e.g., how to teach, what to teach), strategic school decisions (e.g., curriculum, budget, personnel [transfers, hiring, and tenure]), and strategic-operational interface (assignment of students, assignment of teachers, discipline policies, promotion policies). The question is how much influence does each party think it should have on each type of decision?

For example, teachers may feel that they should have a great deal of influence on the assignment of teachers to classes but that school administrators should retain the final authority for such decisions. School administrators, on the other hand, may feel that teachers should have very little influence on this decision. To take another example, administrators may feel that it is their prerogative to supervise teachers closely, assuming sole authority for their evaluation. Teachers and their representatives may feel that peer groups should influence the evaluation process.

These types of conflicts, of course, are at the heart of the tension between the professional ethos and bureaucratic values. To be successful, school-site management implies structuring a process by which negotiation and conflict resolution can occur concerning the amount of influence each party exercises on decisions.

3. *What are the basic tasks of teachers and administrators within the context of decentralized decision making?* Principals have two "core" functions—they are coordinators of organizational resource allocation and reinforcers of organizational values. In this sense, they are instrumental and expressive leaders (Bennis and Nanus, 1985). The assistant principal and department heads carry out linkage functions in the school site, linking the teachers, students, and principals. They also carry out critical support functions, keeping the principal apprised of what is occurring in the school, and providing teachers, often on a daily level, with resources and assistance. Teachers carry out primary delivery activities, providing services on a daily basis to clients (i.e., students).

As stated earlier, school-site management implies a decision-making structure where teachers identify the "line" problems and the resources that are necessary to solve these problems. The middle echelon of the organization (assistant principal and department heads) becomes advocates on behalf of teachers with the principals. The principals, then, become decision makers with regard to the acquisition and allocation of resources within organizational constraints as well as advocates for resources to the upper echelon of the organization on behalf of the school.

One consideration in structuring teacher participation based on the tasks of teachers is the basis of teacher expertise and professional identification. If teachers view their task expertise in terms of their grade level and subject matter, those teachers should probably participate in many decisions that span school boundaries (interorganizational decisions). However, if teachers perceive their task expertise in terms of their clientele (students), those teachers should probably participate in school-level (intraorganizational) decisions. It is likely that elementary school teachers primarily view their expertise in terms of their clientele, whereas secondary teachers primarily view their expertise in terms of subject matter (Bacharach, Bauer, and Conley, 1986). School districts might strategically consider these different orientations in structuring school-site participatory structures.

4. *What is the role of teacher organizations in school-site management?* Clearly, the involvement of teacher organizations is a key strategic issue to consider in structuring systems of teacher participation. It would be all too easy to maintain that, because unions negotiate districtwide contracts, contracts will "tie the hands" of administrators to manage their school site and prohibit them from engaging in the participatory managerial strategies outlined earlier that are critical in school-site management. To this end, unions are viewed as a potential obstacle to professional teachers' involvement in decision making.

Johnson's (1984) study of school districts in New York state, however, showed that, in practice, principals and teachers constantly make exceptions to the contract. Her evidence suggests that it was the contract that actually gave teachers a way of enforcing their own participation in decision making (Shedd, 1988). Prior to collective bargaining, a principal could exercise decision making without involving teachers. With the advent of collective bargaining, however, the contract provided teachers leverage to be involved in decision making. This leverage is based on teachers possessing the option to file a grievance and enter arbitration. Thus, the contract gives teachers a mechanism for ensuring that principals exercise the kind of flexibility in their decision making with which teachers agree.

Furthermore, as discussed earlier, we must realize that collective bargaining and participation in decision making are simply two forms of participatory management. One need not preclude the other. Indeed, they would seem to complement each other, one allowing for involvement in more strategic matters, the other allowing for involvement in issues related to day-to-day school governance.

Thus, it is not exclusively the contract that has forced rigidity in school management. Although on the surface this appears to be the case, in fact, rigidity is also due to two types of managers. The first is the manager (principal) who does not want to make decisions and who uses the phrase "the contract will not let me do it" or "my hands are tied by the contract" as a shield. The second is the principal who does not want to involve teachers and so leaves teachers who wish to participate with little choice but to file a grievance. Again, there is rigidity in such a situation, and the rigidity is partly due to the teacher and the union, but it is also due to the principal's failure to involve the teacher in decision making.[4]

Johnson (1983) demonstrated quite clearly that when there is a willingness on the part of principals to involve teachers in decision making, principals and teachers actively make exceptions to contracts because they are making joint decisions. Union negotiations at the district level do not translate into inflexibility. Rather, a principal's flexibility in school-site management depends on his or her willingness to use a participative or organic managerial strategy and to negotiate changes with his or her professional staff.

CONCLUSION

Current discussions of school-site management must consider the specific relationships that must emerge between teachers and administrators for school-site management to succeed. Recent reports clearly suggest that schools should redesign managerial structures and processes to integrate teachers more fully into school decision-making processes, but we have yet to specify how this will occur.

In outlining strategic questions, we have tried to underscore the need for administrators and teachers to think strategically about implementing school-site management. For example, it is unclear how school-site management, which is based on decentralized notions, will be reconciled with programs from the first wave of reform (e.g., merit pay and career ladders), which are primarily top down in form. Unfortunately, it may well be the case that although academics and researchers are busy discussing school-site management as a basic metaphor for the second wave of reform, school boards and district administrators are still busy implementing the centralized changes suggested by the first wave of reform. The problem that exists for all members of the educational community is how to reconcile the strengths of these earlier suggestions with the participatory management being heralded by the reformers of the second wave. The strategic issues considered in this chapter should hopefully assist in the resolution of this problem.

Endnotes

1. Although this may seem to contradict the notion of teacher identification of necessary resources, it is no different from quality circle operations where line staff make recommendations, but upper echelons retain final decision-making power.
2. A parallel line of research demonstrates that how teachers view students (their belief systems) influences their teaching strategies in classrooms (Richardson, 1988).
3. One way of delineating this knowledge is through detailed job descriptions.
4. The authors are indebted to Joseph Shedd for this point.

References

Bacharach, S. B., Bamberger, P., and Conley, S. (1988). *The see-saw metaphor and managing professionals.* Unpublished paper, Cornell University.

Bacharach, S. B., Bauer, S., and Conley, S. C. (1986). Organizational analysis of stress: The case of secondary and elementary schools. *Journal of Work and Occupations, 13* (1), 7–32.

Bacharach, S. B., Bauer, S., and Shedd, J. (1986). The work environment and school reform. *Teachers College Record, 88* (2), 241–256.

Bacharach, S. B., and Conley, S. (1989). Uncertainty and decision-making in teaching: Implications for managing line professionals. In T. J. Sergiovanni and J. H. Moore (Eds.), *Schooling for tomorrow: Directing reforms to issues that count.* Boston: Allyn and Bacon, pp. 311–329.

Bennis, W., and Nanus, B. (1986). *Leaders: The strategies for taking charge.* New York: Harper & Row.

Burns, T., and Stalker, G. M. (1961). *The management of innovation.* London: Tavistock Publications.

Caldwell, B. J. (1987, March). *Educational reform through school-site management: An international perspective.* Paper presented at the 1987 conference of the American Educational Finance Association, Arlington, VA.

Carnegie Forum on Education and the Economy's Task Force on Teaching as a Profession. (1986). *A nation prepared: Teachers for the 21st century.* Washington, DC: The Forum.

Carter, K., and Doyle, W. (1987). Teachers' knowledge structures and comprehension processes. In James Calderhead (Ed.), *Exploring teachers' thinking.* London: Cassell, pp. 147–160.

Conley, S. C. (1988). Reforming paper pushers and avoiding free agents: The teacher as a constrained decision-maker. *Educational Administration Quarterly, 24* (4), 393–404.

Conley, S. C., Schmidle, T., and Shedd, J. B. (1988). Teacher participation in the management of school systems. *Teachers College Record, 90* (2), 259–280.

Corcoran, T. B. (1987). *Teacher participation in public school decision-making: A discussion paper.* Working paper prepared for the Work in America Institute, mimeographed.

Darling-Hammond, L. (1986). A proposal for evaluation in the teaching profession. *The Elementary School Journal, 86* (4), 531–551.

Doyle, W. (1986). Classroom organization and management. In M. C. Wittrock (Ed.), *Handbook of research on teaching.* New York: Macmillan, pp. 392–431.

Fenstermacher, G. (1987). A reply to my critics. *Educational Theory, 37,* 413–421.

Guthrie, J. W. (1986, December). School-based management: The next needed education reform. *Phi Delta Kappan,* 305–309.

Hall, R. H. (1969). *Occupations and the social structure.* Englewood Cliffs, NJ: Prentice-Hall.

Jackson, P. (1968). *Life in classrooms.* New York: Holt, Rinehart & Winston.

Johnson, S. M. (1984). *Teacher unions in schools.* Philadelphia: Temple University Press.

Lampert, M. (1985, May). How do teachers manage to teach: Perspectives on problems in practice. *Harvard Educational Review, 55,* 178–194.

Lortie, D. (1975). *Schoolteacher: A sociological study.* Chicago: University of Chicago Press.

March, J. G., and Simon, H. A. (1958). *Organizations.* New York: John Wiley & Sons.

Mertens, S., and Yarger, S. J. (1988). Teaching as a profession: Leadership, empowerment and involvement. *Journal of Teacher Education, 39* (1), 32–37.

Metz, M. H. (1978). *Classroom and corridors: The crisis of authority in desegregated secondary schools.* Berkeley: University of California Press.

Mohrman, A. M., Cooke, R. A., and Mohrman, S. (1978). Participation in decision making: A multidimensional perspective. *Educational Administration Quarterly, 14* (1), 13–29.

Mosston, M. (1972). *Teaching: From command to discovery.* Belmont, CA: Wadsworth.

National Education Association. (1988). *Employee participation programs: Considerations for the school site.* Washington, DC: Author.

National Governors' Assocation. (1987). *Time for results: The governor's 1991 report on education.* Washington, DC: National Governors' Association, Center for Policy Research and Analysis.

Perrow, C. (1961). A framework for the comparative analysis of organizations. *American Sociological Review, 32,* 194–208.

Pfeffer, J., and Salancik, G. R. (1983). Organization design: The case for a coalitional model of organizations. In J. R. Hackman, E. E. Lawler, and L. W. Porter (Eds.), *Perspectives on behavior in organizations.* New York: McGraw-Hill, pp. 102–111.

Richardson, V. (1988). *Teachers' beliefs about at-risk students.* Paper presented at the annual meeting of the American Educational Research Association, New Orleans.

Shedd, J. B. (1987). *Involving teachers in school and district decision-making.* Manuscript prepared for the State Education Department, the University of the State of New York, Organizational Analysis and Practice.

Shedd, J. B. (1988). Collective bargaining, school reform and the management of school systems. *Educational Administration Quarterly, 24* (4), 405–415.

Shedd, J. B., and Malanowski, R. (1985). *The work of teaching.* Ithaca, NY: Organizational Analysis and Practice.

Thompson, J. D. (1967). *Organizations in action.* New York: McGraw-Hill.

Chapter Eight

The high-stress environments of urban high schools require especially high teacher dedication. From studies in 11 such schools, Firestone finds that there is more than one kind *of teacher commitment. Some teachers are committed to transmitting knowledge of a particular subject, others are committed to their students' social and psychological development, and still others try to balance their academic and social commitments. Teachers with differing commitments tend to account for student failure differently and to respond differently to school reform attempts. The level of both teacher and student dedication varies among schools, depending on the quality of relationships among the staff, administrative support, expectations for teachers, and staff influence. Teacher commitment can be increased incrementally by paying attention to these factors. However, more fundamental restructuring of urban high schools may be required to make a real difference in teacher commitments to their work and students to schooling.*

Increasing Teacher Commitment in Urban High Schools: Incremental and Restructuring Options

William A. Firestone
Rutgers University

Teaching has been described as a low-commitment occupation (Lortie, 1975). Teachers choose their careers late, they drop in and out of the occupation throughout the life cycle, and they may combine teaching with second jobs. Yet, urban high schools with their poor attendance, high dropout rates, low achievement, and high frequencies of violence and vandalism seem to require especially high commitment (Ekstrom, Goertz, Pollack, and Rock, 1986). Typically, the teachers who work there either leave quickly (Bruno and Doscher, 1981) or suffer from extreme burnout—that is, a sense of entrapment that affects preparation for lessons, relations with students, and absenteeism (Dworkin, 1987).

Teacher commitment affects efforts to improve urban high schools since undercommitted teachers contribute to students' problems and limit efforts to reform those institutions. Teacher commitment is influenced by school characteristics that school and district administrators can change but also by the fundamental mismatch between the ideal of the comprehensive high school and the realities of urban student achievement. Important improvements can be made by incrementally changing school characteristics, but major structural changes will be necessary to address this mismatch. After examining the nature and consequences of teacher commitment, this chapter will identify factors that reduce that commitment and then suggest changes that are likely to enhance teacher commitment.

TWO STUDIES OF URBAN HIGH SCHOOLS

This chapter is based on two studies of urban high schools. The first is a case study of Monroe High School,[1] a small-city high school implementing strategies to cope with a state-mandated minimum competency testing program (Rossman, Corbett, and Firestone, 1988). The school had about 800 students of whom 70 percent were black and 25 percent were Hispanic. Because the school had gone through a period of contraction and staff reductions, most teachers had over ten years' experience in the building. I spent approximately 30 days in the high school interviewing staff; observing in classrooms, corridors, and staff rooms; shadowing administrators; and attending such events as staff meetings and parent-teacher nights. Using a very open-ended approach, I interviewed 57 of the 82 teachers and all five administrators.

The second study grew out of the first. It examined teacher commitment in ten high schools: two each in Baltimore, Newark, Philadelphia, Pittsburgh, and Washington, DC (Firestone, Rosenblum, and Webb, 1987). Each district was asked to pick two urban comprehensive high schools with similar student bodies, one of which reflected the most difficult problems of these schools. The schools were middle sized with a poor, minority population. The median school size was 1,553 with three smaller schools having less than 1,100 students and two very large ones with over 2,500. In seven schools 75 percent or more of the students were black, and in eight schools 40 percent or more received a free lunch. In six schools where data were available, average daily attendance was low, ranging from 72 to 85 percent.

I was part of a team of researchers who spent three days in each building. We interviewed 35 people in each school. Individual interviews were conducted with the principal, two assistant principals, and a counselor. In addition, interviews were conducted with groups of three to four teachers in English, mathematics, social studies, science, and vocational programs; with two groups totaling four to six department heads; and with at least 12 students. These interviews were open-ended with questions generally specified in advance.

THE NATURE AND IMPORTANCE OF TEACHER COMMITMENT

Most definitions of commitment go beyond an affectively neutral exchange of services for rewards to a less rational, more emotional involvement (Etzioni, 1961). For instance, Buchanan (1974, p. 533) defines commitment as "a partisan, affective attachment to the goals and values of an organization, to one's role in relation to goals and values, and to the organization for its own sake apart from its purely instrumental worth." The common theme is the creation of a psychological bond between the individual and the larger system. As a result, the committed person is expected to believe strongly in the system's goals and values, comply with orders and expectations voluntarily, be willing to exert considerable effort—well beyond the minimum expectation—for the good of the system, and strongly desire to stay a part of it (Kanter, 1968). To understand the importance of teacher commitments, it is important to clarify both the specific commitments teachers make and the consequences of those commitments.

Specific Commitments

There is sometimes a tendency to measure the strength of commitment without being clear about its object (Salancik, 1977). Studies often focus on an object of interest to managers or policy makers, like commitment to one's employer or occupation. Yet, people become committed to such diverse things as spouses, hobbies, and specific work objectives. They may be committed to the employing organization but also to their department, their colleagues, and their specialty. The fine-grained nature of these commitments and the way they interact are often important.

In urban high schools, teachers' commitments to teaching and students are separable but interrelated in important ways. Commitment to teaching leads to a sense of fulfillment from exercising craft skills. Sometimes this satisfaction comes from the reaction one sees to a lesson and sometimes from the respect of other teachers, as these comments from teachers in the 10 high schools indicate:

> Teachers want to stay here because they can teach. They want to come back.
>
> [A good day is] when the students learn. There's a good discussion, a challenging discussion. When you test and everyone does well.

Commitment to students comes when teachers get a personal response from students that makes them feel that their work is worthwhile:

> I stay because of the feedback I get from the students I helped. I like to help students. There are times I touch somebody.

> I'm helping students. Just the one or two who say they wish I were teaching geometry.

Interactions with students can also reduce commitment:

> [A bad day is] when you think you're really cooking and they say, "Can I go to the bathroom?" When you look into their eyes and you can see clear out of the backs of their heads.

To assess how the 10 high schools varied on teacher commitment to both teaching and students, the site-visit teams were asked to rate each school on both kinds of commitment.[2] A comparison of school ratings showed that commitment to teaching and to students vary together. (The Kindall's tau—a nonparametric measure of association—for the two variables is .63.)[3]

In fact, teacher commitments are often more specific than to teaching and students. An understanding of microcommitments in each area clarifies the link between the broader commitments. These microcommitments were explored in Monroe High School. There, some teachers were committed to teaching because they found the subjects inherently interesting and enjoyed working on the more challenging issues in the secondary curriculum, saying:

> I enjoy calculus. I can work out Algebra II problems without doing the homework. I *have* to do the problems in calculus. I enjoy the refresher. . . . When I get the answer right, I feel like the kids do.

> I enjoy teaching classical literature because I enjoy it, and I think educated kids need it.

Others were committed more to the psychological development of their students. They wanted to develop students' self-esteem or socialize them to appropriate behavior.

> I work with their self-feelings. I want to drop History II [for special education students] and do more to prepare them for jobs. A lot of these kids don't think they're important. That's bad.

> I think social studies should be about behavior. If I saw my students hassling another teacher, I'd talk to them about their behavior. We talk about behavior a lot.

In between was a group of teachers who balanced academic commitment with a concern for student development. This appeared in a concern to see that the students in the class learn the material, whatever it is:

> Geometry is my favorite. . . . [Another teacher] doesn't like geometry 'cause teaching proofs is tough to these kids. I don't get frustrated. I have tremendous patience.

These microcommitments with their definitions of what constitutes appropriate teaching went along with teachers' openness to low-achieving students. The academic teachers were least patient with low achievers, lamenting a bygone age when the school had its fair share of "real A students." These teachers were most impatient with students who lacked the intellectual preparation for their courses:

> Why should we remediate what should have been taken care of in elementary school? They shouldn't be here if they can't read and write.
>
> You should be able to take things for granted that you can't. When I put the formula, area equals length times width, on the board and assume that students know what I mean when I substitute in numbers, I can run into problems.

They also complained about student behavior:

> Most of them can do the work. They're immature. . . . There are certain stories some of them like, but their habits are chronic. . . . Chronic laziness. They pick and choose what they like.
>
> Attendance is another problem. A lot of kids don't come to school. School is not a priority.

Other teachers objected to these same behaviors, but the academic teachers were the most angry and least willing to treat such behavior as conditions to be worked on rather than prerequisites for high school instruction.

These observations illustrate how the microcommitments that teachers make to teaching affect their commitments to students. Those who adopt a more academic definition of their work generate standards that most urban students cannot meet and believe that these standards should be met *before* students arrive at their classes. Standards are high, but these teachers do not believe it is their job to help students who cannot meet them. Teachers who are more socialization oriented or who balance academic and socialization commitments can respond to behavior that does not meet their preferences more flexibly. Depending on their field, a few even prefer working with lower-achieving students, saying, "I see more lightbulbs going off that way."

The Consequences of Commitment

Commitment is policy relevant because it leads to useful outcomes. Generally, the relationship between commitment, work effort, and quality is complex and difficult to sort out (Mowday, Porter, and Steers, 1982). When that relationship is complex and other variables intervene, associations between teacher commitment and student achievement are extremely weak (Dworkin, 1987). Nevertheless, teacher commitment is important for two reasons. It influences student commitment and it affects teacher willingness to implement administratively sanctioned innovations.

Teacher and Student Commitment. In the 10-school study, we examined student commitment to learning. Some students indicate that they take the school's primary activity seriously:

> In [a special program], you can work independently and help plan your courses. You can suggest projects and topics to work on that interest you.
>
> A good day is when you understand the classwork and you know something new at the end of the day.

Others who are alienated from learning find the instructional activity something to be tolerated or opposed:

> I tolerate teachers. I use "passive resistance" and sleep through class.
>
> A good day is when it goes fast and I get out of here.

Across the 10 schools, the association of student commitment to learning with teacher commitment is high. (Kendall's tau is .78 with commitment to teaching and .77 with commitment to students.)

Interviews from the 10 schools and observations at Monroe High School clarify the relationship between teacher and student commitment. Where teachers' commitment is low, they often blame students' low achievement on their family backgrounds or lack of adequate building and district support (Metz, 1986). By shifting responsibility to others, teachers justify their continuation of valued patterns of behavior from the past even if they prove dysfunctional in the present.

This blaming occurs in the schools with the lowest teacher commitment. Teachers in these schools complain about how uncooperative students and their families are:

> The white kids don't want to go to school. They say, "My Dad's making more money than you working in the mill," and they want to do the same thing. The black kids come from broken homes with a mother and no daddy.

In fact, most students did come from the impoverished backgrounds associated with low achievement, but that was also true in other schools in the study. What distinguished these schools was the attention teachers gave to that background and their use of it to justify poor performance.

Blaming is the opposite of the more frequently discussed high expectations (Brophy and Good, 1974). Blaming is an attitude that leads to changes in teacher behaviors at both the school and classroom levels. For example, one black teacher at Monroe said the curriculum changed:

> After the school became predominantly black, the curriculum changed. I went to an all-black high school, and they had high expectations for me there. I don't see how come a person doesn't expect the same thing from anyone as a black.

The curriculum was adjusted in part through the selection of texts that were easier to read. In addition, assignments were changed. In the English department, the conceptually oriented term paper was replaced by a term report that required students to report facts on a topic but not make judgments.

Other changes occurred in the classroom. One that I observed directly was insulting students in the classroom. Teachers said things like:

> I hope that if I put the date for the War of 1812 on the test, you'll all get it, but knowing some of you. . . .
>
> Some of you in here still can't plot a graph after we've been doing it for so many days. Some people can't even draw a straight line with a ruler. Would you believe it? Would you believe it!

These teachers were likely to make the more negative interpretation of student behavior when more positive ones were equally possible. Thus, when one student asked how one animal family inherited characteristics from another, the teacher said that the student took the idea of cross-species inheritance "literally," drawing a spirited defense from the student rather than noting the effort to draw connections between the current lesson and what had been taught earlier.

According to students, a second response was cryptic teaching—

that is, failing to explain concepts fully and to make sure that students understand:

> Some teachers give homework and don't ask for it or check it. They just go on to other work. Teachers who care check to see if you understand. They ask if you understand.
>
> A [good teacher] is a person who gives you a picture of what she is saying. Some just take 20 minutes and say, "Do your work." Then they get upset when you get a low grade. The better ones take the time to ask if you have questions.

This response was described in both Monroe and in the 10 high schools.

A third response was to get rid of unwanted students. According to one teacher:

> Some teachers send students down [to the office] for frivolities, things that should be handled in the classroom. You'd be amazed at the things kids get sent down for. . . . Some teachers are proud of it. They say, "I got rid of him fast."

The rate of referrals became so high at one point that the administration held a workshop on handling disciplinary problems in the classroom. Students were not just sent to the disciplinarians, however. They were also sent to the library and the cafeteria and simply allowed to roam the halls. Some left the building.

Watering down the curriculum, insulting students, cryptic teaching, and pushing students out of class not only contributed to poor performance but also gave students a clear message that they were not appreciated. It is not surprising that where these behaviors were typical, students' commitment was also low.

Commitments and Change. Commitments also shaped teachers' reponses to district reform. This was most apparent in Monroe High School where the district had to respond to state-mandated minimum competency testing. When this program began almost 10 years before the study, district students had among the lowest scores in the state. Over the years, scores improved steadily. Increasing test scores became one of the district's top priorities, and a variety of approaches were tried. Two are particularly relevant because they illustrate how teachers with different commitments respond in patterned ways to reform efforts.

The first was a curriculum alignment system that began with

a careful comparison of the school's curriculum to both the achievement tests used in the district and the state minimum competency test. Teachers rewrote the curriculum as a series of objectives geared to the tests. Departments that did not normally teach the minimum competencies were to incorporate activities related to them in the curriculum. A complex monitoring system ensured that teachers followed the whole curriculum. Each quarter they were to complete a quarterly topic plan (QTP), indicating which objectives would be addressed using how much time and what materials by what dates. These were reviewed by supervisors and returned to teachers. As each objective was completed, teachers were to record the number of students who got a C or better on a test related to each objective. In addition, teachers were to complete weekly lesson plans that elaborated the QTP and showed what would happen each day. Classroom observations were used to determine whether teachers were on the schedule in the QTP and if the QTP and the lesson plan coincided with in-class activities.

The administrators' rationale for curriculum alignment was that it ensured that students were introduced to all content on which they would be tested at the end of the year. Teachers who balanced commitments to academics and socialization objected to the strict schedule. They argued that if a student did not master the objective in the required time, more assistance was needed. One explained, "I have a student who can't divide. How do you teach him volume and area? Is it better to teach division or follow the objectives?" These teachers shared the administration's goal of teaching students basic skills. However, they were divided on the means. This division could create friction:

> I don't gear myself to the quarterly. I gear myself to the class. It doesn't matter to me if the date I'm supposed to finish is February 22 and I finish on February 28. If the administration wants to reprimand me, that's their prerogative, but I won't change.

The academically oriented teachers objected to the requirement that they include basic skills instruction in classes not dealing with those skills directly, saying it was "silly" to deal with English basic skills in a Spanish class that was all basic skills. However, their major concern was with what they called "teaching to the test." In the weeks before the competency tests were given, English, reading, and mathematics teachers had students practice taking old tests. When the state switched to a more difficult test, the district bought copies of a practice book developed by a professor in a nearby university. Teachers in those three areas were required to use the book to drill students for a major portion of every day.

The teachers with academic commitments did not view this drill as a legitimate form of instruction, and they objected that the instructional end (passing the test) was inappropriate.

> We aren't teaching them how to think. We're teaching them to take tests.
>
> We're test-oriented here. No teacher objects to that. Our emphasis is too much on some areas though. We spend so much time reviewing grammar in the eleventh and twelfth grades. There should be more reading and developing of thought processes and interpretation skills. Our children aren't being prepared for college in terms of what they read.

In effect, the minimum competency testing focus was pushing the academically oriented teachers to a lower level of cognitive activity than they wanted.

"Resistance to change" has been seen as a major barrier to reform efforts, and viewed as a kind of knee-jerk conservatism on the part of teachers (Giacquinta, 1973). These observations suggest that resistance must be reinterpreted. In part, it can very well be a principled opposition based on deep-seated commitments. Such commitments may be inappropriate in specific instances—as the strong academic commitment was in Monroe—but they are often a product, at least in part, of thought and training. They reflect teachers' honest efforts to do what they consider to be the best job possible.

SOURCES OF TEACHER COMMITMENT

One can approach the problem of teacher commitment by looking for differences in school management that relate to variation in teacher commitment. Such differences do exist and point to ways to increase teacher commitment by managing urban schools better. However, there are limits to this approach. The recurring problems of urban schools suggest that their design is fundamentally flawed and needs to be changed. Evidence is presented here that speaks to both the better management and the restructuring option.

Variation among Schools

Among the 10 schools, four characteristics differentiate those with high and low teacher commitment. The first of these is the *quality of teachers' social relations* with other adults in the school. Teachers are often isolated from both their peers and administrators. Yet, they are more committed when norms and working conditions promote interpersonal attachment. Moreover, teachers learn from each other so their teaching skills develop more with frequent opportunities for interaction (Rosenholtz, 1985). Teachers' relationships with the administration are more ambiguous. They want to maintain enough distance to preserve independence. Yet, since the principal is the only adult in regular contact with them who can appreciate their performance, they would like to have more contact. Overall, the evidence suggests that isolation from administrators reduces commitment (Zielinski and Hoy, 1983).

Among the 10 schools where commitment is low, teachers believe they are not respected. They look for respect from two sources—the building administration and colleagues. Teachers perceive a wide range of reactions from administrators. In one building a teacher reported that "teachers don't get anything from the administration here or uptown that makes them feel important." In another, a teacher reported that "the administration administers this building with love and caring" and made clear that such caring applied to teachers as much as students. This was one of the buildings where teachers were the most committed.

Teachers also prize the respect of and interaction with their colleagues. There is considerable range from one school where teachers complain extensively that colleagues no longer try to maintain discipline, to those with a surface friendliness where teachers report that "We're friendly towards each other, and we always say, 'Good morning,'" to a positive extreme in a school where teachers share about instructionally relevant matters:

> The degree of professionalism here is exceptional. At the school I worked at before, the main topic of discussion was retirement. Here people talk about educational issues. What works. Its intellectually stimulating.

Here too, where teachers are most collegial, commitment is highest.

The second characteristic is *administrative support*, which contributes to teachers' performance and willingness to stay in the field. Teachers identify a number of barriers to their work that administrators can minimize. These include poor discipline, excessive paperwork, disputes with parents, and interruptions to their classroom routine. Consistent application of rules creates a more predictable environment so teachers know how to get things done. It also helps with discipline and reduces role ambiguity (Schwab and Iwanicki, 1982).

The concerns about discipline, rule enforcement, role ambiguity, and fairness in combination provide a sense of consistency in the 10 schools. Fairness is what takes consistency beyond tough discipline. Low consistency occurs when administrators say one thing one time and something else later or when two administrators handle the same event quite differently. A consistent environment is one where order is maintained, roles are clear, and rules are enforced fairly and rigorously, but not harshly:

> Discipline problems are easier now. It comes down from the top here. The fact that the principal makes it a priority is important. He backs up teachers.

There is also a more personalized support that has less to do with consistency than individualized consideration and kindness. Part of the issue here is whether superiors listen to subordinates or simply impose their own way:

> The administration is great. It allows us to be creative. . . . The requests teachers have are looked into and taken to heart. . . . The administration administers with love and caring, and we can still disagree.

Although these administrative actions are especially important, the question of physical support also arises. This includes the quality of both buildings and materials. The buildings in the study range from those that have extensive graffiti, bathrooms with broken fixtures, heating systems that do not function, and roofs that leak, to others that have recent remodeling and are a pleasure to be in. For example, in one school, teachers complained that they only had one complete set of texts so students could not take books out to do homework. In another, a teacher hid the venetian blinds at the end of the school year because, if stolen, they would never be replaced. Yet, in other buildings, laboratories were new and supplies were adequate. Generally, where buildings were well maintained and supplied, teachers were more committed; however, such physical support had less to do with commitment than did organizational consistency and administrative support.

The third characteristic is *expectations for teachers.* When individuals become committed to a performance objective, they will strive to attain it (Salancik, 1977). They will accomplish less when no objective is set or when the objective is too low. However, persistent failure to reach a goal will reduce commitment. The implication of this view is that support ought to be accompanied by a certain amount of stress in the form of high expectations to have commitment to improve performance.

Teachers' expectations of students have been studied extensively. High expectations contribute to student success, often because teachers praise and give more attention to the students they expect to perform at higher levels (Brophy and Good, 1974). Administrative expectations for teachers have been studied less. Still, when a principal holds high expectations for teachers, they should perform better (Wellisch, Macqueen, Carriere, and Duck, 1978).

Expectations vary considerably among the 10 schools. The schools fit into three relatively distinct groups. In most schools there is little pressure for good teaching and student achievement. Sometimes goals are unclear. One principal, when asked about his goals, gave a rambling, ambiguous answer and then said, "You have to excuse me. Its been a long time since I've been asked to think about my goals." Sometimes goals are incomplete, as in one school where a principal stressed attendance without clearly linking it to student achievement.

A second, smaller group tries to create support for instruction. In one school, teachers and administrators agree that "this is a place where teachers can teach" because of the way the school is managed, but there is no special training or pressure for them to teach better. These schools also provide incentives for students who succeed academically. Finally, one school combines strong management and incentives for students with extensive teacher training and inservice programs. These efforts contribute to an unusually high level of reflectiveness and interest in teaching among the staff. Generally, commitment is highest where expectations for teachers are highest.

The final characteristic is *staff influence.* Individuals are most highly committed to jobs that give them autonomy and discretion, partly because they have a sense of making a greater contribution to the organization (Steers, 1977). In education, there has been considerable debate about what kinds of issues teachers want influence over. Although they clearly value classroom autonomy, they are willing to forgo participation in major policy deliberations that take time from teaching (Corbett, Dawson, and Firestone, 1984). Thus, influence over day-to-day decisions rather than strategic choices is most important.

Teachers' lack of interest in major policy decisions is striking in these schools. Teachers rarely discuss the major questions of budget, curriculum, and new programs. Instead, their sense of control is enhanced when they help set a school's discipline code, when they have the support to try new things, and when they can work out their own schedules collectively within their department. Their interest in budgetary issues emerges primarily when they cannot get the materials and supplies they need to function adequately in the classroom.

Nevertheless, opportunity for teacher influence has a substantial impact on teacher commitment. Some schools establish participation structures for teachers in the form of committees or "open-door policies" that encourage teacher consultation with the principal. Low participation is indicated where neither of these is present or where a formal committee is in place, but the principal vetoes all of its decisions.

Moderate participation occurs when the principal circumvents the existing structure or when effective committees are established but teacher input is not well utilized outside those committees. Strong participation structures do not always include special committees. In one school, the principal delegates decisions to the lowest level and gives teachers considerable support for their ideas. Clear opportunities for teacher influence contribute substantially to teacher commitment.

The Common Problem

Although school characteristics contribute to teacher commitment, there are limits to what can be achieved within the structure of the typical urban high school. In fact, teachers and students alike appear trapped in an institution designed with a different clientele and different set of educational concerns in mind. To understand these, it is necessary to turn to the idea of the comprehensive high school.

Originally, the U.S. high school was an elite institution for upper-class children going on to college. First, efforts to standardize the organization of high schools in the 1890s employed a college-preparatory model, even when it was recognized that this would be the final educational experience for many students. Later, vocational and other programs for noncollegiate students were appended to the basic framework (Tyack, 1974). Presently, high schools are staffed by subject-matter specialists in areas like English, foreign languages, mathematics, science, physical education, shop, the arts, and so on. Each teacher may see 150 or more students each day for tightly regulated time periods in order to teach a specified "content area" like world history, remedial English, or Advanced Placement calculus. Students see six or more teachers each day. Personal problems with courses are to be discussed with counselors who are seen even less often than the teachers. This subject-matter specialization and limited personal contact between teachers and students lead to the popular observation that elementary teachers teach students and high school teachers teach subjects.

Moreover, the high school is designed to give students a great deal of choice in what subject areas they will take and therefore what teachers they will see (Powell, Farrar, and Cohen, 1985). Although the amount of choice has been reduced substantially since the 1970s (see Clune, 1988), students, with the advice of counselors, generally have the option of taking a college preparatory, regular, or vocational sequence of courses. This choice further loosens the bond between student and teacher. It contributes to a situation where teachers can say that students "should not be in my class" because they do not have the requisite skills.

One assumption behind the comprehensive high school is that the achievement levels of its clientele will be approximately normally distributed. A few will do college-preparatory work, most will take a "general" track, a few will take vocational courses, and some others will take remedial courses (Conant, 1959). A related assumption is that students will be assigned to tracks that fit their achievement level and that by far the largest proportion will be able to progress through school as a cohort with very few failing a grade or even having to retake a course.

These assumptions do not apply in many urban high schools. The numbers of students achieving at advanced and even average levels are extremely low. Many lack the skills assumed by even the regular high school curriculum. Yet, only modest accommodations to the basic structures are made. In some ways, Monroe High School was unusual in that it had a reading department separate from its English department with a specially trained staff to work with ninth-graders and those who failed the state competency test. Still, in spite of that school's special effort to ensure that students passed the state test, no more than a third of the teachers (including reading, remedial math, special education, and other specialists) were seriously assigned to that task.

The result is a serious mismatch between organizational structure and clientele. Students and teachers deal with this mismatch in different ways, depending on how bad it is. Students who have the greatest academic problems typically drop out (Ekstrom et al., 1986). Those who do not (or have not yet) deny the relevance of the high school curriculum, saying:

> I don't see the purpose of algebra. All you need is English and math. The rest just fills time.

> In English you need to learn to speak and read right, but reading stories is pointless.

These students often question the legitimacy of the educational enterprise as if the game they are losing is not worth playing. Still, these students will accept one standard of relevance—the relationship of academics to future work:

> I'm in a dental technician program. . . . It's pretty relevant. We make dentures and partials. . . . I tell my friends to get in it. They like the pay. It's pretty decent. There's a place in ______ that will start you out at ten dollars an hour.

Students in such special vocational programs see a direct connection between what they are doing and their posthigh school careers that is not apparent when they "read stories" or take algebra.

For teachers, the magnitude of the mismatch between the comprehensive ideal and their students depends on the specific view of teaching to which they are committed. Those with a more academic perspective are the most frustrated. These appear most frequently in the standard college preparatory subjects like English, foreign languages, the sciences, and mathematics. They are the most dependent for their work on the high-achieving students who are disproportionately underrepresented in these schools. Hence, they are the most likely to blame students and engage in behavior that reduces student commitment.

Students who are not committed to the school and who think that it lacks relevance respond in a variety of ways. Many drop out. Others act out, retaliating in little or big ways, from not bringing books to class, to not doing homework, to disrupting the class. These behaviors make a teacher's life even more difficult. What happens, then, is a vicious cycle in which a school with a curriculum and staff prepared for one skill level meets a student body with a different one. Many students become frustrated and do things to make teachers' lives more difficult, so some teachers respond in hostile ways, thereby reinforcing the problem. This vicious cycle can be a major impediment to teacher commitment.

It is important here to comment on the distance between teachers and students created by specialization and frequent class changes. Under existing conditions this distance may contribute to the surface level of decorum that exists in these buildings most of the time. Since a teacher's investment in any student is limited, so is the resulting frustration. Similarly, a student with one blaming teacher is likely to find others who are at least more neutral. However, there is evidence that under some conditions, closer ties between teachers and students can contribute to student commitment and willingness to work, thereby reducing a major impediment to teacher commitment (Wehlage, Stone, Lesteo, Nawman, and Page, 1982).

ADDRESSING THE PROBLEM

Efforts to increase teacher commitment can be made either through incremental attempts to manage urban high schools better or by considering major structural reforms. Both options will be explored here.

The Incremental Alternative

Within the existing structure of urban high schools, a great deal can be done to build teacher commitment. Although the 10-school study did not focus on exemplary schools, it suggests a number of actions that administrators can take to shape the school characteristics that affect teacher commitment. A few are dramatic departures from existing practice, but others are quite mundane. Indeed, many are commonplace in moderately well-run suburban high schools. This is in fact a positive development. It is not necessary to invent new strategies to manage urban high schools better. Instead, the question is one of will and capacity to ensure a sort of equity between urban and other high schools.

Table 1 illustrates some ways to change the school characteristics that shape teacher commitment. These actions can be taken by principals through their daily interactions with teachers and through formal decisions that have long-term consequences for the school's organization. District administrators can also make decisions that affect teacher commitment. Each approach will be discussed separately. Yet, a glance at the table illustrates one important point. Principals have their impact not so much through the big decisions they make as through their day-to-day interaction with staff. The district office works primarily through formal actions.

Through daily behavior, the principal has a number of ways to build teacher commitment. Personal contact with teachers, for instance, is very important for enhancing teachers' sense of respect. The largest school studied had over 3,500 students and over 180 teachers. The principal managed the school through a cabinet of vice-principals and department heads. Everyone understood and accepted the procedures for taking problems to a first-

Table 1 Actions that Promote Student or Teacher Commitment Organized by School Factor

	Principal Microbehavior	Principal Formal Actions	District Formal Actions
Respect	Direct teacher contact with principal who respects teachers. Principal exhibits respect for teachers.	Space for teacher interaction. Events to promote collegiality.	Space for interaction.
Support	Administrative consistency and concern.		Adequate buildings and materials.
Expectations	Principal attention to academics and communication of expectations.	Staff inservice and teacher training programs.	Curriculum alignment and testing programs. Staff inservice and teacher training programs.
Influence	Demonstrated principal belief in shared decision making.	Special committees for teacher input. Delegation of decisions to departments.	Teacher input into curriculum alignment and testing programs.

level official and only bringing to the principal those issues that could not be resolved lower down. However, the department heads who were in regular contact with the principal (and whose efforts he consistently praised) had a greater sense that they were respected and therefore had a greater commitment to the school than did other teachers. As the example of this school indicates, contact must be accompanied by demonstrations of respect and personal consideration. Praise, an elaborate code of politeness, and personalized interaction—all of these things illustrate to teachers that they are not "treated the way we treat some of the kids."

In some schools, demonstrations of respect expand into more concrete forms of support. The absence of such support leads to a bureaucratized environment where the principal is concerned mainly about "when deficiency notices go out, when the forms are due, and with faculty meetings." The positive side of support is reflected in consistency, especially in maintaining order and dealing with staff. In consistently managed schools, where, as one teacher puts it, "the principal is mostly concerned with when teachers know that a particular kind of student problem will be handled the same way every time, that administrators will be fair," teachers will be more committed.

Principals can also exemplify high academic expectations although as a rule they did not. The principals in the schools where commitment was highest appeared to give more attention to building a safe, hospitable, even warm climate than to stressing high academic achievement. In other schools, however, the principal may even have undercut high expectations. In one school, a teacher complained that when the principal brought a visiting dignitary into her room, he did not comment on her teaching, but instead pointed out one of his city all-star athletes in the room. Such behavior sends a clear message to staff.

Finally, principals can enhance teacher influence by demonstrating their own belief in teacher decision making. This is often done by the way individual requests are handled. To one set of curricularly adventurous teachers, it was important that "this is a place where you can try anything you like," where the principal would approve a wide range of individual teacher initiatives.

Principals can also take formal actions that enhance teachers' sense of respect and influence. In fact, observations in the 10 high schools illustrate how principals can do a fair amount to facilitate collegial interaction among teachers. Some make decisions to develop "collegiality structures" or arrangements that facilitate interaction among teachers. First, efforts are at a social level: Christmas and end-of-the-year parties. Others go deeper. In one school where collegiality was limited, the principals held a week-end, off-campus retreat with outside facilitators to build stronger ties, and later rearranged space in the building to increase the number and pleasantness of departmental work spaces. They can also allocate space to help teachers get together by ensuring that there are comfortable teachers' lounges and adequate departmental work spaces. As simple as these things seem, they are very important for giving teachers the chance to get together.

Principals can also establish influence-sharing structures. In one school, the principal rarely makes a major decision without establishing a committee of teachers to study the matter and formulate options. In another, departments, working with vice-principals, establish their own rosters and schedules. Establishing one's own schedule—even through negotiation with others—is a powerful, if mundane, symbol that teachers control their fate.

District actions can reinforce those of the principal. For instance, changing spatial arrangements to give teachers opportunities to interact may require central office assistance. Basic plant maintenance and provision of materials is an important source of support. Leaking roofs and over- and underheated classrooms can be a major distraction. Without enough books, teachers cannot assign homework. Moreover, all of these problems send a not-so-subtle symbolic message about how important the inhabitants of these buildings are to the larger public.

District actions are the predominant source of academic expectations in these schools. The most common form is the district curriculum alignment project. Three of the districts studied have recently developed such projects. These typically include some combination of a common criterion-referenced testing program for students and citywide curriculum development efforts (often linked to the testing program). Where implemented in ways that do not promote teacher-district antagonism, they draw attention to academic concerns. One district accompanied its curriculum alignment project with a massive staff-development program that brought all high school teachers in the district to one school to receive special instruction from a cadre of master teachers. That school was included in this study. The ferment created by the master teachers self-consciously thinking about their own instructional approach added substantially to the commitment to teaching in the school.

Finally, the district can enhance teacher influence. The most extensive experiments in this area are currently being carried out in cities like Miami and Rochester (New York) where new collective bargaining agreements are providing a context for school-based management approaches that have a great deal of promise. Among these 10 schools, the most obvious example of district influence sharing was including teachers when building citywide testing programs. Where teachers believed they were integrated into the planning, they were more accepting of the results.

The incremental option can make a real difference in teachers' commitments to their work, especially when principal and district actions are coordinated. In two or three of the schools visited, teachers were seriously demoralized and often angry about their schools. In the two schools where commitment was highest, teachers exhibited either a strong loyalty to the school and engagement with students or a deep concern about the quality of their teaching. Nevertheless, high teacher commitment is especially rare in urban high schools. For that reason, it is important to consider the restructuring option.

The Restructuring Option

The restructuring option begins with the contradictions of the comprehensive high school organization in the urban setting and suggests that a major redesign is in order. Without such a redesign, the vicious cycles developing between students and teachers will be difficult to break.

This analysis of the problems with the comprehensive high school suggests design criteria from the point of view of both students and teachers. For students, arrangements are needed that enhance their sense that school work is relevant and that they, like teachers, are respected as individuals. Teachers need arrangements that enhance their autonomy and collegial relationships with their colleagues—criteria often recommended by those seeking to professionalize teaching. Some other criteria suggested by this analysis have received less attention. That is, arrangements must be developed that break the self-defeating specialization of high school teachers and put them into closer relationships with students, that in fact make them responsible for student learning rather than subject-matter instruction. This may require changes in the high school curriculum; it will clearly require adjustments in the delivery mode.

These criteria suggest a very different model for the internal organization of high schools. The central element of such a model is to reorganize the high school into small teams that have considerably more cohesion than current departments. As few as three or four teachers might be responsible for 90 to 150 students. The teachers' task might be to get students to some level of learning competence (e.g., from "tenth to eleventh grade level" or even all through high school). Placing responsibility for student progress with the team would enhance collegiality; teachers even with different specialties would be forced to work together. Giving them materials, space, and access to specialists (e.g., counselors, gym teachers, etc.) but removing the constraints of the daily schedule would enhance their autonomy. Even if teachers were subject-matter specialists, the nature of the assignment would focus their attention on the group of students and encourage them to think in broader terms than their areas.

A team structure could also provide the basis for meeting student criteria. Relevance could be provided by authorizing and encouraging the teacher team to organize career-oriented learning opportunities. In fact, teams could be organized around themes that would lead to out-of-class learning activities.

There is no guarantee that such a structural rearrangement will lead to a different quality of respect between students and teachers. However, the long-term coassociation of students and teachers increases the likelihood that the role distance, alienation, and antagonism that now often characterize teacher-student relationships would be reduced. As students and teachers interact in a variety of situations, there is a greater probability that mutual understanding and respect will grow. Such changes are not likely, however, without extensive training and role modeling of new relationships.

Such a team structure is almost unprecedented in "regular" U.S. high schools, both urban and otherwise. Moreover, it runs against the professional subject-matter-based commitments of high school teachers. Thus, this analysis clearly indicates the difficulties in convincing existing teachers to suggest such a major change. A difficult sales job is ahead for anyone who seriously considers it. Nevertheless, there are three precedents for such a change. These precedents provide reason to believe that such a restructuring is feasible and offer concrete guidance on how it should be organized.

One precedent comes from experiments with work redesign in industry (Hampton, Sumner, and Webber, 1978). These include job enlargement, enrichment, and quality circles that create autonomous work groups. Examples include the creation of teams to assemble whole engines and chassis at Saab and Volvo plants in Scandinavia, assignment of responsibility for production planning to groups of electronic instrument assemblers at Texas Instruments, and creating pet food packing units in a General Foods factory. In these and similar cases, work became less boring and more meaningful. These changes, plus the social interaction of team planning, increased commitment. Economic benefits included cost savings, reduced numbers of employees, and higher productivity.

The industrial model of autonomous work groups is applicable to educational settings. It is exemplified by many alternative programs for at-risk youth. Almost all of the 10 high schools had business academies, electronics magnet programs, special music programs, junior ROTC, or some other kind of programs that appeared extremely motivating for the students in them. Studies of exemplary programs for at-risk youth indicate that they,are small, often run by teams of teachers, and provide greater opportunity for interaction between adults and students than regular high schools. These programs "take care of their own." Moreover, the multiperiod schedules and tyranny of the bells are absent. Many programs include an experiential education piece, such as rebuilding a house or an outward bound-type experience (Wehlage et al., 1982). These programs are designed to engage students in the instructional process and are usually evaluated on that basis. However, there are indications in the reports that they have similar effects on teachers.

The problem with these special programs is that they serve so few students. The programs observed in the 10 high schools were frequently drawn to the visitor's attention, but it was clear that only a fraction of the students in any school benefited from them. Can a whole high school be organized on such a basis? A provisionally positive answer comes from a study of exemplary middle schools (Lipsitz, 1984). All these schools divided students into groups of 110 to 155 students with a team of teachers assigned to each group. The length of these joint assignments varied; some lasted for the students' middle school career. According to the author:

> The groups of students are small enough that . . . [teachers] know the students' moods and do not make the interpersonal mistakes that would be unavoidable in large, more impersonal settings. The students are secure in being known, and staff members are relaxed because of their deep familiarity with the students and their confidence in dealing with them. . . . *Antisocial behavior that results from the randomness and brevity of student groupings in most secondary schools is substantially reduced in these schools* (italics in original) (Lipsitz, 1984, p. 182).

Teacher isolation is also reduced. Here again, although the focus is on students, there are indications in the text that modified structural arrangements build teacher commitment as well.

These examples suggest the general value of the team approach for motivating students and teachers. They do not address the problem of student variability. The comprehensive high school assumes an approximately normal distribution of student academic ability. Furthermore, through free-choice options, students can cope with the academic demands of the curriculum. The team approach is recommended specifically because in urban schools large number of students lack the prerequisite skills for the comprehensive high school. These students need instructional assistance, social support, and an understanding of what the payoffs of effort are in order to succeed. Without such assistance, they will continue to act in ways with which teachers in the current system cannot cope. Thus, for low-achieving students such a change may be critical. However, it is quite likely that the same structure with its combination of flexibility and student support would help teachers work with average and high-achieving students as well.

CONCLUSION

This analysis illustrates the importance of thinking of teacher commitments as separate but interrelated. Teachers' commitment to teaching and definition of appropriate teaching have a lot to do with their assessment of and commitment to students. Where teachers are committed to teaching the students they have (rather than some unavailable ideal), they at least avoid the blaming and negative behavior that reduces student commitment. Moreover, the nature of their commitments affects their responses to administratively initiated changes. Changes congruent with those commitments will be most easily implemented with the least conflict.

The sources of teacher commitment are to be found in the world of adults and also in the interaction between adults and students. Adult interactions are what is often referred to as participatory management (see Chapter Seven). This analysis of school characteristics focuses on many of the issues central to that literature like influence, support, and respect (often referred to as affiliation), while adding a concern for high expectations. The 10-school study illustrates that, through a combination of principal microbehavior and district policy, a great deal can be done to change these characteristics in ways that promote teacher commitment. The steps that need to be taken are not tried as often as they should be, but the knowledge of what to do is there. Well-managed urban high schools do not exhibit major surprises.

Less attention has been given to the influence of students on teacher commitment (even though Lortie's [1975] observations on student control of the incentives critical to teachers are now well known). What is striking in some of these schools is the prevalence of vicious cycles where teachers depress student commitment and students depress that of teachers. Although good management can help to break these cycles, the basic structure of urban high schools contributes to the problem. What appears necessary is a new model for high schools that does not try to be all things to all students (like the comprehensive high school) but does do justice to the students who are there. A central element of such a structure should be a more student-centered arrangement based on teams of teachers and students working together for long enough periods of time to get to know each other.

This team approach is congruent with the reformers who are currently interested in professionalizing teaching through such changes as career ladders and merit pay. However, it is likely to appear "soft" to reformers intent on improving high schools by "tightening them up" through higher course requirements and tougher tests. The proposed restructuring violates the public's conceptions of what high schools are supposed to be like as well as teachers' current professional commitments. The political climate may not be right for advocating such a change on a massive scale. Nevertheless, experimenting with such developments appears highly promising. Limited pilots to perfect a team-based approach and identify its strengths are clearly in order.

Endnotes

1. This is a pseudonym.
2. The team met together first to be presented with definitions and to do initial ratings on these and additional variables. Then each team member was given the ratings generated in the meetings and a list of variable definitions and asked to look for justification of the rating in field notes taken during the visit. Often ratings were changed after the review of the field notes. Where raters disagreed by one point on the seven-point scale employed, the two ratings were averaged. Where the disagreement was more than one point, the raters were asked to discuss the reasons for their ratings and reach an agreement on the number. Once this process was completed it was determined that raters agreed on 40 percent of the ratings, differed by one point on 32 percent of the ratings, and by more than one point on 9 percent of the ratings.
3. Where raters disagreed by one point on the seven-point scale employed, the two ratings were averaged. Where the disagreement was more than one point, the raters were asked to discuss the reasons for their ratings and reach an agreement on a number. Once this process was completed it was determined that the raters agreed on 40 percent of the ratings, differed by one point on 32 percent of the ratings, and by more than one point on 9 percent of the ratings.

References

Brophy, J. E., and Good, T. L. (1974). *Teacher-student relationships: Causes and consequences.* New York: Holt, Rinehart, & Winston.

Bruno, J. E., and Doscher, M. L. (1981). Contributing to the harms of racial isolation: Analysis of requests for teacher transfers in a large urban school district. *Educational Administration Quarterly, 17* (2), 93–108.

Buchanan, B. (1974). Building organizational commitment: The socialization of managers in work organizations. *Administrative Science Quarterly, 17* (2), 93–108.

Clune, W. (1988). *Graduating from high school: New standards in the states.* New Brunswick, NJ: Center for Policy Research in Education.

Conant, J. B. (1959). *The American high school today.* New York: McGraw-Hill.

Corbett, H. D., Dawson, J. L., & Firestone, W. A. (1984). *School context and school change.* New York: Teachers College Press.

Dworkin, A. G. (1987). *Teacher burnout in the public schools: Structural causes and consequences for children.* Albany, NY: SUNY Press.

Ekstrom, R. B., Goertz, M. E., Pollack, J. M., and Rock, D. A. (1986). Who drops out of high school and why? Findings from a national study. *Teachers College Record, 87* (3), 356–375.

Etzioni, A. (1961). *A comparative analysis of complex organizations.* New York: Free Press.

Firestone, W. A., Rosenblum, S., and Webb, A. (1987). *Building commitment among students and teachers: An exploratory study of ten urban high schools.* Philadelphia: Research for Better Schools.

Giacquinta, J. B. (1973). The process of organizational change in schools. In F. N. Kerlinger (Ed.), *Review of research in education* (volume 1). Itasca, IL: F. E. Peacock.

Hampton, D. R., Sumner, C. E., and Webber, R. A. (1978). *Organizational behavior and the practice of management* (3rd ed.). Glenview, IL: Scott, Foresman.

Kanter, R. M. (1968). Commitment and social organization: Study of commitment mechanisms in utopian communities. *American Sociological Review, 33* (4),499–517.

Lipsitz, J. (1984). *Successful schools for young adolescents.* New Brunswick: Transaction Books.

Lortie, D. C. (1975). *School teacher: A sociological study.* Chicago: University of Chicago Press.

Metz, M. H. (1986). *Different by design: The context and character of three magnet schools.* London: Routledge & Kegan Paul.

Mowday, R. T., Porter, L. W., and Steers, R. M. (1982). *Employee-organization linkages: The psychology of commitment, absenteeism, and turnover.* New York: Academic Press.

Powell, A. G., Farrar, E., and Cohen, D. K. (1985). *The shopping mall high school: Winners and losers in the educational market place.* Boston: Houghton Mifflin.

Rosenholtz, S. J. (1985). Effective schools: Interpreting the evidence. *American Journal of Education, 93* (3), 352–388.

Rossman, G. B., Corbett, H. D., and Firestone, W. A. (1988). *Change and effectiveness in high schools: A cultural perspective.* Albany, NY: SUNY Press.

Salancik, G. R. (1977). Commitment and the control of organizational behavior and belief. In B. Staw and G. Salancik (Eds.), *New directions in organizational behavior.* Chicago: St. Clair Press.

Schwab, R. L., & Iwanicki, E. F. (1982). Perceived role conflict, role ambiguity, and teacher burnout. *Educational Administration Quarterly, 18* (1), 60–74.

Steers, R. M. (1977). Antecedents and outcomes of organizational commitment. *Administration Science Quarterly, 22* (1), 46–56.

Tyack, D. B. (1974). *The one best system: A history of American urban education.* Cambridge, MA; Harvard University.

Wehlage, G., Stone, C., Lesteo, N., Nawman, G., and Page, R. (1982). *Effective programs for the marginal high school students: A report to the Wisconsin Govenor's Employment and Training Office.* Madison: Wisconsin Center for Education Research, University of Wisconsin–Madison.

Wellisch, J. B., Macqueen, A. H., Carriere, R. A., and Duck, G. A. (1978). School management and organization in successful secondary schools. *Sociology of Education, 51* (3), 211–227.

Zielinski, A. G., and Hoy, W. K. (1983). Isolation and alienation in elementary schools. *Educational Administration Quarterly, 19* (2), 27–45.

PART III

Changing the Teacher Work Environment: Practices and Programs

Chapter Nine

In response to reform proposals from the Holmes Group and Carnegie Forum, some institutions have adopted extended teacher preparation programs combining a four-year bachelor's degree with a year-long clinical internship. Schwab argues that extended programs have many advantages over the traditional four-year program. One advantage may be that such programs prepare new teachers better for the stresses of their work, and thus prevent early burnout. Schwab examines one aspect of a research program evaluating a five-year teacher preparation program at the University of New Hampshire. In this survey study, the author probes for variations in stress levels of intern teachers, their satisfaction with the extended program, and functions of the social support network created through the program. The findings suggest that a support network for intern teachers is better fostered when several placements are clustered in the same school, though, as the author explains, this is sometimes logistically and financially difficult. Research on and political controversy over extended teacher preparation programs seem likely to continue.

Stress and the Intern Teacher: An Exploratory Study

Richard L. Schwab
Drake University

BACKGROUND

Learning to teach is a complex and, at times, stressful process. The problems individuals face in the transition from being a "student of learning how to teach" to being an effective and professional teacher are well documented. Problems that cause stress for student teachers, teaching interns, and beginning teachers frequently mentioned in research are: reality shock (when the idealistic expectations of the new teacher conflict with the realities of classroom life), role conflict, role ambiguity, role overload (too much to do and little time to do it), isolation, and lack of practical training in such areas as discipline and curriculum development (Veenman, 1984; Schwab and Iwanicki, 1982; Corcoran, 1981, 1989; Corcoran and Andrew, 1988; Bullough, 1989). New teachers who are unable to cope with the stresses caused by these problems may experience symptoms of job burnout early in their career. Characteristics of job burnout in teaching include chronic feelings of emotional exhaustion and fatigue, the development of negative attitudes toward students, and a loss of feelings of accomplishment from teaching (Maslach, Jackson, and Schwab, 1986). Research by Schwab and Iwanicki (1982) and Gold (1985) found younger teachers experienced these feelings more frequently than older teachers.

New teachers who experience these negative feelings are likely to be less effective in the classroom and eventually leave the profession. In some cases individuals may decide to stay on the job but detach themselves from responsibility for dealing with the problems they were unable to resolve (Jackson, Schwab, and Schuler, 1986; Dworkin, 1987). In any case, everyone loses—the system, the students, and the new teacher.

A major goal of the reform movement in teacher education is to redesign teacher preparation programs so that teachers are better able to handle these stressors in both their practice and first regular teaching assignments. One of the most controversial reforms advocated to address these problems is the establishment of extended teacher preparation programs (Holmes Group, 1986; Carnegie Forum, 1986). Extended programs (often referred to as *five* or *fifth-year programs*) require the completion of a bachelor's degree in an academic field outside of education and a year-long clinical experience dedicated to mastering the complexities of learning how to teach. To date, many teacher training institutions have expended a great deal of energy debating the virtues of extended programs, but few have abandoned undergraduate four-year programs to adopt them. One reason for the reluctance to change is that many educators argue that little or no research exists to support the contention that extended programs prepare better teachers. It is also argued that such programs will allow only the most financially able students to pursue teaching as a career (Wilkinson, 1989; Howey and Zimpher, 1986).

A research base has evolved over the last few years that has begun to address these concerns. This research has been conducted at the University of New Hampshire by faculty members involved in their Five-Year Teacher Education Program, which was implemented in 1973. Studies by Andrew (1983, 1986, 1990), Corcoran (1981), Corcoran and Andrew (1988), and Oja (1988) have indicated that extended programs have several advantages over four-year programs. One of the more important findings of these research studies is that graduates over a ten-year period have come from more academically talented backgrounds and are more likely to stay in teaching than students in traditional four-year programs (Andrew, 1990).

The UNH program is an integrated program that begins at the undergraduate level and extends into a fifth year. All students must complete broad-based general education requirements, an academic major outside of education, professional coursework, a graduate concentration in a particular area, and a year-long internship in a local school. The Five-Year Program culminates in a master's degree and certification at the elementary or secondary level. Several articles provide an in-depth discussion of the program (Andrew, 1974, 1983, 1986; Corcoran and Andrew, 1988; Schwab, 1990).

The year-long clinical experience (hereafter referred to as *internship*) is the focal point of learning how to teach in extended programs. Experience and research show that the internship has several advantages over the traditional one semester of student teaching. First, there is more time for the intern to learn about teaching through reflection and supervision from the cooperating teacher and university supervisor. Second, interns are assigned a classroom from the start of the school year to the end, thus gaining the opportunity to witness the growth and development of their students over time. A third advantage is that interns have more opportunity to undertake supervised risks and experiment with new ideas since they have a year to prove their competence, not 14 weeks as in the case of student teachers. A fourth benefit is that there is enough time and opportunity to establish more sophisticated clinical supervision models among school-based cooperating teachers and university supervisors. Finally (though I am sure more exist), there is the opportunity to build support networks among interns to help them handle the stresses involved with learning to teach (Andrew, 1990; Corcoran and Andrew, 1988; Schwab, 1990).

Effective support networks are important factors in helping teachers handle job stress. Studies by Dworkin (1987), Schwab, Jackson, and Schuler (1986), and Jackson, Schwab, and Schuler (1986) found that teachers who do not have an effective social support network are more likely to experience burnout. Support networks are groups of people who help the individual by providing emotional sustenance, assistance, resources, and feedback in times of need (Caplan, 1974; Pines, Aronson, and Kafry, 1981). Pines, Aronson, and Kafry (1981) identify six functions that people in a support network serve for the individual:

1. *Listening.* People actively listen without offering advice or making judgments.
2. *Technical appreciation.* People provide appreciation for the work someone does. People serving this function must be seen as experts in the field and they must be seen as honest and having integrity by the individual.
3. *Technical challenge.* People are more knowledgeable about the job than the individual, and challenge the individual to improve and grow in his or her profession.
4. *Emotional support.* People will be on the individual's side in a difficult situation even if they don't agree with the individual. Unlike technical support and challenge, people outside the job can serve this purpose.

5. *Emotional challenge.* People confront the individual when he or she is not doing his or her best or is complacent. Emotional challenge differs from technical challenge in that people do not have to be experts in the field the individual is in; they only need to be trusted by him or her.
6. *Sharing social reality.* People share similar priorities, values, and views.

Social support can emanate from supervisors, coworkers, and people outside of the organization. The UNH Five-Year program has stressed the development of support networks for interns at all three levels. Efforts to build support networks for interns include mandatory peer observation, peer videotaping and analysis, and attendance at a weekly seminar led by the university supervisor. The first half of the seminar concentrates on individual problem solving, which provides the listener with emotional support, emotional challenge, and a shared sense of reality functions of the support group. The second half of the seminar emphasizes what Shulman (1987) refers to as pedagogical content knowledge. During this part of the seminar, the emphasis is on the technical support and challenge functions of the support network. In addition to seminars, university supervisors and cooperating teachers serve various support functions on an individuals basis. Interns are observed in the classroom at least six times a semester and participate in two three-way conferences with the university supervisor and cooperating teacher. To help cooperating teachers develop supervisory skills, the university offers a four-credit graduate course and workshops in clinical supervision specifically for cooperating teachers.

During the 17 years that the Five-Year program has been in existence, several different approaches to organizing the internship and seminar have been tried and either refined or abandoned. Currently, the placement can be broadly classified into two types: cluster placement and noncluster placement.

In the most basic sense, a cluster school has at least three interns, and opportunities are available for both cooperating teachers and interns to meet on a regular basis. Cluster sites offer greater opportunities for developing school-based support networks for both interns and cooperating teachers. They allow both interns and cooperating teachers to build peer support systems on site. In most cluster sites cooperating teachers meet on a regular basis (often during the day while the interns cover their class) to discuss issues relating to the internship and clinical supervision. The university supervisor usually attends these meetings as a resource person and as a link between the university-based teacher education program and the cluster site. At the present time all cluster sites are at the elementary level. Though many of the secondary interns are in schools with three or more interns, they do not meet together or interact on a regular basis. This is because university supervisors have preferred to work with interns in the same discipline. Consequently, interns in the same school will have different supervisors and seminars. Currently more than half of the elementary placements are in cluster placements.

Students who are not in cluster sites are placed in schools within a 45-minute driving radius of campus. Over the 17 years that the internship has been in existence, a good relationship has been developed with a cadre of excellent teachers at these schools, many of whom are graduates of the Five-Year Program. School district teachers and administrators are eager for assignment of interns. In some cases, stipends are offered, thereby providing incentives for attracting the best interns to their schools. Usually only one or two interns end up in these schools. Although these settings make establishing on-site support networks more difficult, the university has been reluctant to abandon the sites and wholeheartedly adopt the cluster concept. As is well known, finding master teachers who are good cooperating teachers is a difficult and time-consuming task. In many cases, trial and error are the only valid ways to identify these teachers.

STUDY DESIGN

The exploratory study reported in this chapter was designed to provide some baseline information on the effectiveness of the internship program. It was developed to determine (1) the interns' levels of stress and satisfaction as they neared the end of their placement; (2) if internship setting, age of the intern, or level of experience of the cooperating teacher had any influence on the levels of stress and satisfaction; and (3) if the type of internship placement had any relationship with the development of an effective support network. Because research is limited in these areas, the focus of this exploratory study was to generate hypotheses for future research and to provide insights that may result in changes to the internship. The general research questions that guided this study were:

1. What are the stress levels of interns as they near the end of their year-long placement? Do levels vary by type of

placement, age of intern, or experiential background of the cooperating teacher?

2. How do interns rate their experiences in the internship as they near completion? Do these ratings vary by age of intern, type of placement, or experiential background of the cooperating teacher?
3. What functions of a social support network do people in the role set of the intern serve? Do cluster placements encourage the development of more effective support networks?

The participants in this study were interns in the University of New Hampshire Five-Year Teacher Education Program during the academic year 1988–1989. The survey was administered in midpoint of the second semester of their internship. Interns were asked to complete the surveys anonymously and place them in a sealed business envelope, which were then returned to the author. Of the 84 interns enrolled in the program, 82 completed the survey, for a return rate of 98 percent. A description of the sample is presented in Table 1.

Table 1 Description of Sample $N=82$

Interns					
Sex		*Age*		*Grade Level Taught*	
Male:	24.4%	Mean:	27.6	Elementary:	52.4%
Female:	75.6%	Median:	24	Middle/jr. high:	13.4%
		Mode:	22	High school:	34.1%
		Range:	21–52		

Experience Level of Cooperating Teacher		
Years of experience as a classroom teacher:	Mean:	14.48 years
	Median:	15 years
	Mode:	15 years
	Range:	3–40 years
Previous experience as cooperating teacher with interns:	First time:	43.6%
	One before:	20.5%
	Two or more	35.9%

The five-page survey contained several questions to determine background characteristics of respondents and degrees of satisfaction with various aspects of the internship. The second section of the survey asked respondents to complete the Maslach Burnout Inventory: Educator's Edition, which is a valid and reliable instrument to measure three aspects of educator burnout: Emotional Exhaustion, Depersonalization, and Personal Accomplishment (Maslach, Jackson, and Schwab, 1986). The final section contained questions adapted from Pines, Aronson, and Kafry's (1981) instrument to assess functions of an individual's support network. Though the instrument has face validity, caution will be taken in reporting findings using this instrument since validity and reliability information were not available.

The subgroups used in the following analyses were categorized based on the author's 10 years of experience of working with the internship.

- *Age:*

  Group one: From 21 to 24 years of age. Interns were grouped this way because it is likely that they are entering the five-year program directly out of undergraduate school.

  Group two: From 25 to 30 years of age. This group has likely spent some time after college gaining experience in some occupation, or has entered college after limited outside experience. They are not yet at the point of a major career change.

  Group three: From 30 years of age and older. This group most likely represents adults who are seeking career changes and/or women who are returning to finish studies after starting families.

- *Cluster placement versus noncluster placement:*

  Group one: Interns who are in cluster placements at the elementary school level (minimum of three interns per school).

  Group two: All other elementary interns not placed in clusters.

- *Experiential background of cooperating teacher:*

  Group one: First-year cooperating teachers.

  Group two: Cooperating teachers who have had one previous intern.

  Group three: Cooperating teachers who have had two or more interns.

FINDINGS

The first research question addressed the stress levels of interns. Table 2 shows the subscale scores for the Maslach Burnout Inventory: Educator's Edition (MBI:ED). The first scale, Emotional Exhaustion, shows the frequency that interns feel emotionally exhausted and drained from teaching. The second subscale, Depersonalization, measures attitudes toward students. The third subscale, Personal Accomplishment, indicates the frequency that the person feels a sense of accomplishment from his or her work. A person who is experiencing burnout will score high on the Emotional Exhaustion and Depersonalization subscales and low on Personal Accomplishment. As shown on Table 2, interns score much lower on Emotional Exhaustion and Depersonalization and higher on Personal Accomplishment than teachers in the national sample. This clearly indicates that interns are experiencing very low levels of job-related stress, as measured by this inventory. The MBI:ED also has range scores based on the national norms. Interns are in the average range for Emotional Exhaustion, and in the low range for Depersonalization and Personal Accomplishment.

Table 3 presents the results of one-way analysis of variance for age, internship placement, and experience of cooperating teachers. As one can see, there are no significant differences at the conventional $p \leq .05$ level of significance. One can only hypothesize why no differences were found. First, since interns are experiencing very low levels of burnout there is not much

Table 2 Intern Levels of Perceived Burnout Compared with National Teacher Norms

Factors	**Interns' Mean ($N = 82$)**	**National Teachers' Mean ($N = 4, 163$)**
Emotional Exhaustion	18.30	21.25
*range	average	average
Depersonalization	3.52	11.00
*range	low	average
Personal Accomplishment	39.09	33.54
*range	low	average

*National means and range scores from: *Maslach Burnout Inventory: Educator's Edition Manual* (Maslach, Jackson, and Schwab, 1986).

Table 3 One-Way Analysis of Variance of Selected Background Variables and Frequency of Perceived Burnout

Variable	*Groups*	*Group Means*	*Anova F*	*Sig. Level*
Emotional Exhaustion				
Age	21–23 years	17.59	.19	.82
	24–29 years	18.52		
	30 plus	19.44		
Internship setting	Cluster	14.56	2.9	.09
	Noncluster	19.62		
Experience of cooperating teacher	First intern	19.31	.39	.68
	One other	16.92		
	Two or more	18.52		
Depersonalization				
Age	21–23 years	3.94	.09	.90
	24–29 years	3.48		
	30 plus	3.78		
Internship setting	Cluster	2.87	.04	.95
	Noncluster	2.80		
Experience of cooperating teacher	First intern	4.18	.71	.49
	One other	2.96		
	Two or more	3.67		
Personal Accomplishment				
Age	21–23 years	40.2	2.28	.11
	24–29 years	36.86		
	30 plus	39.58		
Internship setting	Cluster	38.7	1.21	.28
	Noncluster	40.70		
Experience of cooperating teacher	First intern	39.54	1.86	.16
	One other	39.9		
	Two or more	36.77		

variance to explain. Second, other factors not examined, such as responsibilities outside the internship (i.e., family responsibilities), relationships with cooperating teachers, and amount of financial support, may be better predictors. The third possible reason may be due to the small cell size that emerges when the groups are formed, thus making significance levels very difficult to attain.

Since the purpose of this study was to generate hypotheses for future studies, a higher significance level or simple trends could be used to generate questions (Borg and Gall, 1983). Given this assumption, one can make some interesting observations. First, elementary interns in cluster placements have lower levels of emotional exhaustion than elementary interns not in cluster placements ($p = .09$). This score moves the cluster placement group from the average range to the low range in Emotional Exhaustion. A second observation is that the interns right out of undergraduate programs and those over age 30 feel the greatest amount of personal accomplishment from teaching. A third observation is that interns working with cooperating teachers who have had the most experience have lower levels of personal accomplishment ($p = .11$). This lower score is enough to move this group from the low range up to the average range for this aspect of burnout.

The second research question addressed general attitudes toward the internship and seminar. In general, interns viewed their intern experience very positively. Some 56 percent rated their internship experience as excellent, 39 percent rated it as good, 4 percent rated it as fair, and no one (0) percent rated it as poor. The seminar component of the internship was viewed somewhat more mixed but still on a positive note: 33 percent rated their seminar as excellent, 51 percent as good, 13 percent as fair, and 1 percent as poor.

Table 4 presents the results of one-way analysis of variance that looked for relationships between age, internship setting, experience level of the cooperating teacher, and satisfaction with the internship and seminar. Again, no significant differences were found using $p \leq .05$. As in the previous question, 95 percent of the interns rated their internship experience as good or excellent, which makes for very little variance to explain. Since none of the significance levels was near $p \leq .10$ level, it is difficult to detect trends as we were able to in the first question.

The third research question addressed the issue of whether the functions of a support group are better enhanced by cluster placement of interns. Table 5 again shows no significant differences among groups but it does show some interesting trends. Though the differences overall are slight, the mean scores for each function of the support group are higher for cluster placements. The two areas where the most significant differences occur are in technical challenge and emotional challenge categories.

Table 4 One-Way Analysis of Variance for Background Variables and Internship and Seminar Satisfaction

Variable	*Groups*	*Group Means*	*Overall Means*	*Anova F*	*Sig. Level*
	***Overall Internship Satisfaction**				
Age	21–23 years	1.34	1.46	1.24	.29
	24–29 years	1.53			
	30 plus	1.55			
Internship setting	Cluster	1.44	1.47	.26	.61
	Noncluster	1.53			
Experience of cooperating teacher	First intern	1.38	1.46	.97	.38
	One other	1.62			
	Two or more	1.46			
	***Satisfaction with Seminar**				
Age	21–23 years	1.81	1.81	1.32	.27
	24–29 years	1.96			
	30 plus	1.61			
Internship setting	Cluster	2.00	1.90	.49	.49
	Noncluster	1.84			
Experience of cooperating teacher	First intern	1.85	1.84	.64	.53
	One other	2.00			
	Two or more	1.75			

***Ratings: 1 = Excellent; 2 = Good; 3 = Fair; 4 = Poor.**

CONCLUSION

The results of this study provide information that is useful on two dimensions. The overall positive response to the internship aspect of the UNH program provides one more piece of information to support the adoption of extended programs to prepare teachers. The overall low levels of job-related stress indicate that the supportive yet technically challenging climate that can be developed over the year has achieved its goal of helping practice teachers enter their profession on a positive note. These findings

Table 5 Functions of a Support Group by Cluster and Noncluster Groups

		Listener		
Groups	*Group Means*	*Overall Means*	*Anova F*	*Sig. Level*
Noncluster ($N = 15$)	20.53	20.76	.08	.77
Cluster ($N = 23$)	20.92			
		Technical Appreciation		
Noncluster ($N = 15$)	20.00	20.29	.07	.79
Cluster ($N = 23$)	20.45			
		Technical Challenge		
Noncluster ($N = 15$)	17.57	18.80	1.52	.23
Cluster ($N = 23$)	19.59			
		Emotional Support		
Noncluster ($N = 15$)	19.60	20.38	.76	.39
Cluster ($N = 23$)	20.87			
		Emotional Challenge		
Noncluster ($N = 15$)	15.38	16.8	1.56	.22
Cluster ($N = 23$)	17.64			
		Shared Sense of Reality		
Noncluster ($N = 15$)	21.20	21.29	.01	.91
Cluster ($N = 23$)	21.34			

support those found by Andrew (1990) in a followup study of 10 years of graduates from the Five-Year Program. His study found that 92 percent of graduates take teaching jobs and that 75 percent of them stay in teaching five years or more. These statistics are much higher than those found in studies that have looked at teacher entrance to the profession and retention rates across the country (Benton, 1985; Geer, 1966; Mark and Anderson, 1977).

To add more credibility to the findings that the year-long internship is more successful at helping new teachers handle job-related stress, a future study should take a relatively similar group of student teachers near the end of their placement and compare their scores on the MBI:ED with those found in this study. Another needed study would be to follow interns into the first two years of their regular teaching positions to compare their ability to handle job-related stress with that of student teachers. In such a study great care would have to be made in controlling for organizational conditions, as these have been linked to burnout levels in the previous research (Jackson, Schwab, and Schuler, 1986; Schwab, 1983; Maslach, Jackson, and Schwab, 1986). One way to control for this is to use individual schools as the unit of analysis, as advocated by Hubert and Iwanicki (1989).

The results of this study also offer information that is useful for universities that have begun to implement five-year programs and are designing their clinical experiences. This study has shown that interns in cluster placements experience lower levels of emotional exhaustion and fatigue and have the opportunity to develop more effective support networks. From the university's perspective, it is much easier for supervisors to spend time in schools if they do not have to travel great distances between placements. It is also possible to build a better rapport with cooperating teachers if one can work with them in their schools on a more regular basis. However, developing effective cluster sites requires more than just placing three or more interns in the same school.

Cluster sites must be developed in collaboration with the administrators and cooperating teachers if they are to succeed. Consequently, each develops its own personality, reflecting the nature of the school organization and philosophical outlooks of teachers and administration. Oja (1988) found that although cluster sites were unique, they did share some common traits. Among the most important were:

1. Time is made available for cooperating teachers to meet together.

2. The university supervisor and cooperating teacher collaborate in making decisions that directly affect the intern.
3. Emphasis is placed on making a good match between the cooperating teacher and intern in the placement process.
4. The university supervisor acts as a liaison between the school and the university teacher education program.

Although it is difficult to find fault with the cluster placement concept, there are factors that need to be overcome before moving in that direction. In all but our largest high schools it is very difficult to place three or more interns in a single academic department and expect to make good matches between cooperating teachers and interns. In order for the concept of cluster placement to work at the secondary level, university supervisors must be amenable to supervise more than one discipline. Rather than be a subject-area specialist, it is more important that the university supervisor be well grounded in general pedagogical knowledge that is applicable to all disciplines. Consequently, the university supervisor must depend on the subject-area expertise of the cooperating teacher and also serve as a liaison with university-based content experts when necessary. Since interns in extended programs all have a strong background in their subject area, this is less of a problem than in traditional four-year programs.

A second issue blocking cluster placement is that many of our interns are financially strapped. School districts are often able to find money to provide stipends for one or two interns per district but funding three or more per school is next to impossible. Previous experience has shown that having paid and unpaid interns in the same school is not a good idea because a two-class citizen of intern develops. Until states, local schools, or the federal government provide funding to support clusters of interns, it is unlikely that a five-year program will be able to totally abandon placing individual interns in schools except in our large urban and suburban schools.

In summary, this study has also raised some additional research questions that need examination. Two of these are raised by the findings in the Personal Accomplishment aspect of job burnout. These questions are:

1. Do the interns who are working with the most experienced-cooperating teachers experience lower feelings of accomplishment from their work? If so, why?

2. Do interns in the 24- to 29-year-old age bracket experience lower levels of personal accomplishment? If so, why?

A number of questions not examined in this study may also be interesting for future investigations. Among the more important are:

1. Are interns more likely than student teachers to develop and maintain support networks on their own when they enter full-time teaching?
2. Are interns more likely to have more positive attitudes toward supervision activities once they are in their first full-time teaching assignments?
3. Can support groups be developed during the student teaching experience that have the same long-term effects as those in the internship?

The development of extended programs in teacher education is one of the most positive outcomes of the reform movement in education. Although research has begun to provide information that will help both program planners and those already involved in extended programs, much more is needed. Hopefully, this study has helped to provide some potential areas of inquiry.

References

Andrew, M. D. (1974). *Teacher leadership: A model for change.* Washington, DC: Association of Teacher Educators. (ERIC No. ED 096288).

Andrew, M. D. (1981). A five-year teacher education program: Successes and challenges. *Journal of Teacher Education, 32* (3), 41–43.

Andrew, M. D. (1983). The characteristics of students in a five-year teacher education program. *Journal of Teacher Education, 34* (1), 20–23.

Andrew, M. D. (1986). Restructuring teacher education: The University of New Hampshire's five-year program. In T. J. Lasley (Ed.), *The dynamics of change in teacher education* (Vol. 1). Background papers from the National Commission on Excellence in teacher education. (AACTE-ERIC Teacher Education Monograph No. 5).

Andrew, M. D. (1990). Differences between graduates of 4-year and 5-year teacher preparation programs. *Journal of Teacher Education, 41* (2), 45–51.

Benton, C. J. (1985, April). *Predicting occupational persistence: A comparison of teachers and five other occupational groups.* Paper presented at the Annual Meeting of the American Educational Research Association.

Borg, W. R., and Gall, M. D. (1983). *Educational research: An introduction.* New York: Longman.

Bullough, R. L. (1989). *First year teacher: A case study.* New York: Teachers College Press.

Caplan, G. (1974). *Social support systems and community mental health.* New York: Behavioral Publications.

Carnegie Forum on Education and the Economy. (1986). *A nation prepared: Teachers for the 21st century.* New York: Author.

Corcoran, E. (1981). Transition shock: The beginning teacher's paradox. *Journal of Teacher Education, 32* (3), 19–24.

Corcoran, E. (1989). *Critical issues for intern teachers during the clinical experience.* Paper presented at the American Educational Research Association Annual Conference, San Francisco.

Corcoran, E. and Andrew, M. (1988). A full year internship: An example of school/university collaboration. *Journal of Teacher Education, 39* (3), 17–35.

Dworkin, A. G. (1987). *Teacher burnout in the public schools.* Albany: State University of New York Press.

Geer, B. (1966). Occupational commitment and the teacher profession. *School Review, 74,* 31–47.

Gold, Y. (1984). The factorial validity of the Maslach Burnout Inventory in a sample of California elementary and junior high school classroom teachers. *Educational and Psychological Measurement, 44,* 1009–1016.

Gold, Y. (1985). The relationship of six personal and life history variables to standing on three dimensions of the Maslach Burnout Inventory in a sample of elementary and junior high school teachers. *Educational and Psychological Measurements, 45,* 377–387.

Holmes Group. (1986). *Tomorrow's teachers: A report of the Holmes Group.* East Lansing, MI: Author.

Howey, K. R., and Zimpher, N. L. (1986). The current debate on teacher preparation. *Journal of Teacher Education, 37* (5), 41–49.

Hubert, J., Gable, R., and Iwanicki, E. F. (1989). The relationship of school organizational health to teacher stress. In S. B. Bacharach, S. Conley, and B. Cooper (Eds.), *Advances in research and theories of school management* (Vol. 1). Greenwich, CT: JAI Press.

Iwanicki, E. F., and Schwab, R. L. (1981) A cross-validational study of the Maslach Burnout Inventory. *Educational and Psychological Measurement, 41*, 1167–1174.

Jackson, S. E., Schwab, R. L., and Schuler, R. A. (1986). Toward an understanding of the burnout phenomenon. *Journal of Applied Psychology, 71* (4), 630–639.

Mark, J. L. and Anderson, B. D. (1977). Teacher survival rates: A current look. *American Educational Research Journal, 15* (3), 379–383.

Maslach, C., Jackson, S. E., with Schwab, R. L. (1986). *The Maslach Burnout Inventory Manual.* Palo Alto, CA: Consulting Psychologists Press.

Oja, S. N. (1988). *A collaborative approach to leadership in supervision.* Final Report to the Office of Educational Research and Improvement. U. S. Department of Education.

Pines, A., Aronson, E., and Kafry, D. (1981). *Burnout: From tedium to personal growth.* New York: Free Press.

Schwab, R. L. (1983). Teacher burnout: Moving beyond psychobabble. *Theory into Practice, 22* (1), 21–25.

Schwab, R. L. (1990). Extended teacher education programs: Lessons from experience. In S. Bacharach (Ed.), *The educational reform movement: Making sense of it all.* San Francisco: Jossey Bass.

Schwab, R. L., and Iwanicki, E. F. (1982). Who are our burned out teachers? *Educational Research Quarterly,* 7 (2), 5–16.

Schwab, R. L., Jackson, S. E., and Schuler, R. A. (1986). Educator burnout: Sources and consequences. *Educational Research Quarterly, 10* (3), 14–29.

Shulman, L. S. (1987). Knowledge and teaching: Foundations of the new reform. *Harvard Educational Review, 57.*

Veenman, S. (1984). Perceived problems of beginning teachers. *Review of Educational Research, 54* (2), 143–178.

Wilkinson, L. (1989). Prospects for graduate preparation of teachers. In A. Woolfolk (Ed.), *Research perspectives on the graduate preparation of teachers.* Englewood Cliffs, NJ: Prentice-Hall.

Chapter Ten

In a natural companion piece to Schwab's chapter on teacher preparation (Chapter Nine), the authors assert that beginning teachers need more support to survive the challenges they face. Roper and colleagues report on a consortium for improving teacher induction made up of representatives from a rural school district, a college of education, and a regional research laboratory. The consortium's accomplishments included interchanges and mentoring between veteran and beginning teachers, a principal checklist on orienting new teachers, and a comprehensive evaluation, which pointed the way to further program refinements. There were problems: initial suspicion, unclear expectations, unequal effort among the three-member groups, and low priority of teacher induction activities in the district. A collaborative effort must overcome the effects of years of isolation, both among consortium partners and among teachers. Roper and colleagues advise that trust building, recognition of legitimate differences of orientation, flexibility, frequent communication, and, above all, patience are required to succeed with such an effort.

Consortium Support for Teachers in Rural Oregon

Susan Stavert Roper
Southern Oregon State College
with
John Mahaffy, Northwest Regional Educational Laboratory
Charles Barker, Josephine County School District
Burl Brim, Southern Oregon State College
Neil McDowell, Southern Oregon State College

This chapter will examine typical problems of beginning teachers and describe one case where administrators, teachers, and college faculty attempted a collaborative approach to teacher induction. This effort, which made use of a "consortium" for providing a program for beginning teachers, revealed several successes and problems. These experiences are instructive for improving collaboration generally.

PROBLEMS ENCOUNTERED BY BEGINNING TEACHERS

All teachers need support; beginning teachers need it the most. Although the range of need varies to the extreme of first-year teachers experiencing "blind panic" (Griffin, 1982), far from all neophytes report their initiation into teaching as traumatic. Even so, teaching is not always smooth sailing; the maiden voyage can be rocky indeed.

> The condition of not knowing is common to beginning teachers. No matter how extensive the beginner's preservice education, beginning teachers are faced by and accountable for or to—sometimes it is not clear which—unknown students, teaching colleagues, administrators, university supervisors, and parents. In the midst of so many strangers, it is difficult to know to whom to turn or where to begin. In addition, the school and community environments have norms

> and rituals that most probably are new and strange. The large number of factual and procedural unknowns can send the beginning teacher into a state of shock wherein it becomes impossible to transfer previously mastered concepts and skills from the university to the public school classroom. (Corcoran, 1981)

Regardless of the level or nature of the physical, mental, and emotional difficulties encountered, however, all beginning teachers must face three kinds of challenges:

1. *Managing instructional demands.* Beginning teachers have reported a fairly consistent set of problems related to classroom instruction. Two of the most persistent problems concern issues related to classroom management and student behavior, and to teaching students with wide-ranging motivation and ability. New teachers also tend to find themselves relatively unprepared to deal with issues related to assessing student learning. Planning instruction, whether lessons or units, can be intimidating. These teachers, unlike their veteran counterparts, do not have files full of lesson plans, handouts, tests, activities, and overhead transparencies on which to rely. They lack the experience to know which materials will be most effective for a given lesson. Developing and producing needed instructional materials often becomes a formidable task. A more mundane, though too common, frustration is difficulty in identifying, locating, and securing instructional resources. Finally, first-year teachers frequently receive too many different preparations and the least desirable assignments (e.g., the "difficult" students other teachers don't want). In some cases this practice has become institutionalized through teachers' unions insisting that seniority earns teachers the right to a choice of assignments (analogous to having first-year surgeons attempt heart transplants while their experienced senior colleagues perform appendectomies.)

2. *Managing noninstructional demands.* Though in some respects not as taxing as managing instructional demands, new teachers may be less prepared to cope with some noninstructional areas. Foremost among these are the social and professional relationships. New teachers have few guidelines for establishing relationships with students, fellow teachers, administrators, parents, and the community. Some teachers will handle these well (intuitively), others will learn the hard way, and some will seek safety in isolation. If a school improvement or major staff development effort is underway, participation will require yet more time and energy. Added to all this are other noninstructional demands in the form of cocurricular assignments. Rather than

being sheltered from such responsibilities, beginning teachers often find themselves overcommitted. This is particularly a problem in rural schools where there are fewer teachers to assume responsibility for after-school activities.

3. *Managing personal demands.* The personal demands faced by beginning teachers emanate both from many of the instructional and noninstructional responsibilities just mentioned, and from significant lifestyle changes (e.g., living alone for the first time, starting a family, full-time employment, etc.) that many are experiencing.

In the case of new rural teachers, many come from urban and suburban backgrounds and must adjust to living a different lifestyle as well as starting a new career. The isolation, limited opportunity for social contacts, and "fish-bowl" existence of their new environment add to the stress that is endemic to the first year of teaching (Guenther and Weible, 1983).

The press of time, however, may be the most demanding factor of all. New teachers are doing many tasks simultaneously for the first time, both in and out of school. Lacking a cache of instructional materials, much time is spent preparing for class and the preparation process is likely less efficient than for their more experienced colleagues. Devoting so much energy to teaching leaves relatively little time for life outside school; balancing personal and professional time can be trying.

All beginning teachers, but particularly those in rural areas, need the opportunity to visit outstanding colleagues in schools similar to their own and time to get together with other novices. Long distances between schools and the small size of school faculties in rural areas are formidable obstacles to bringing teachers together. Transportation costs and time on the road make it difficult for novice teachers to participate in a support network. They miss out on the reassurance that their anxiety, exhaustion, and feelings of inadequacy are the common lot of first-year teachers, not proof that they have chosen the wrong career. It should be no surprise that the attrition rate of new teachers in rural areas is a continuing problem.

RESPONDING TO THE PROBLEM: FORMING A CONSORTIUM

In response to the problems just mentioned, administrators in Josephine County, Oregon, a district covering 3,200 square miles and including 15 schools with as much as 70 miles between them, began searching for a way to do a better job of supporting their new teachers.

At the same time, education faculty members at Southern Oregon State College were looking for a district that would allow them to work with beginning teachers. As part of a grant from the Northwest Regional Educational Laboratory for Educational Research (NWREL), faculty in the education department studied the literature about the plight of beginning teachers. When they came across Kevin Ryan's description of the abandonment of new teachers by teacher educators, the faculty agreed that it was all too accurate a description of themselves. Ryan stated:

> The way teacher training institutions send new teachers out to the field always brings to my mind scenes from those old World War II movies. An idealistic recruit volunteers for the paratrooper corps. Veterans of former battles prepare them for the coming invasion. Chock-full of skills and weaponry after a few practice jumps, they are loaded aboard planes that take off and head into the skies over enemy territory. Once behind the lines, their instructors, with thumbs up and a gentle push, send them off into the inky blackness. Some float down, land gracefully, join the battle, and become heroes. Some have a gentle landing amid minefields and go up in a puff of smoke. Some get hung up in trees and church spires, easy prey to enemy guns. A few have a fast ride down and a short military career because their chutes don't open. And while all this bedlam and mayhem is happening, the trusty trainers are flying back to the base to induct another group of recruits. They rarely learn what happens to their recruits and how effective their training turned out to be. (Ryan, 1985, p. 240)

The Southern Oregon State College faculty returned from the Lab convinced that it was time to find out how their recruits and graduates from other training programs were doing in action.

Professional development staff of the Northwest Regional Educational Laboratory were also on the lookout for colleges and schools interested in induction. The Lab had been awarded a grant to develop three models for inducting new teachers: one in an urban area, another in a Pacific rim community, and a third in a rural area. The interest of Southern Oregon State College and Josephine County in the plight of new teachers convinced the NWREL staff to locate the rural model in southern Oregon.

In the summer of 1986, representatives from Southern Oregon State College, the Northwest Regional Educational Laboratory, and the Josephine County School District formed a consortium for the purpose of designing an induction program. Each member had something of real value to contribute.

College faculty brought information from the literature regarding the needs of beginning teachers and lessons from exemplary induction programs. They presented special courses to address particular problems new teachers encountered. These courses were offered on-site in the district and for graduate credit—no small incentive for a first-year teacher. In addition, faculty and college administrators served as group facilitators for the new teachers, encouraging them to share their concerns and assist one another in a nonevaluative setting.

Working concurrently with the urban, Pacific rim, and rural induction projects, NWREL staff suggested strategies to the consortium that were working in the other sites. The NWREL staff designed a comprehensive mentor handbook and a formative evaluation report of the first year of the project. Through the Lab connection, consortium members were able to meet with experts in the fields of induction and collaboration.

School district staff provided access to teachers and administrators and allowed released-time for beginning teachers to visit top-rated teachers. The personnel director/curriculum coordinator of the school district was the prime mover in the project. He called all the meetings of the consortium, selected mentor teachers, planned visitations for beginning teachers, arranged for mentor teachers to observe and be observed, and negotiated with the college and NWREL for their respective services.

CONSORTIUM SUCCESSES

Through these joint efforts, consortium members can point to a number of successes. All beginning teachers visited some outstanding teachers within and outside the district. One of the best activities was a group observation and meeting with a few of the district's "super stars." During that meeting one experienced teacher admitted to frequently feeling overwhelmed by the job. She confessed that just the previous week she was so tired of awakening early and worrying about unfinished work that she hopped in her car and drove over to the school at four o'clock in the morning. She worried that a cruising police officer might think she was breaking in. The beginning teachers were able to laugh with her and feel comfortable enough to share their own anxieties. As one said, "I'm so glad I'm not married. The only one I have time for at home is my cat" (Personal communication, Josephine County School District, December 3, 1986).

Perhaps the most worthwhile interchange of this session was when the veteran teachers told the beginners that sometimes it is okay to do what is easiest for the teacher. They suggested that new teachers look for activities that give students more responsibility (e.g., debates, group projects and panel presentations) instead of continually making more work for themselves. The beginners left this session knowing that even the very best in their profession occasionally feel overwhelmed, but there are ways to gain more control over their time.

Although the group visits and conferences were inspirational and cathartic, the essential mechanism for improving curriculum knowledge and instructional skills was the mentor-protege relationship. Each new teacher was assigned a mentor, usually in the same building. Mentors frequently observed their proteges and shared a host of practical suggestions with them. Mentors also demonstrated exemplary lessons for the protege to observe.

The professional development staff of the Northwest Lab and the Oregon State Department of Education provided training to the mentors. The NWREL Mentor Handbook served as a useful tool in acquainting mentors with their responsibilities and suggesting ways to support new teachers.

Beginning teachers also met together without their mentors. This was a time for sharing their woes, airing personal as well as professional problems, and giving each other ideas for surviving the first year.

The year before the consortium was formed, an education professor interviewed over 40 new teachers and asked what they wished they had known on their first day on the job. Their responses were organized into a checklist for administrators. The checklist was provided to the principals in Josephine County. It reminded principals to acquaint their new teachers with everything a novice might need to know—from the mundane (e.g., bus schedules, dress codes, fire alarm drills) to the sublime (e.g., school philosophy, community profile, district curriculum guide).

Before the end of the first year of operation, the consortium members agreed to make a comprehensive evaluation of the project. Many induction strategies that were tried came from this evaluation and were implemented to help new teachers in the second year of the program. Seven areas emerged as the major areas of concerns:

- Understanding school policies and procedures
- Managing time effectively
- Finding instructional materials and resources
- Learning about the informal organization of the school
- Interacting successfully with parents

- Motivating students
- Teaching a wide range of students

For each of these areas, beginning teachers provided a list of specific problems they encountered and recommendations to address each problem. For example, new teachers were presented with district policies and procedures via handbooks mailed prior to the beginning of school, coupled with three or four orientation meetings scheduled throughout the first two months. This suggestion seemed to work much better than the previous practice of trying to cover all orientation items in one long districtwide meeting held before school began—during the time that new teachers are anxious to get their classrooms organized.

The evaluation sessions were particularly helpful to college faculty in shaping the inservice agenda for new teachers. In response to concerns about parent interaction, student motivation, and teaching a wide range of students, college faculty designed a special course. The Classroom Survival Skills course focused on parent-teacher conferences, mainstreaming, motivating the reluctant learner, and teaching students to be independent learners.

The result of all this activity is that the life of a first-year teacher in Josephine County, Oregon, has become a little easier and consortium members are a little smarter about how to help people make the transition from student to teacher.

CONSORTIUM PROBLEMS

Despite these accomplishments, this consortium-based approach to the induction of rural teachers is by no means an unqualified success story. Problems endemic to interorganizational collaboration limit the scope and quality of the consortium's efforts. They include initial suspicion of one another, unclear expectations, unequal effort, difficulty of making induction a priority, and the professional isolation of teachers and educational institutions.

Initial Suspicion

Our consortium was fortunate in that the individuals representing each organization knew one another and had worked together on other projects. Nevertheless, anyone who has attempted to make collaboration work between higher education and schools knows that initial suspicions are inevitable. College faculty typically have little experience working as colleagues with public school personnel. Their contacts are usually limited to conducting research projects and supervising student teachers. Many college faculty believe that school people are so immersed in day-to-day problems that they are hostile to ideas and uninterested in developing long-range goals and programs. On the other hand, school-based educators often believe that college professors live in an unreal world of highly motivated students, impractical theories, and dry statistics (Hagberg and Walker, 1977).

Both groups had some doubts about the value of working with NWREL and with one another. They asked each other, "Will the staff from the Lab really understand the problems unique to our area?" "Will they assume that they have all the answers and we are unsophisticated 'country cousins'?" "Will they impose a research agenda that is irrelevant to our problems?"

Although initial suspicion is eventually overcome by time and good will, it makes for a slow start.

Unclear Expectations

Unclear expectations remain a difficult problem to overcome. To this day, college and Lab staff wait to be invited to a consortium meeting or activity in the district. This is the case even though the consortium has never formally agreed that the district members are expected to call meetings and set agendas.

Although consortium members communicate frequently, misunderstandings can still arise. For example, at the conclusion of the first year of the project, the school district member of the consortium asked college faculty and staff to facilitate an evaluation meeting with the district's beginning teachers. In the course of this meeting, some comments were made that were construed by one experienced teacher as critical of district policies. The district administrator was upset and skeptical about the value of the session. Fortunately, he immediately called consortium members from the college and Lab to voice his concerns. After reviewing the written report on the evaluation meetings, he became convinced that the criticism was constructive. In fact, the consortium used the report as a planning document for the following year's activities.

This incident had a happy ending but it could have been disastrous. College faculty and NWREL staff who facilitated the meeting were totally surprised by the district administrator's reaction. They thought they understood what was expected of them as facilitators and performed that role successfully. In retrospect, the facilitators realized that they were expected to be more sensitive to the district administrator's reluctance to have dirty laundry aired in public.

Unequal Effort

Unequal effort continues to plague the project. With the lack of funds to hire a project coordinator, the district's personnel director/curriculum coordinator has assumed this responsibility. To some degree this has happened because consortium members from the college and Lab see the district as "his territory" and are reluctant to intervene without his permission.

Sheer physical distances have also played a part in the unequal participation of consortium members. The college is an hour's drive from the district office and as much as two hours from some of the schools. The region served by the district is a four and one-half-hour drive from the Northwest Lab.

The reward system in higher education does not encourage college faculty members to devote substantial effort to collaborative activity. Time spent in research that will lead to publications is a better investment for promotion and tenure than the considerable time commitment required to participate in a consortium with school personnel.

Low Priority of Induction

Although the district consortium member has spent more time on the project than have the members from the college and Northwest Lab, even he finds it difficult to make the induction program a priority. The district has suffered from political unrest and financial instability. Dealing with an attempt to recall school board members, suspension of busing, and potentially severe reductions in force leave little leeway for one more service to be managed from the director's office.

College faculty members have also had their attention absorbed by the instructional and institutional demands of their jobs. The Northwest Lab member spends a good part of his time overseeing a variety of programs, both domestic and abroad. This is only one of several programs in which he is involved. It often seems that the induction program does not top anyone's list of priorities.

Professional Isolation

Over 20 years ago, Seymour Sarason and colleagues (1966) described teaching as "a lonely profession." It is paradoxical that teachers work in buildings filled with people and have nearly constant contact with people the whole day. The contact, however, is with students; little substantive interaction occurs with colleagues during a school day. Until very recently the condition of isolation observed by Sarason had changed little. Professional isolation is slowly giving way to professional collaboration (Little, 1982).

Consortium members were involved in both collaborative and isolated schools. Introducing the induction program in the "isolated" schools, we faced an absence of support systems for the program and staff norms, which mitigated against collaboration. While formidable, this problem represented both the "good news" and the "bad news." Not surprisingly, the bad news was that chances for success in isolated schools were diminished and participants had to pay a higher price to achieve meaningful benefits.

The good news was that the induction program proved to be a foot-in-the-door toward more collaboration among staff. We found that relative isolation and collegiality were perceptions of the workplace environment reflecting the cumulative values, attitudes, and beliefs of the teachers (and other staff members). These perceptions resulted from daily activities and behaviors in which teachers engaged. Collaborative activity led teachers to value collegiality, but the activity had to come first. The induction program introduced collaborative activity—the opportunity for teachers to experience new ways of doing things and, thereby, to develop new norms.

IMPROVING COLLABORATION

In reviewing the literature on collaboration, it has been reassuring to know that the problems the consortium encountered were not unique. That literature, and the successes and problems described earlier, suggest that there are specific guidelines for achieving collaboration among higher education faculty, public school teachers, and administrators interested in improving the lives of beginning teachers.

First, to assist with teacher induction, college faculty must gain credibility and trust. Professors build credibility by being visible in the schools, getting acquainted with teachers, and demonstrating their expertise in classrooms. A large part of gaining trust is simply to be there—not only in the classrooms but also at school functions, in faculty meetings, in the lunchroom, and at social occasions.

A second useful guideline concerns the impact of different goals on collaborative endeavors. A review of Gerald Pine's insightful paper, "The Certainty of Change Theory: An Analysis of Change Ideologies," warns that partners in collaborative educational projects rarely share the same goals. He points out that conflict and resistance to change are no strangers to interorganizational collaboration, partly because of "the clash of legitimately different interests" (Pine, 1980).

In our consortium, the main goal of members from the school district was to improve the quality and retention of new teachers in their district. College representatives were not as concerned with that particular group of teachers as they were with learning more about the needs of beginning teachers in general. The college faculty wanted to know about the problems their graduates were likely to face in the near future so they could adjust their pre-service program to minimize those problems. The Lab's interests differed to some degree from those of the school district; the college NWREL staff were interested in learning about the concerns of new teachers that were rooted in the rural experience and how they differed from problems new teachers in other environments were facing.

Partners in interorganizational collaboration endeavors should not ignore these legitimate differences in goal orientation. A full and frank discussion of differing goals should be held before any commitment is made to participate in a consortium. Once these differences of goals and interests are known, it becomes much easier to negotiate compromises and to anticipate potential conflict situations.

A third and related guideline is that goals and activities must be modified to meet the needs of all participants, but in cases where teachers and students are directly involved, school district members must make the final decisions (Hagberg and Walker, 1977). Consortium members from an institution of higher education or any other agency need to understand that collective bargaining, public relations, or financial constraints in the district impose limitations on consortium plans.

A fourth guideline is that frequent communication is essential. Regularly scheduled meetings with clear agendas, minutes, and written agreements for each inservice activity will keep consortium members informed and avoid misunderstandings. In some consortiums, members hammer out expectations for all participants and put these expectations in writing.

A final guideline for successful consortiums is that each member of a collaborative effort must learn that most difficult of all virtues—to be patient (Roper and Jung, 1980). The investment of time and effort necessary for a truly successful consortium is a big one, but so are the payoffs. Every teacher who went through the induction program designed by the consortium in 1986–87 returned the following year to teach in the same school district. School administrators report that these teachers are more knowledgeable about their school, district, and community; more willing to become involved in school governance and activities; and appear happier and more comfortable in their jobs than beginning teachers from previous years.

College faculty are seeing an immediate payoff from their participation in the consortium as they plan a new teacher education program. Partly as a result of the concerns voiced by Josephine County's new teachers, the new Southern Oregon State College program will have a longer period of student teaching, more carefully selected placements, and better trained supervisors.

The payoff for the Northwest Lab is the contribution they are making to the knowledge base about beginning teachers. NWREL staff are presently comparing the needs reported by new teachers in the urban, rural, and Pacific rim sites. They are also examining the characteristics of schools and districts that support or hinder induction efforts in these different settings.

The impact of the consortium's work is apparent in more confident first-year teachers, a better designed teacher education program, and increased knowledge about the lives of beginning teachers. The hope of all consortium members is that together we can help ensure that the "fittest"—not merely the most persistent—will survive in the teaching profession.

References

Corcoran, E. (1981, May-June). Transition shock: The beginning teacher's paradox. *Journal of Teacher Education, 32* (3), 19–23.

Griffin G. (1982). *Induction—An overview. Beginning teacher induction—Five dilemmas.* Invited Symposium, AERA.

Guenther, J., and Weible, T. (1983, Winter). Preparing teachers for rural schools. *Research in Rural Education, 1.*

Hagberg, H., and Walker, D. (1977, October). The problems of collaboration. In D. Duke (Ed.), *When teachers and researchers cooperate.* Stanford Center for Research on a Development in Teaching.

Little, J. W. (1982). Norms of collegiality and experimentation: Workplace conditions of school success. *American Education Research Journal, 19* (3), 325–340.

Pine, Gerald. (1980, April). *The certainty of change theory: An analysis of change ideologies.* Paper presented at the Teacher Corps Research Adaptation Cluster Conference, Boston.

Roper, S., and Jung, R. (1980, July). Initiating staff development under fire: A project learns to adapt. *A Journal of Research Adaptation,* Teacher Corps, Journal II.

Ryan, K. (1985). Beginning teachers: Parachutists behind the lines may be in need of a chaplain. In S. M. Hord, S. F. O'Neil, and M. Smith (Eds.), *Beyond the looking glass: Papers from a national symposium on teacher education policies, practices and research.* Austin: The Research and Development Center for Teacher Education, The University of Texas.

Sarason, S., Levine, M., and others. (1966). Teaching is a lonely profession. In *Psychology in community settings: Clinical, educational, vocational, social aspects.* New York: John Wiley and Sons.

Chapter Eleven

Architects of career ladders propose that such systems will foster teacher motivation and professional growth. However, failures of career ladders in states like Tennessee have been due, the authors maintain, to increased competition among teachers, teacher isolation, and standardization of teachers' work. Freiberg and Knight examine two different types of teacher incentive programs operating simultaneously within a district in the state of Texas. The authors find that a prescribed career ladder for all teachers and districts in a state reduces the ability of incentive programs to match local needs and abilities. They suggest the Professional Incentive Program or similar models be considered as alternatives for local school districts. Such programs allow teachers to improve their work environment and provide them with some professional autonomy.

Career Ladder Programs as Incentives for Teachers

H. Jerome Freiberg
University of Houston

Stephanie L. Knight
Texas A&M University

Tomorrow's Teachers: A Report of the Holmes Group (Holmes Group, 1986) and *A Nation Prepared: Teachers for the 21st Century* (Carnegie Forum, 1986) challenged the educational establishment to restructure the teaching profession in order to give teachers more opportunity for growth and recognition—not to mention greater financial rewards. One theme, beginning in the initial reports and continued in the Holmes and Carnegie commission reports, was the need for career paths for teachers.

The terms *career teacher, master teacher,* and *lead teacher* used in the two reports signaled a need to provide differentiated levels of professionalism. Career ladders were to be part of a new credentialing system for teachers to distinguish between beginning teachers who are learning their craft and experienced teachers who have mastered it. The career paths or ladders were designed to provide alternatives for career development, allowing teachers to stay in the classroom and receive higher salaries and greater prestige. (To this point in time, most teachers have had to leave the classroom or profession in order to advance.) In addition, career ladders provide teachers with a choice of roles; stimulate teachers to be critical of their teaching; promote competition consistent with the free enterprise system; and incorporate a pay-for-performance approach, which has taxpayer support (Frieberg, 1985).

Several forces created a climate conducive to career ladder programs in school districts across the nation. Career ladder programs were developed and implemented during the early 1980s as a means of attracting and retaining teachers, since many teachers were considering leaving the teaching profession. Federal reports during the mid-1980s predicted a 34 percent shortage of teachers by 1992. A crisis atmosphere was created in which school boards and district administrators envisioned classrooms of students without teachers. A 1985 Gallup Poll (Gallup, 1985) indicated that 60 percent of these adults questioned favored a career ladder plan for teachers to be adopted by school districts in their own communities. And the mood of the country at the time also supported a more businesslike approach to education, which included greater competition as a method for achieving advancement within the profession.

Reaction to the perceived crisis came in the form of sweeping legislative mandates, often bypassing the teaching professionals who would implement the programs. Rewards and incentives were mandated in the form of career ladder and master teacher programs designed to break the lockstep salary schedule and provide new ways to encourage competent people to remain in teaching.

CAREER LADDER DESIGNS

Tennessee, the first comprehensive statewide career ladder plan for the 1980s, provided advancement for teachers within a five-tier system based on information gained from seven data sources for six areas of competence (Furtwengler, 1985). Initial data sources included classroom observation, development of a portfolio by the teacher, a written examination, and questionnaires administered to peers, students, and supervisors. Peer teachers who have reached higher levels of the ladder are used to implement each phase of the evaluation. Teachers who qualify for movement on the ladder receive monetary rewards ranging from $1,000 to $7,000 and participate in professional incentives such as extended contract duties and mentoring new teachers.

Although the specifics of the new wave of career ladder programs vary from state to state (i.e., a number of steps on the ladder, rewards and duties of participating teachers, areas of evaluation, and number and type of data sources), the frameworks of current programs are similar enough to provide models of comparison with the programs of the 1960s and 70s. Descriptions of these initial programs (Freiberg, 1985; Moore, 1984; Stedman, 1983) reveal that incentive models of the 1980s are repeating many of the same mistakes made by models of the 60s and 70s, as well as adding new problems, without incorporating some of the recognized strengths of first-generation plans.

Lessons from the Past

The designers of recent incentive programs failed to analyze the demise of career ladder programs from the 1960s. The conditions that led to the termination of initially successful programs such as those implemented in Temple City (California) in the late 1960s have not changed in the 1990s. The Temple City plan was one of the most widely cited and disseminated career ladder programs of the 1960s. The plan, with a hierarchy of four career paths, including Associate Teacher, Staff Teacher, Senior Teacher, and Master Teacher, was designed to financially reward those who reached the Master Teacher level with a salary that was greater than the superintendent of schools. The plan went beyond financial support to create a differentiated staffing pattern that would allow teachers to have greater decision-making authority as they moved along the career ladder (Freiberg, 1987). Although the Temple City plan lasted for seven years, problems with continued financing (as more teachers became eligible for higher levels of the career ladder) ultimately ended the program. However, problems related to funding limitations were not the sole reason for the demise of career ladder programs during the 1960s (see Freiberg, 1985, for a historical overview of master teacher programs). The egalitarian nature of teaching and the motivations of those entering the profession may actually have contributed more to the downfall of teacher incentive programs than the spectre of a financial time bomb for cost-conscious districts. Competitive reward systems, inherent in most career ladder plans, may foster greater teacher isolation and diminished collegiality, which run counter to the best interests of both teachers and students.

Teacher Cooperation versus Competition

Career ladder programs can foster competition among teachers, particularly those programs that focus on individual rewards, limiting advancement to a select few (e.g., Master Teachers). Proponents of competitive systems often point to business as proof that the competitive, pay-for-performance concept works. This is a misconception, however, since the business world has learned during the last decade that successful businesses foster internal cooperation, not competition (Sergiovanni, 1985). Competition in the business realm works best when it is "interorganizational" rather than "intraorganizational." As is true in business, intraorganizational competition in the teaching profession may have undesirable effects. A research study on educational reform related to merit pay, career ladder, and teacher incentives, which was commissioned by the Education Commission of the States, Denver, reports the following (Rosenholtz, 1985):

1. Research suggests that the schools with the greatest student learning gains are those which do not isolate teachers, but instead encourage professional dialogue and collaboration. Teaching in effective schools is a collective, rather than individual, enterprise.
2. Competitive rewards tend (a) to close rather than open communication and sharing among those who work together, (b) to bias comprehension of different viewpoints, and (c) to destroy trust among group workers.
3. Mutual encouragement and support by group members are substantially reduced in group settings, and their problem-solving capacity is diminished. In fact, competitive conditions may lead people to deliberately frustrate the attempts of others to succeed (p. 351).

In summary, a teacher development program that requires teachers to compete for limited rungs on a career ladder will not foster cooperation and communication or reduce the isolation faced by some teachers in the classroom.

Norm-Referenced versus Criterion-Referenced Career Ladders

Presently, two types of career ladder programs are in operation (Freiberg, 1987): norm referenced and criterion referenced (see Figures 1 and 2). Each type of career ladder has a significantly different effect on the issue of cooperation and competition.

The career ladder concept by nature, produces a hierarchy in teaching. A norm-referenced career ladder plan (e.g., Temple City, the original career ladder components of the Tennessee Plan, and the current Texas and Florida plans), by design, limits the number of teachers at the top of the ladder through funding limitations or fixed quotas. The norm-referenced career ladder relegates the majority of teachers to a future of limited opportunities, forced competition, and greater isolation.

Similar concerns were expressed in a 1973 report of the American Institute for Research report of the Temple City plan cited by English (1985): "The concept of a career ladder, which allows teachers to advance to higher levels of responsibility and income within the teaching profession, has proved largely impractical due to a lack of teacher turnover and absence of openings to which teachers can, in fact, advance" (pp. 23–24).

Figure 1
Norm-Referenced Career Ladder

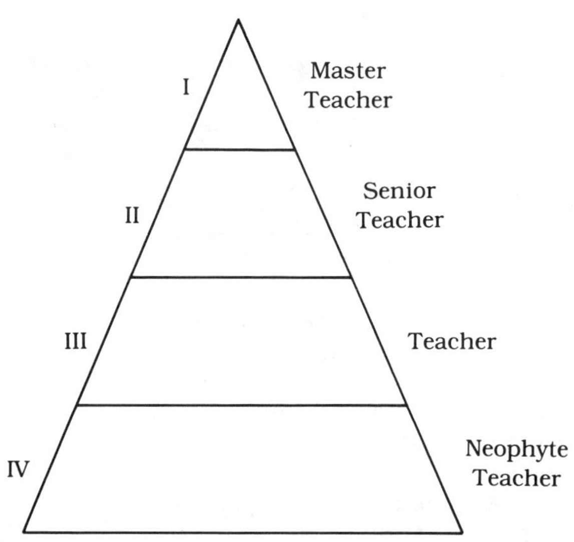

Figure 2
Criterion-Referenced Career Ladder

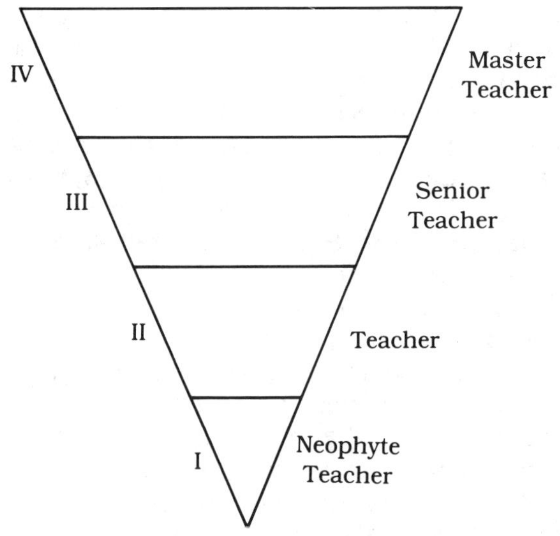

Conversely, a criterion-referenced career ladder plan, which uses, for example, advanced degrees, years of experience, or favorable classroom evaluations as bases for promotion, allows many more teachers to advance through the hierarchy. In addition, this system reduces competition by focusing teachers' time and energy on the criteria to be obtained rather than on each other. However, after a few years, the inverted pyramid may become a financial time bomb for the school district or state funding agency if a fixed stipend is provided for each teacher who fulfills the requirements. Furthermore, the motivational factors for teachers may become diminished over time.

Current Trends

In 1986, 43 states were considering or implementing career ladder, merit pay, or incentive programs, in part to respond to a pending teacher supply crisis (Darling-Hammond and Berry, 1988). Actual teacher employment figures for 1989, however, showed that the dire predictions for teacher shortages have not been realized. Some shortages exist in growth areas of the country (e.g., southern California), in inner-city schools, and in selected content areas (mathematics and science), but widespread shortages have not emerged. Real increases in teacher salaries (Darling-Hammond and Berry, 1988) during the last several years have drawn more college students into teaching (AACTE, 1988) and brought certified teachers out of retirement. The addition of alternative certification programs has also added to the supply of teachers (particularly in mathematics and science).

Leaving the Profession

The initial intent of career ladder programs was to recruit and keep the best teachers. A recent poll conducted for Metropolitan Life by Harris (1988) indicates that 26 percent of teachers polled are planning to leave the profession. Teachers most likely to leave the profession are small-town teachers (29 percent) and inner-city teachers (28 percent). When one compares years of experience with intent to leave the profession, teachers with 10 to 19 years' experience indicate the least likelihood of leaving; however, 34 percent of new teachers (0 to 5 years' teaching experience) and veteran teachers (20+ years) indicate they will be leaving during the next five years. The veterans presumably plan to leave for retirement. For new teachers, the rate is 14 percent higher than a similar poll taken during 1987. Additionally, 40 percent of minority teachers at all levels of experience indicate they will be leaving in the next five years. Since more minority teachers teach in inner-city schools than nonminority teachers (29 percent versus 9 percent), working conditions may contribute to their desire to leave teaching. The conditions of inner-city schools require a greater degree of effort on the part of the teacher to meet more demanding needs of the students.

However, the number of teachers actually quitting their jobs is considerably less than those wanting to leave teaching. The issue may be one of entrapment. Without realistic alternatives, teachers remain locked into their current positions. Dworkin (1987), in a study of teacher burnout in a large inner-city district, concludes that entrapment and teacher burnout could be alleviated by higher pay, greater professional autonomy, and a more collegial style among school administrators (p. 171).

Teacher salaries have increased significantly during the last several years as a result of reform efforts to attract and keep quality teachers. Changes in the style of principals have become a focal point of administrative reform based on the effective schools' research. In contrast, teacher professional autonomy has lagged behind the other two areas. Career ladder and other teacher incentive programs were designed to provide new leadership roles (e.g., Master Teacher) and additional resources to enhance teacher self-worth. However, this intent has not been found in practice. Most of the incentive programs have been top-down state-mandated programs that built on business and industry models that had little applicability to the egalitarian nature of the teaching profession (Lortie, 1975). Additionally, current career ladder programs have tied teacher evaluation to advancement on the ladder. With teacher evaluation comes the dilemma of who should assess the effectiveness of the teacher and what role this evaluation should play in the teacher's or principal's everyday work.

Teacher Evaluation

Tennessee has recognized the problems that evaluation creates in relation to school climate. The use of school principals as primary evaluators conflicts with the role of the principal as creator of staff cohesion and impedes the use of formative evaluation to improve teacher performance. Principals have a difficult time "ranking" teachers for career ladders and, at the same time, maintaining the atmosphere of trust, openness, and cooperation that characterizes many effective schools. The use of peer evaluators, on the other hand, is favored by teachers (French, Malo, and Rakow, 1988) and would appear to be the answer to the principal's problem. However, peer evaluation creates other areas of concern.

Evaluation by peers may not create an atmosphere of cooperation among teachers and may eventually heighten teacher isolation. Successful business models have made educators aware of the advantages of "intergroup" competition as oposed to "intragroup" competition. In addition, peer evaluation is not popular with many teacher organizations and unions. The Tennessee Education Association, for example, has continued to be a vocal and influential opponent of the program (Furtwengler, 1987).

Funding

Funding problems continue to exist today, as in the past. Innovations such as career ladder plans partly rest on financial rewards for excellence in teaching. School districts depend on legislative largesse for the additional funds to provide the salary increments that differentiate steps on the ladder. Since legislatures are subject to turnover of key personnel and, as a result, changing priorities, and since general economic conditions dictate the availability of funds, many states are faced with the withdrawal or reduction of funding for career ladder plans. The general economic slowdown in Texas in the mid- and late 80s, for example, has placed continuation of funding for the Texas Career Ladder in jeopardy. Recent legislative actions require local school districts to pay a greater share of career ladder costs. Districts that are unable to supplement increments with district resources will be faced with the dilemma of drastically reducing the number of participants in the program or complying with the state mandate in name only. As a result, school climate problems associated with the competition for scarce resources to maintain career ladders may create more problems than were initially solved by introduction of the "incentive."

Incentives by Mandate

Perhaps the most serious flaw in many of the current programs is mandating career ladder programs from the "top down." Tennessee admits that the perception that teachers were only minimally involved in the planning process is a sensitive issue (Furtwengler, 1987). One of the greatest strengths of the Temple City model was the involvement of teachers in all phases of program development and implementation. Models that are not initiated within the contexts in which they will be carried out are unlikely to be sensitive or even compatible with local goals and needs. In fact, the mere mention of a mandate often creates suspicion among personnel to the extent that the plan is marked for failure before it has even been fully implemented. Furthermore, districts are less likely to keep allocating scarce funds since the commitment and need for the programs are often tenuous.

Local Initiatives

Two exceptions to this pattern of top-down mandates have recently emerged. In 1987, a large urban school district in Rochester (New York) initiated a plan to increase the roles, responsibilities, and salaries of teachers to address problems facing urban schools today (Sheive, 1988). The Rochester Contract is based on the idea of "shared governance," reminiscent of the shared decision-making processes initially so successful in Temple City. However, it is too early to determine if Rochester can overcome the threats to administrators involved in decentralization of power. In fact, the district has already been involved in litigation brought against them and the teachers' union by the Administrators' and Supervisors' Association of Rochester (Urbanski, 1988).

The second exception is drawn from a small rural school district in Texas. Although the district is part of a state-mandated career ladder program, it began its own locally developed program prior to the state's. A study was conducted by the authors to examine the effects of two types of teacher incentive programs operating simultaneously (Freiberg and Knight, 1988).

CAREER LADDER STUDY

Participants in this study were approximately 170 teachers from a small rural school district in southeast Texas. Teachers were administered a school climate questionnaire in April of 1985, 1986, and 1987 to obtain their perceptions of six dimensions of school climate, as well as the recent state-mandated Career Ladder Program, over a three-year period. Prior to the development of the state career ladder, the district introduced the nonmonetary Professional Incentive Program (PIP), which has been designed by a committee of district teachers and administrators. Teachers' perceptions of this program were assessed in conjunction with the 1986 and 1987 school climate survey.

Incentive Program

In the summer of 1984, teachers were administered a questionnaire to assess their current satisfaction with teaching and to identify nonmonetary professional incentives that could be implemented by the district. Teachers were asked to identify (1) those elements that add or detract from their satisfaction with teaching as a profession and (2) their level of interest in certain items as professional incentives. A task force composed of 10 teachers and 2 administrators studied these data and made recommendations on development and implementation of an incentive program for teachers in the district. Using the interview results, the committee hoped to gain additional information to enable them to define and structure a program based on teacher needs, and to uncover possible issues, problems, or misconceptions to facilitate successful implementation of the program.

Teachers surveyed indicated greatest interest in the following professional incentives:

1. Participating in school improvement programs (79 percent)
2. Participating in demonstration teaching programs (72 percent)
3. Receiving a computer for classroom use (69 percent)
4. Attending professional conferences (69 percent)
5. Participating in teacher self-assessment programs to improve teaching skills (67 percent)

The followup interview data revealed attending professional conferences, participation in summer institutes, and participation on school improvement teams as the top three choices. The increased popularity of the summer institute concept was, perhaps, the key incentive after the interviewer explained that teachers would have the opportunity to define and structure these sessions themselves. Interest in participating in demonstration teaching programs decreased when participants realized that they, personally, might be asked to allow other teachers to observe them in the classroom. Most of the negative respondents cited their dislike of being observed by their peers as their main reason.

After reviewing these results, the committee divided into subgroups to discuss the findings and prioritize the incentives using both survey and interview data. The Superintendent and Director of Instruction worked closely with the group to contribute their knowledge of the resources of the district. The committee forged a plan that was flexible enough to appeal to kindergarten as well as high school teachers and that would respond to the needs of a changing staff. Finally, less than a year after the formation of the working committee, the Board of Trustees adopted the recommended Professional Incentive Plan. The plan included the following three components, which were available to individuals, groups, grade levels, or departments:

1. *Special project grants.* A special project can be defined as a nonroutine, different, or innovative approach to teaching a particular unit, skill, or concept. A request for a special project grant may include funds for materials, for the use of special equipment for a specified period of time, or for paraprofessional assistance for a specified period of time. Additionally, special project grants may include funds for attendance at summer institutes, workshops, or conferences during the year that provide training that is related to the implementation of the project.
2. *Grants for summer institutes.* Grants for summer institutes are available for the purpose of funding participation in summer institutes related to the teaching assignment.
3. *Grants for conferences or workshops.* These grants are available for the purpose of funding participation in conferences or workshops during the school year or during the summer months that are related to the teaching assignment.

A committee comprised of teachers and administrators representing all the schools in the district was responsible for considering grant applications and determining the level of funding to be awarded. During the 1985–86 academic school year, 22 grants involving 37 teachers were funded in the district. For the 1986–87 school year, 25 grants were awarded involving 51 teachers. The average award per grant in 1985 was $304, while the average award per teacher was $181. The average award per grant in 1986 increased to $323, while the average award per teacher was $158, indicating group efforts.

The School Climate Questionnaire for Teachers (Freiberg, Pyper, Ginsburg, Spuck, and Forsbach, 1980), administered on the span of each year, contains six scales, each consisting of five items designed to assess teachers' opinions of the principal's role in their schools; teacher interactions with peers, administrators, parents, and students; and the physical environment. The specific scales include: Leadership Qualities of the Principal, Teacher-Peer Relations, Parent-Teacher Relations, Student-Teacher Interpersonal Relations, Student-Teacher Instructionally Related Interactions, and School Building and Facilities. These scales have been found to be reliable, with alpha coefficients ranging from .55 to .85 (Pyper, Freiberg, Ginsburg, and Spuck, 1981). Additional scales were included to determine teachers' perceptions of the effects of the statewide career ladder program on school climate in 1985 and 1986. In addition, the 1986 and 1987 climate questionnaires included scales consisting of items to assess (1) teachers' opinions of the effects of the program on school climate and (2) their actual or intended participation in the Professional Incentive Program implemented during the previous year by the district.

Teachers responded to each item on the questionnaire by indicating their level of agreement with statements on a Likert-type scale. Mean scores for each item and subscale were computed. A mean value near 1 means that teachers strongly agreed with that item or the items in the subscale and had a positive opinion of that dimension, whereas a value close to 5 reveals that teachers strongly disagreed with the statement or statements comprising the subscale and exhibited a negative perception of that dimension. A value near 3 can be regarded as an expression of uncertainty or neutrality for that item or subscale. Additionally, a series of open-ended questions relating specifically to the Texas career ladder were added to the end-of-school climate questionnaire. Some 151 questionnaires were returned, yielding an 88 percent response rate.

Results and Discussion

Descriptive statistics were calculated for all subscales. Table 1 presents the means and standard deviations of the six climate indicators and three external influences indicators (the career ladder subscale for 1985, 1986, and 1987, and the two incentive program subscales for 1986 and 1987). Results revealed that teachers rated the six climate indicators positively for all three years. Also, for the three time periods, teachers viewed student-teacher interpersonal relations as the most positive indicator of school climate. The career ladder itself, however, was the only scale that was viewed negatively by the teachers for all three years. Teachers' perceptions of the Professional Incentive Program and their participation in it during 1986 were uncertain or neutral, perhaps suggesting a "wait-and-see" attitude. For 1987, teachers' views of the PIP and their participation in it were more positive.

Open-Ended Responses

A content analysis was conducted on the open-ended responses to the item: "The effects of the career ladder components of HB72

Table 1 **Means and Standard Deviations of School Climate and External Influences Variables by Year**

	1985 (N = 172)		1986 (N = 148)		1987 (N = 116)	
	M	*SD*	*M*	*SD*	*M*	*SD*
School Climate Variables						
Leadership qualities of the principal	2.25	.71	2.33	.80	2.21	.74
Teacher-peer relations	2.52	.54	2.62	.54	2.48	.51
Parent-teacher relations	2.41	.56	2.21	.53	2.25	.59
Student-teacher interpersonal relations	2.19	.47	2.11	.49	2.04	.45
Student-teacher instructionally related interactions	2.69	.77	2.85	.87	2.80	.78
Variables						
Career ladder	4.26	.87	4.26	.87	3.81	1.04
Professional Incentive Program (PIP)	—	—	3.01	.96	2.66	1.08
Participation in PIP	—	—	3.31	1.06	2.98	1.14

Note: **Mean values near 1 indicate a positive perception of the subscale. Mean values closer to 5 exhibit a negative perception of the subscale.**

have had a positive effect on school climate. Please explain." Teachers' responses sorted into 11 categories. Table 2 shows these categories and their frequencies. Of 101 responses, 100 could be identified as disagreeing with the statement and one written response agreed with the statement. Responses relating to low morale/dissatisfaction, competition between teachers, and the fairness of the career ladder represented over 50 percent of the responses.

Discussion

The intent of the Texas Career Ladder is to improve the career paths of teachers, provide greater motivation to teach and remain in teaching, and improve the quality and conditions of teaching. The negative responses from teachers over a three-year period on the school climate questionnaires would indicate that the intent of the career ladder in Texas is not being realized. Although the general society realizes the importance of providing support and incentives for teachers to stay in the profession, the actions by state legislatures, governors, and other representatives of the people have taken a paternalistic view of what teachers need. Mandating a career ladder without input from those teachers or administrators who are recipients is destined to meet resistance and failure.

Table 2 The Effects of the Career Ladder Component of HB72 on School Climate: Content Analysis of Open-Ended Responses

	Frequency
Causes low moral/dissatisfaction	26
Causes competition between teachers	15
Career ladder is applied unfairly	15
Evaluation instrument is unfair	13
People are on the career ladder who should not be	13
Causes competition between teachers and administration	8
Uncertainty of requirement	7
Criteria not worth the effort and money	2
More teacher input is needed	1
Creates no problems	1
No responses	50

Using proven management practices from business or industry, future incentive programs should establish governance panels composed of teachers and administrators who would develop and implement incentive programs and monitor their effectiveness. Incentive programs should have common goals but flexibility in the routes teachers and administrators can take in achieving those goals. Prescribing a career ladder for all teachers and districts in a state reduces the ability of incentive programs to match local needs and abilities. The Professional Incentive Program and other similar models (see Freiberg, 1987) should be provided as alternative routes for local school districts.

The implications for school districts seeking to balance local, state, and federal mandates are important. Districts need to provide greater opportunities for teachers and administrators to share decision making on local programs, perhaps resulting in a reduction of the negative side of state or federal mandates. It is evident from the data collected from this district that good intentions on the part of lawmakers do not always achieve their intended results.

References

American Association of Colleges for Teacher Education. (1988). *Teacher education pipeline: SCDE enrollments by race and ethnicity.* Washington, DC: Author.

Association for Supervision and Curriculum Development. (1985). *Incentives for excellence in America's schools.* The ASCD Task Force Report on Merit Pay and Career Ladders.

Brookover, W. B., Beady, C., Flood, P., Schweitzer, J., and Wisenbaker, J. (1979). *School social systems and student achievement: Schools can make a difference.* New York: Praeger.

Brookover, W. B., and Lezotte, L. W. (1977). *Changes in school characteristics coincident with changes in student achievement.* East Lansing: Michigan State University, College of Urban Development.

Burden, P. (1985). Career ladders and Japanese management styles. *Teacher Education and Practice, 2* (1), 15–23.

Burke, B. T. (1982). Round Valley School District. *Phi Delta Kappan, 64* (4), 265–266.

Carnegie Forum on Education and Economy. (1986). *A nation prepared: Teachers for the 21st century.* New York: Author.

Darling-Hammond, L., and Berry, B. (1988). *The evolution of teacher policy.* Santa Monica, CA: Rand.

Dronka, P. (1984). Pay incentive programs begin in four states. *ASCD Update, 26* (8), 1, 3, 6–7.

Dworkin, A. G. (1987). *Teacher burnout in the public schools: Structional causes and consequences for children.* Albany: State University of New York Press.

English, F. W. (1985). We need the ghostbusters! A response to Jerome Freiberg. *Educational Leadership, 42* (4), 22–25.

Freiberg, H. J. (1984, April). *A case study of school climate improvement at an urban junior high school.* Paper presented at the American Educational Research Association meeting, New Orleans.

Freiberg, H. J. (1985). Master teacher programs: Lessons from the past. *Educational Leadership, 42* (4), 16–21.

Freiberg, H. J. (1987). Career ladders: Messages gleaned from experience. *Journal of Teacher Education, 38* (4), 49–56.

Freiberg, H. J., and Knight, S. L. (1988). A longitudinal study of the effects of the career ladder on school climate in one district. *Teacher Education & Practice, 5* (1), 17–23.

Freiberg, H. J., Pyper, J., Ginsburg, M., Spuck, D., and Forsbach, J. (1980). *Teacher Corps School Climate Questionnaire.* Houston: University of Houston Teacher Corps Project.

Freiberg, H. J., Townsend, K., and Buckley, P. (1982). Does inservice make a difference? *British Journal of In-Service Education, 8* (3), 189–200.

Freiberg, H. J., Waxman, H. C., and Knight, S. L. (1985). Teacher incentive survey. Unpublished data.

French, R. L., Malo, G. E., and Rakow, E. A. (1988). What we have learned from Tennessee's career ladder experience. *Educational Leadership, 46* (3), 70–73.

Furtwengler, C. B. (1985). Tennessee's career ladder plan: They said it couldn't be done. *Educational Leadership, 43* (3), 50–56.

Furtwengler, C. B. (1987). Lessons from Tennessee's career ladder program. *Educational Leadership, 44* (7), 66–67.

Gallup, G. H. (1984). The 16th annual Gallup poll of the public's attitudes toward the public schools. *Phi Delta Kappan, 66* (1), 23–38.

Gallup, G. H. (1985). The 17th annual Gallup poll of the public's attitudes toward the public schools. *Phi Delta Kappan, 67* (1), 35–41.

Harris, L. (1988). The Metropolitan Life Survey. *The American Teacher.* New York: Metropolitan Life.

Holmes Group. (1986). *Tomorrow's teachers: A report of the Holmes Group.* East Lansing: Michigan State.

Lortie, D. (1975). *School teacher.* Chicago: University of Chicago Press.

Moore, R. W. (1984). *Master teachers (Fastback 201).* Bloomington, IN: Phi Delta Kappa Educational Foundation.

National Commission on Excellence in Education. (1983). *A nation at risk.* Washington, DC: U.S. Department of Education.

Pate-Bain, H. (1983). A teacher's point of view on the Tennessee master teacher plan. *Phi Delta Kappan, 65* (1), 725–726.

Peters, T. J., and Waterman, R. H. (1982). *In search of excellence.* New York: Harper & Row.

Purkey, S. C., and Smith, M. S. (1983). Effective schools: A review. *The Elementary School Journal, 83* (4), 427–452.

Pyper, J. R., Freiberg, H. J., Ginsburg, M. B., and Spuck, D. W. (1981, April). *School climate questionnaire: Instruments to measure teacher, parent and student perceptions of school climate.* Paper presented at the annual meeting of the American Educational Research Association, Los Angeles.

Rosenholtz, S. J. (1985). Political myths about education reform: Lessons from research on teaching. *Phi Delta Kappan, 66* (5), 349–355.

Rutter, M., Maughan, B., Mortimore, P., Ouston, J., and Smith, A. (1979). *Fifteen thousand hours: Secondary schools and their effects on children.* Cambridge, MA: Harvard University Press.

Sergiovanni, T. J. (1985). Teacher career ladders: Myths and realities in implementation. *Teacher Education and Practice, 2* (1), 5–11.

Sheive, L. T. (1988). New roles for administrators in Rochester. *Educational Leadership, 46* (3), 53–55.

Stedman, C. H. (1983). Tennessee's master plans for teachers, supervisors, and principals. *Journal of Teacher Education, 34* (2), 55–58.

Texas Association of School Boards. (1984). *Legislative report: Summary of House Bill 72,* 3–4.

Urbanski, A. (1988). The Rochester contract: A status report. *Educational Leadership, 46* (3), 48–52.

Chapter Twelve

A study of 75 teachers challenges the "risk-averse profile" that stereotypically describes the occupation. The teachers interviewed assumed leadership roles to be actively engaged in changing their work conditions. According to Trachtman, these teacher leaders helped formulate policies that would determine practice, evaluated first-year teachers, helped make decisions on funds distribution, and conducted classroom research. In addition, student, personal, professional, and school-site benefits accrued from their leadership activities. Few, however, reported real, shared participatory management in their schools. Decision making is still primarily "top down."

Voices of Empowerment: Teachers Talk about Leadership

Roberta Trachtman
Fordham University
School of Education

Education reform is no longer news. Yet, in a familiarly ironic way, while the rhetoric about the expansion of teachers' roles and leadership opportunities was growing during the mid-1980s, teachers' voices were decidedly missing. In the spring of 1987, we decided to ask teachers to speak for themselves, about themselves. Through conversations with teachers, we sought to examine whether or not the rhetoric of teacher leadership and expanded roles (Carnegie Forum, 1986; Holmes Group, 1986; Committee for Economic Development, 1985; National Governors' Association, 1986) matched the realities of public schools. Specifically, we asked those teachers designated as teacher leaders to discuss their expanded roles, describe what motivated them to accept leadership opportunities, and discuss whether these activities contributed to school improvement. This is the story of teachers who chose to step beyond their classroom doors into the wider world of their own schools and even beyond.

We found examples of new roles for teachers, personal satisfaction, powerful collegial relationships, and a pervasive professional glow. As we listened to teacher leaders, we became aware that they had obtained the rewards and recognition previously lacking in their work lives.

This chapter will discuss the activities and perceptions of

This research was supported by the American Federation of Teachers. From its inception, it has benefited from Marsha Levine's good conversation and critical review. Errors of fact or interpretation, however, are the author's responsibility.

teacher leaders by the staff of the American Federation of Teachers (AFT) as teachers who were performing activities beyond their traditional job descriptions. These activities included supervising new teachers, developing districtwide curricula, formulating school policies, and working with the external school community. In total, 75 teachers were interviewed by telephone, 50 selected from an AFT roster of teacher leaders, and 25 others recommended by the first group. These teachers were employed in large urban or medium-sized suburban school districts throughout the country. The study focused on defining their roles and examining their perceptions of the benefits and limitations of these expanded responsibilities.

FROM THE BOTTOM UP

Most career ladders (Freiberg and Knight, this volume; Darling-Hammond, 1987; Hawley, 1985; Malen and Hart, 1987) assign teachers to their roles on a competitive basis. In this "model" of teacher leadership, however, many teacher leaders were part of an initiative whereby no preestablished limits governed the number of potential leadership roles at a school site. In interviews, these teachers supported the absence of competitive structures that reward the few and ignore the many (Doyle and Hartle, 1985). Although it was clear that not every teacher would seek positions of leadership and that some "have had their decisions made for them for so long that their self-confidence has atrophied" (Dillon-Peterson, 1986, p. 32), there were no reported quotas on opportunities for teacher leadership roles. In speaking about the selection process, one teacher said, "I wanted to participate. I made it clear that I wanted to be part of that group." Another said, "Any teacher who wanted to be on it [districtwide curriculum committee] could have volunteered." In most cases, principals were not directly involved in the creation of these roles; consequently, the power that teachers derived was not viewed as *ceded power* but as *added organizational power.* The self-initiation of these roles enabled the teacher leaders to achieve a sense of control that had been previously lacking in their organizational lives. While they had historically controlled their life in the classroom, their success in carving out an added dimension to their work lives seemed to invest these initiatives with a different meaning. Clearly, the internal generation of these roles provided for a unique form of ownership and commitment from the teachers involved.

Career ladders attempt to change schools from the outside (Boyd, 1987). However, as Freiburg and Knight argue in Chapter Eleven, considerable evidence indicates that outside changes imposed on schools are consistently ignored, circumvented, or defeated at the local level (Berman and McLaughlin, 1978; McLaughlin, 1987). When asked how they were chosen, about one-third of these teacher leaders indicated that they were self-selected; they saw an opportunity for meaningful participation and they seized it. Over two-thirds of the teachers filled formal organizational positions. They indicated that their selection was based on "being known" to building administrators, to colleagues, or to the leadership of the local teachers' organization. As stated previously, they emphasized that no quota for teacher leadership existed. (*Author's note:* Nonteacher leaders might be interviewed at some future time to determine whether this is a consistent perception in the schools.) Regardless of whether the teacher leaders filled formal or informal organizational roles, the decision to participate reflected a desire to change the existing norms.

The teacher leaders rarely mentioned the selectivity and exclusivity problems reported by some of those in districts where teacher leadership roles have been externally introduced through the implementation of career ladders (Johnson, 1987; Kasten, 1986; Warren-Little, 1987). Instead, the data indicate that teachers as individuals, union leaders, or collaborators with administrators created opportunities for career growth, role expansion, and increased involvement in decision making.

Teachers Are Different

Teaching is an occupation traditionally characterized by privacy and isolation (Lortie, 1975). Teachers are urged not to look beyond the classroom door (Warren-Little, 1982; Rosenholtz, 1985). "When their [teachers'] work is finished they have nothing tangible to show off as a fruit of their labor" (Jackson, 1986, p. 55). Yet, on average, the 75 teachers in this study reported that they were participating in about *four* outside classroom activities each. They thus seemed to contrast clearly with the conservative, passive teacher described in the research literature (Lortie, 1975; Waller, 1961).

Like those who attempted to teacher-proof the school curriculum in the 1970s, or those who devised complicated accountability schemes in the early 1980s, recent reform proponents may be skewing their recommendations to reflect a stereotypical image of the teacher as resistant to change (Richardson, this volume). Teacher leaders in this study portray quite a different image of the professional teacher. Specifically, these data indicate that teacher leaders are active, engaged, and determined to change their working conditions. As a group, they are very experienced; over 90 percent have taught for longer than 10 years. They are also highly educated; about 75 percent hold at least a master's degree. They voice the same needs for task autonomy, discretion, and psychic rewards described by other experienced teachers (Rosenholtz and McAninch, 1987). Given the traditional "stagelessness" of teaching, with its rather flat opportunity structure, many of the teacher leaders in this study chose to stage their own careers and empower themselves. As one teacher leader said, "I [now] see my career differently too. I'm no longer focused on one classroom."

Through their many leadership roles, teachers in this study created networks and structures for increasing effective communication with colleagues and with those outside of the school community. Teacher leadership activities were also characterized by significant teacher-to-teacher exchanges. They required a frequency and quality of interaction that had been absent in most schools. For example, a Kansas City teacher said, "[Through these leadership opportunities] I've seen people who used to be afraid to express their opinions doing it. People are working together a lot more. Teachers are working more collaboratively."

All of these roles are consonant with the clarion calls for professionalism and empowerment; they include expanded decision-making responsibilities, increases in collegial activities, and more visible roles for teachers in the broader school community.

Professional Development and Training. Teacher leaders are engaged in significant professional development activities that brought them into frequent and systematic contact with their peers. Such activities included demonstrating instructional techniques to colleagues, presenting workshops to building and district teachers, and designing inservice activities. As one teacher in a midwestern city remarked, "[Through our efforts] we are training teachers at the building level to be leaders."

Teachers also provided training to their colleagues on specific topics determined by local need. For example, several teachers offered preparation sessions for the National Teachers' Exam, and others provided knowledge on curriculum development, such as student critical thinking skills.

Teacher Centers. Many teachers participated in teacher centers created by the local teachers' organization. The Teacher

Center is a districtwide entity that addresses the professional development needs of all teachers. Staffed by teacher leaders, the center has moved the delivery of professional development from an ad hoc, sporadic effort to one that is regular, consistent, and available. Given its separate location in the district, the Teacher Center provides teachers with a communal place for sharing ideas and strategies for the improvement of student learning.

Curriculum Development. Teachers were also working with their colleagues to develop curricula and monitor their implementation. In the words of one teacher from the Midwest, "We wanted to make the school different. When I first became involved . . . I felt that I was doing a hit and miss job [as a teacher]. I was concerned about the lowest level of kids who were not getting what they needed."

Department Chairs/Grade-Level Leaders. Teacher leaders were also participating in nonevaluative administrative roles. Through these activities, they provided colleagues with information, relayed teacher perspectives to the building administration, and served as ongoing liaisons between teachers and their supervisors.

Different Kinds of Leadership Roles

Many of the roles described by these teachers might be considered "second generation" in nature; they moved teacher leaders into an arena in which they were helping to set education policy, participating in financial decision making, assuming responsibility for coaching new and veteran teachers, and conducting research. Such activities served to increase teachers' understanding and participation in the broader organization of the school. The following paragraphs describe these roles.

Policy Roles. Teachers participated in policy-setting committees at the school building, district, state, and national levels. In this context, they helped formulate the policies that would determine teaching practice. For example, one New York teacher was involved in the selection of new colleagues and administrators, and a West Coast teacher was a member of a statewide standards and practices commission that established regulations regarding teacher assignment, certification, and training. (The Commission was also empowered to monitor compliance with its policies and to levy fines against those districts not in compliance.) Another teacher leader worked with teachers and administrators to create two new schools that would be collaboratively managed. Finally, a teacher from the Southwest worked with colleagues and administrators to design and implement new student evaluation procedures.

Mentoring/Coaching. Teachers evaluated first-year teachers and supervised (but did not evaluate) veteran teachers whose performance had been designated unsatisfactory. Many of the teacher leaders, as mentors and coaches, actually voted on the retention of first-year teachers, as well as veteran teachers who required intervention. While teachers' roles were previously limited to "coaching" colleagues, they were now participating in the final evaluation and promotion decisions.

Community Outreach. Teachers were systematically engaged with members of the external school community, including parents and members of the public and private sectors. This role proved particularly important in districts experiencing enrollment declines and the "graying" of the community. In such places, parental concern was no longer securing the passage of education budgets. Instead, in one teacher's words, teachers were "going out on Saturday, knocking on doors, and inviting the community to come to the school." Through these activities, teachers hoped to improve the image of the public school in the community and to develop greater support for education.

Research and Political Activism. Teacher leaders conducted classroom research on questions of direct interest to themselves and their colleagues. Others served information dissemination functions, often to further political goals. For example, one teacher stated that he "wanted to gain a political presence [so] we participated in endorsing candidates for the school board."

BENEFITS OF TEACHER LEADERSHIP

The teachers identified four major benefits accrued from leadership activities, including benefits for their students, for themselves, for their profession, and for the school. These coincided with previously identified teacher leadership benefits (Warren-Little, 1987; Rosenholtz and McAninch, 1987; Jacullo-Noto, 1987).

Teacher leaders in this study were unable to relate their work directly to increased student learning; only a small minority (8 percent) reported changes of any kind. Although researchers report that educationally effective schools are characterized by greater teacher collegiality and professional autonomy (Rosenholtz, 1985), at the time of this study, there may have been too few teacher leaders at each site to make this happen or the activities may have been too new. An alternative explanation, however, is that when the professionalization of teaching is confined to limited changes in teachers' working conditions, we have a long way to go toward changing learning in schools.

The Benefits to Students

It is most important to teachers that students learn. As described by Lortie (1975), work satisfaction for teachers is directly tied to task-related student outcomes; thus, teachers experience satisfaction when they feel they have positively influenced students' learning. This study was consistent with these observations. One teacher said, "I've learned to be a coach and to allow the student to be in charge of his or her learning." Another reported, "[Through this role] other teachers have learned to relate to kids as individuals. They've sought out ways to integrate curricula. . . . They enjoy and celebrate working with someone else." A third indicated that "It [the leadership role] forces me to see the larger picture. It helps me to understand that things affecting the kids are way out of my hands as a teacher." However, as indicated earlier, only a small number of teachers were able to report these kinds of changes.

The Benefits to Teachers

Teachers were asked to estimate the amount of compensation attached to these activities. Some 75 percent of the teachers received no money at all. As previously described by Lortie (1975) and Rosenholtz (1985), and apparently confirmed by these teachers, the availability of additional compensation did not predict teacher participation.

Professional and Personal Gains

Almost two-thirds of the teachers reported that they had experienced "changes" from these activities. Many of the respondents indicated that they and their colleagues had learned new skills through these roles, including a better understanding of group dynamics, improved leadership skills, and better instructional delivery techniques.

These additional roles appear to have provided teachers with the recognition and prestige that were otherwise missing from their work lives (Gallup Poll, 1985; Waller, 1961). Many reported that, as a result of these roles, they and other teachers had gained access to elites—district administrators, community leaders, and politicians. The gains teacher leaders described spoke directly to the issues of isolation and low self-esteem, which the literature offers as explanations for teacher burnout and disengagement (Lortie, 1975; Schug, 1983; Sergiovanni, 1976; Waller, 1961). As Purkey and Smith advised, "In both schools and industry, shared decisionmaking leads to increased job satisfaction, which has obvious ramifications for the quality of life in schools regardless of its impact on student achievement" (1985, p. 360).

There are some important implications to consider relating to the benefits identified by these teachers. A teacher shortage currently exists in certain subject areas in the inner cities and rural communities. Over the next 10 years, these shortages threaten to increase geometrically as veteran teachers throughout the country retire (Darling-Hammond, 1987). Accordingly, efforts that serve to attract and retain teachers are not to be undervalued. Since we know that teaching is characterized by self-imposed isolation (Flinders, 1987) and that it occurs in loosely coupled bureaucracies (Weick, 1976) where resource limitations encourage a greater reliance on work-processing strategies than on client needs (Flinders, 1987; Sizer, 1984), why are we surprised when new teachers exit quickly? Why do we continue to ask first-year teachers to perform the same duties and meet the same obligations as their most experienced peers?

The movement toward valuing veteran teachers by asking them to mentor first-year teachers is well conceived and long overdue. As one mentor described, "I was concerned about these new teachers getting off to a good start. I saw them as having potential; I didn't want their first year to be so hard that they didn't want to continue." Furthermore, by formalizing the assistance to experienced colleagues who are in need of help, teachers have begun to take responsibility for policing themselves—the hallmark of professionalism. Although we recognize that the introduction of these roles will shift the relations among educators and introduce predictable and considerable strain (Warren-Little, 1987), we must seek ways to mediate these changes.

LIMITS OF TEACHER LEADERSHIP

Teacher leaders in this study described some problems created by new leadership roles. More than 25 percent indicated that this role made serious demands on their time. About 10 percent reported that their participation had interrupted the continuity of instruction in their classes. Other teacher leaders indicated conflicts with peers and administrators. For several, the greatest conflict resulted from the general ambiguity of their roles and their discomfort with "having a foot in two worlds (teacher and administrator)." One teacher cautioned, "There's an energy developing [here]. We're broadening the base of power . . . [but] some teachers are having a bad time adjusting to the role . . . they're not sure what to do." Another said, "When I was chosen to be a member [of the district's faculty and administrator search committee] the younger teachers congratulated me. But it alienated me from the senior teachers for several years." A third teacher said, "Some issues have been favorably resolved. But sometimes the teachers undermine themselves—our committee makes decisions and the [other] teachers run to the principal." And finally, "Administrators and teachers out of my own district are interested and enthusiastic about what I share. Within my own school, I fear for my appraisal."

Others spoke about the responses of administrators. In some places, administrators have continued to block the process: "In my school nothing has changed. The principal doesn't abide by our recommendations." Or, as another teacher described her administrators' perspective, "Teachers think that they run the school. But, *we do*."

These comments are consistent with observations that suggest we need to reconceptualize schools so that they are communities characterized by a "culture of caring" (Noddings, 1988). Such communities are characterized by teamwork, by serious and intense dialogue among members, and by collegial, collaborative work. Indeed, these teacher leaders sought to introduce this kind of exchange within their settings. Three-quarters of them were able to remain in their classrooms while creating networks of collegiality. They did not distance themselves from students while engaged in efforts to expand their professional autonomy and power. They recognized the benefits, including increased credibility among colleagues, that accrue from retaining their primary roles as service providers to students. As they reported, they felt more influential and more effective at making things happen. The respondents indicated they were sought out as experts, recognized by their peers, and more generally visible in the school setting. Teacher leadership roles evoked feelings of personal meaningfulness. In Kanter's terms (1977), these teachers had gained organizational power through increased visibility.

We have witnessed the creation of new structures to provide for the perspectives and the participation of teachers. As evidenced by these teachers, participants derive much personal satisfaction from these roles. However, as discussed previously, while teachers seek means that confirm their efficacy with students, teacher leadership has not yet forced implementation of changes. Without such confirmation in the form of measurable achievements for their students, teachers may retreat from their participation in these activities as they recognize the limits of their involvement.

A Norm of Collaboration

Currently, teachers are not accustomed to working in collegial schools (Warren-Little, 1982); in fact, DeSanctis and Blumberg (1979) found that, on average, teachers interact with each other for less than two minutes each day! Thus, they must "unlearn" the norms of privacy and isolation as they develop new interpersonal, managerial, curricular, and instructional skills through leadership roles. Griffin writes, "The ideal classroom teacher sees teaching as more than meeting with students, and works with peers on identifying and acting on problems at classroom and school levels of the system" (1987, p. 33). Yet, we are sobered by the knowledge that, for the most part, teachers do not feel that the school is theirs, or that their individual success is tied to the success of the whole school (Sizer, 1984).

To nourish the potential for leadership in more teachers, colleges and universities will be required to provide preservice teacher candidates with appropriate knowledge and skills (Brownlee, 1979; Jacullo-Noto, 1987). Further, principals will need to learn the skills of collaboration and collegiality to accommodate these changes (Kasten, 1986). We already know that when management treats participation as a gift rather than a right, the threat of removing that gift is always present. Thus, as we continue to press for greater and more substantive teacher participation, we must remember Kanter's (1982) caution that gifts keep the giver in control.

SUMMARY

Presently, many school cultures do not establish teachers as leaders. In Schein's (1985) terms, teachers in leadership roles are not yet part of the basic assumptions and beliefs that are shared by school professionals. Even in places where teachers have established a presence in the school community that enables them to interact with colleagues and meet with parents and school administrators, decision making within school buildings is still primarily "top-down": fewer than 30 percent of teacher leaders reported that there was real shared, participatory management in their schools (see also Glasman, this volume).

In 1987, the teachers' views on teacher leadership corresponded to the views in the policy community at that time. This discussion has attempted to illuminate a stage in the current period of reform by describing the ways in which some teachers were thinking. Since two years have passed, it would be informative to determine whether teachers' conversations today are significantly different. Given that the policy community is now talking about reforming schools to improve student learning, it would be useful to find out whether "teacher talk" is now reflective of this shift.

For us, it is clear that expanding teachers' roles and creating opportunities for collegiality are important precursors to the ultimate goal of improved student learning. They are enabling structures—necessary but not sufficient for reforming schools.

References

Bacharach, S. B., Bauer, S. C., and Conley, S. (1986). Organizational analysis of stress. *Work and Occupations, 13* (1), 7–32.

Berman, P., and McLaughlin, M. (1978). *Federal programs supporting educational change. Vol. VIII. Implementing and sustaining innovations.* Santa Monica, CA: Rand.

Boyd, W. L. (1987). Public education's last hurrah? Schizophrenia, amnesia, and ignorance in school politics. *Educational Evaluation and Policy Analysis, 9* (2), 85–100.

Brownlee, G. D. (1979). Characteristics of teacher leaders. *Educational Horizons, 57,* 112–122.

Carnegie Forum on Education and the Economy. (1986, May). *A nation prepared: Teachers for the 21st century. The Report of the Task Force on Teaching as a Profession.* New York: Carnegie Corporation.

Committee for Economic Development. (1985). *Investing in our children.* New York: Committee for Economic Development.

Darling-Hammond, L. (1987). Schools for tomorrow's teachers. *Teachers College Record, 88* (3), 354–358.

DeSanctis, M., and Blumberg, A. (1979). *An exploratory study into the nature of teacher interactions with other adults in the schools.* Paper presented at the annual meeting of the American Educational Research Association, San Francisco.

Dillon-Peterson, B. (1986). Trusting teachers to know what's good for them. In *Improving Teaching.* Alexandria, VA: ASCD Yearbook.

Doyle, D. P., and Hartle, T. W. (1985). Leadership in education: Governors, legislators and teachers. *Phi Delta Kappan, 67* (1), 21–27.

Flinders, D. S. (1987). *How teachers survive teaching: Themes drawn from educational criticism.* Paper presented at the annual meeting of the American Educational Research Association, Washington, DC.

Frymier, J. (1987). Bureacracy and the neutering of teachers. *Phi Delta Kappan, 69* (1), 9–16.

Gallup Poll. (1985). *Phi Delta Kappan, 66* (5), 35–47.

Goodman, J. (1987). Key factors in becoming (or not becoming) an empowered elementary school teacher: A preliminary study of selected novices. Revised copy to be published in the *Journal of Education for Teaching, 13* (3), 121–130.

Griffin, G. (1987). Clinical teacher education. *Journal of Curriculum and Supervision, 2* (3), 248–274.

Hart, A. W. (1987). A career ladder's effect on teacher career and work attitudes. *American Educational Research Journal, 24* (4), 479–503.

Hawley, W. (1985). Designing and implementing performance-based career ladder plans. *Educational Leadership, 43* (3), 57–61.

Holmes Group, The. (1986, April). *Tomorrow's teachers: A report of the Holmes Group.* East Lansing, MI: Author.

Jackson, P. (1986). *The practice of teaching.* New York: Teachers College Press.

Jacullo-Noto, J. (1987). *Teachers: Behavioral characteristics of emerging leaders.* Paper presented at the annual meeting of the American Educational Research Association, Washington, DC.

Johnson, S. M. (1987). Teaching reform in an active voice. *Phi Delta Kappan, 68* (8), 591–598.

Kanter, R. M. (1977). *Men and women of the corporation.* Philadelphia: Basic Books.

Kanter, R. M. (1982). Dilemmas of managing participation. *American Management Association Journal, 11.*

Kasten, K. (1986). Redesigning teachers' work. *Issues in Education, IV* (3), 272–286.

Levine, M. (1986). Excellence in education: Lessons from America's best run companies and schools. *Peabody Journal of Education, 63* (2), 156–186.

Lortie, D. C. (1975). *Schoolteacher: A sociological study.* Chicago: University of Chicago Press.

Malen, B., and Hart, A. H. (1987). Career ladder reform: A multi-level analysis of initial efforts. *Educational Evaluation and Policy Analysis, 9* (1), 9–23.

McLaughlin, M. W. (1987). Learning from experience: Lessons from policy implementation. *Educational Evaluation and Policy Analysis, 9* (2), 171–178.

National Governors' Association. (1986). *A time for results.* National Governor's Association.

Noddings, N. (1988, March). Toward a culture of caring. Presentation made at Hofstra University, New York.

Purkey, S. C., and Smith, M. S. (1985). School reform: The district policy implications of the effective schools literature. *The Elementary School Journal, 85* (3), 353–389.

Rosenholtz, S. (1985). Political myths about education reform: Lessons from research on teaching. *Phi Delta Kappan, 66* (5), 349–355.

Rosenholtz, S., and McAninch, A. C. (1987). *Workplace conditions and the rise and fall of teacher commitment.* Revised version of a paper presented at the annual meeting of the American Educational Research Association, Washington, DC.

Schein, E. H. (1985). *Organizational culture and leadership.* San Francisco: Jossey-Bass.

Schug, M. C. (1983). Teacher burn-out and professionalism. *Issues in Education, 1* (2,3).

Sergiovanni, T. (1976). Factors which affect satisfaction and dissatisfaction of teachers. *The Journal of Educational Administration, 27* (1), 14–31.

Sizer, T. (1984). *Horace's compromise.* New York: Houghton Mifflin.

Waller, W. (1961). *The sociology of teaching.* New York: John Wiley.

Ward, B., Pascarelli, J., and Carnes, J. (1985). The expanding role of the teacher: A synthesis of practice and research. In L. Crohn (Ed.), *Pathways to growth.* Portland, OR: Northwest Regional Educational Labs. ED 265160.

Warren-Little, J. (1982). Norms of collegiality and experimentation: Workplace conditions of school success. *American Educational Research Journal, 19* (3), 325–340.

Warren- Little, J. (1984). Seductive images and organizational realities in professional development. *Teachers College Record, 86* (1), 84–102.

Warren-Little, J. (1987). *Assessing the prospect for teacher leadership.* Paper presented at the annual meeting of the American Educational Research Association, Washington, DC.

Weick, K. (1976). Educational organizations as loosely coupled systems. *Administrative Science Quarterly, 21* (1), 1–19.

Chapter Thirteen

New collective bargaining arrangements, called policy trust agreements, *are opening the door to significantly expanded teacher work roles. Kerchner and Koppich examine trust agreements in three school districts in California. The agreements provide a way for teachers and administrators to meet on pressing problems identified in the trust agreements. The agendas span the topics of curriculum, student discipline, and teacher evaluation. According to the authors, the trust agreement is a new idea, and its propriety and legitimacy are uncertain. Furthermore, reaching agreements requires team members to work through several uncertainties. However, the trust agreement's delineation of specific problems, resources, and goals appears to be providing a structure for one form of shared governance in schools.*

Redefining Teacher Work Roles through the Educational Policy Trust Agreement

Charles Taylor Kerchner
The Clarement
Graduate School

Julia E. Koppich
University of California,
Berkeley

WHAT IS A TRUST AGREEMENT?

An Educational Policy Trust Agreement both expands and alters the relationship between unionized teachers and their employers. A trust agreement is a negotiated compact that covers educational items generally not addressed in collective bargaining. It expands teachers' participatory and decision-making activities. By expanding decision making and participation, trust agreements also broaden responsibility for educational problems. The districts that negotiate trust agreements recognize that it is no longer sufficient for teachers to say, "That's management's problem," or "That's the teachers' interest."

In the larger context, trust agreements redefine teacher work roles. In a decade of labor relations research, role prescription or identification presented itself as the single most important commonality in norms and values individuals brought to education (Kerchner and Mitchell, 1988). Work role was more important than gender, race, geography, or political predisposition in determining attitudes about education. Teachers *did* think like teachers. Thus, a policy vehicle, such as the Educational Policy Trust Agreement, that offers teachers the possibility of redefining historic role relationships is potentially powerful.

A trust agreement was originally proposed to the California Commission on the Teaching Professions as a means for involving teachers in the reform of their own occupation (Kerchner and Mitchell, 1986). Trust agreements anticipate joint action on problems such as curriculum reform, achievement, teaching careers, school restructuring, and teacher evaluation.

These problems differ from conventional labor relations in both technical and substantive ways. Technically, they are frequently beyond the scope of bargaining for labor contracts. Although the legal definition of what may or may not be bargained is often imprecise, each school district usually has a working tradition of what it negotiates and what it does not. Substantively, conventional contractual agreements are designed to deal with subjects where the outcome can be clearly known. It is readily apparent, for instance, whether someone is being paid and at what rate. One recognizes who has the right to continued employment during times of layoff. And there is no unsureness about the football coach's supplemental salary, or the steps that should be taken to resolve a grievance.

Problems of school reform are not so certain. Although teachers and administrators may be certain they need a better mechanism for socializing and evaluating new teachers, they may be quite unsure about what will work best for them. How should administrators and experienced teachers work with novices? Should there be occasions when all new teachers are brought together for in-service education? Who should visit classrooms and how often? Does intensifying efforts with new teachers pay substantial dividends in terms of teacher performance? How can student success be determined?

As in most problems associated with schools, the problem to be solved is relatively clear, but the solution is not certain. What is needed is not a specification of the solution so that individual rights and obligations are made clear but a stipulation that people agree to work on the problem and to set aside resources so that they can jointly attack it. This is the setting of which the Educational Policy Trust Agreement is intended.

What's in a Name?

One of the best ways to understand an Educational Policy Trust Agreement is to look at the words in its name:

Educational Policy. These agreements are intended to focus on the teaching-learning process, the central function of schooling. Entering into a trust agreement mode of labor relations establishes a new arena. Both administrators and teachers can raise questions that are explicitly educational but are not frequently discussed in conventional collective bargaining.

Explicitly involving organized teachers in policy making involves rethinking organizational roles. Classically, policy is thought to be the exclusive domain of school managers and the school board, but we have come to recognize that, in practice, the division between policy and practice is not nearly so tidy. Organized teachers are already involved in policy making. Collectively bargained contracts distribute the vast majority of a district's operating resources, and labor relations dramatically affect the institutional culture of a school and the ways in which teachers define their occupation. Trust agreements merely make explicit that which we have known all along.

Two Kinds of Trust. The word *trust*, as we use it, has two meanings. The first involves the reliability and truthfulness of the other party. A certain level of this common, ordinary type of trust is a necessary ingredient in trust agreement negotiations. However, the uniqueness of the trust agreement is formed around the definition of *trust* as things of value entrusted to a person with instructions to use them for the benefit of another. These are the kinds of trusts that parents establish for their offspring, that philanthropists create for the benefit of society, and that governments found to protect national treasures.

In education, we intend that the well-being of children and youth should be the object of trusts that are established by school districts and teachers. Each of these parties controls valuable resources—money, time, authority, commitment—that can be applied to further the condition of the school's clients and the larger community.

The Trust Agreement Project

With financial support from the Stuart Foundations, an action research project has been undertaken to facilitate trust agreements and to document their implementation. The project is cosponsored by the California Federation of Teachers, the California Teachers Association, the Association of California School Administrators, and the California School Boards Association, and it is operated under the auspices of Policy Analysis for California Education (PACE), headquartered at the University of California, Berkeley.[1]

Shortly after release of recommendation on cooperative labor-management agreements by the California Commission on the Teaching Professions, Miles Myers, president of the California Federation of Teachers, expressed interest in a pilot project

(California Commission, 1985). With foundation assistance, the initial pilot project expanded, first to 6 and then to 12 districts, ranging in enrollment from 2,500 to more than 60,000 students.

Trust agreements have no subject matter. Districts are faced with diagnosing their own situation rather than adopting solutions to someone else's problems. Each district also establishes its own form of organization. Like conventional "bargaining teams," the trust agreement teams are composed of teachers and management members, but there are no preexisting rules about who, how many, or how often.

AMBIGUITY IN THREE DISTRICTS

The three school districts—here called Able, Baker, and Charlie—display three different uncertainty problems regarding the legitimacy of the trust agreement, its purpose, and leadership toward it. Interestingly, whenever two of the three uncertainties are managed, at least tacit agreement and implementation are possible. These chronologies describe the three districts' trust agreement experience through the 1988–1989 school year.

Able District

Able is a large and growing suburban district with a history of fractious labor relations. As a case, Able District represents a very firm topical focus that has yielded a well-implemented project. But through accident of history, the trust agreement as a negotiating setting remains illegitimate, and the agreement remains unsigned.

Interest in peer evaluation predates Able District's involvement in the trust agreement project or their acceptance of the idea that educational policy questions might be the subject of labor-management agreements. One teacher, Martha Joyce, had become interested in peer review and had applied to become a Mentor Teacher.[2] She was an active member of the Able Teachers Union and was familiar with the teacher supervision and evaluation program in Toledo. The outlines of the Able evaluation program were strongly influenced by the Toledo structure.

The district was interested in the project for two quite different reasons. First, rapid growth necessitated implementation of a new evaluation plan. After several years of stable to declining enrollments, the district anticipated increasing its teaching force as much as 10 percent a year for several years. In the first year of Joyce's evaluation plan, there were to be 125 new teachers—far more than principals could effectively socialize. Joyce's plan was perceived as a way to continue the district's tradition of providing high levels of teacher socialization to common teaching and classroom management practices.

Second, the district, and particularly superintendent Sam Adams, was interested in forming a new relationship with teachers. The district had been plagued by difficult labor relations, which resulted from a historic inability to reach closure in negotiations. The district negotiated continuously, finally signing one contract just in time to begin bargaining the next. Angry meetings and public protests were part of the ritual. In Joyce's words, concerted action short of a strike became "the foreplay to an agreement." Superintendent Adams saw providing other avenues for teacher expression and involvement as alternatives to what he called "union tactics." The teacher improvement project was not administratively perceived as a union venture, even though it was led by a union activist, and Able Teacher Union president Roberta Sanchez controlled the majority of appointments to the governing board. As the Able Teacher Improvement Project started (see Table 1), teachers and administrators were at impasse in contract negotiations.

Three senior teachers began work in September helping to orient new teachers: finding supplies, introducing them to other teachers, and sharing classroom survival techniques. Contract negotiations continued at a standstill. Excepting the new teachers, the ATU ordered teachers not to attend back-to-school meetings scheduled by the district. The boycott had taken the form of an annual ritual. This act, and other minor examples of civil disobedience, nettled Superintendent Adams, encouraging the union to repeat them. It was agreed that any substantive discussion of reducing the teacher evaluation system to a union-management agreement would have to wait until after the contract was signed.

The teacher socialization project was far more successful than expected. The three supervising teachers, who virtually created their new jobs, encountered no serious problems. The superintendent openly supported the program but wisely did not mandate schools to participate. This act, alone, probably prevented initial failure. The supervising teachers were saved from battling with reluctant principals, and their case load became manageable. They began formative evaluations in October and summative ones by year's end.

By January, contract negotiations were still stalled, but union president Sanchez was actively participating in the governing board committee overseeing the new teacher program. She, the superintendent, and a board member also participated in a trust

Table 1 Able School District

June	July	Aug.	Sept.	Oct.	Nov.	Dec.
Evaluation Project						
Concept complete. Basic text of agreement written. Contact with Toledo about its evaluation plan.		Teachers hired.	Supervision begins. School opening activities.		Evaluation begins.	
Bargaining Negotiations						
Negotiations at impasse.			Boycott of back-to-school events. New teachers are exempted from boycott.		No progress in negotia-tions.	Unfair labor practices, filings, and hearings with hearing officer.
Union agrees to use $100,000 previously negotiated for new teacher evaluation project.						
Trust Agreement Negotiations						
District becomes aware of and interested in trust agreement concept.			Trust agreement negotiations postponed until contract settled.			

agreement retreat at which the district's program was presented. Shortly after this retreat, an unprecedented three-year contract was signed, thus assuring Able of starting a new school year without the cloud of contract negotiations.

Simultaneously, however, the ATU filed several unfair labor practice charges against the district over questions that the district, and some union members, considered frivolous. Interpersonal relations between Sanchez and Adams remained frosty, and trust agreement negotiations never began. By year's end, Adams had simply declined to memorialize the already operating agreement with teachers.

However, both parties were actively discussing next steps. The ATU had reservations about extending the evaluation plan to include intervention with tenured teachers whose performance had deteriorated. Adams wanted expansion. The teachers wanted a career development plan for the vast majority of staff who were neither new nor "at-risk" (low performers). The stage was set for a fruitful negotiation, but there was no apparent way to begin.

Baker District

Baker District came to the trust agreement project with a history quite different from Able's. It had a tradition of friendly labor relations, and the new superintendent, who had been in charge of personnel for several years, prided himself on being in the forefront of labor relations. Similarly, the new union president, who had replaced a union founder, looked to the trust agreement as a means of establishing a progressive, activist stance for the organization.

Baker was not a rich district, and under the veneer of peaceful relationships were the seeds of political and organizational instability. There were factions within the union and within the administration that were spoiling for a fight. Moreover, the Baker Teachers Association had only narrowly won a decertification challenge from another union, and the school district had narrowly lost a tax election.

In this context, trust agreement negotiations started with great enthusiasm and goodwill (see Table 2). Participants from the central office and the union leadership held brainstorming sessions and easily agreed to an ambitious three-part agreement covering evaluation, teacher participation in school-site decision making, and staff development. They decided to write the staff development agreement first because it was seen as relatively noncontroversial and could be most easily launched.

A staff development agreement gained concreteness both because it was built on a known, internal model and because it cap-

Table 2 Baker School District

Year 1	Year 2	Year 3
Organizational and Political Environment		
New superintendent and new union leader—image of solidarity—at odds with underlying instability. Tax election turned down; union decertification attempt narrowly fails.	Principal suspicious of trust agreement.	New union president. Dissident board member elected. System shock disasters.
Trust Agreement Negotiations		
Preliminary meetings yield three-part structure: (1) staff development, (2) evaluation, and (3) site participation. Staff development agreement reached; put into effect	Begin work on evaluation agreement: —progress frustration —develop instrument —opposition surfaces	Evaluation project shelved: Site decision-making agreement developed agreement not very specific. Internal tension about meaning and intent.

tured the momentum of an existing project. After the second brainstorming session, when the idea of staff development was agreed upon, Patricia Deaton, a deputy superintendent, joined the trust agreement meetings. She and union activist, Thomas Dreyfus, had already been working with a teacher-administration committee to develop a new mode of staff development, and this process became identified with the trust agreement. Deaton became an important spokesperson for the trust agreement and the virtual implementor of the staff development agreement.

A successful agreement was reached early in the spring, presented to the school board, and efforts under its aegis began almost immediately. All agreed that the staff development agreement was not particularly heroic—its redistribution of resources and authority were quite modest—but the agreement was seen as a forerunner of larger ventures.

During the next summer, work began in earnest on an evaluation agreement, but there were problems almost immediately. The participants had quite different ideas about what an evaluation system should be, what the proper role for teachers should be, and the apparent symbolism involved in evaluation. Some wanted to address the "total evaluation system" to create a new mechanism whereby virtually everyone evaluates everyone else. Some wanted clear distinction between assistance and coaching programs and summative evaluation.

At this point, the problem of incompetent employees began to surface, obliquely at first, then quite pointedly. There was a growing paradox between statements about a humanistic, open, and supporting evaluation system and the apparent need to fire incompetents. Participants had grave difficulties deciding whether they would cross that line. Both management and teacher representatives voiced doubts about whether a labor-management agreement should be written in an area that might involve dismissal of a teacher or administrator. Still, the need for reworking the system was strongly felt.

The group, which had now expanded to 10 members, began to have substantive process difficulty. No stable natural leadership evolved. Members complained about having to "start over" at every meeting because there had been little preparation and no one had taken on a committee "staff" function. The superintendent felt torn between a need to make forward progress and a fear that assertiveness on his part would simply smother the process.

After several months of no apparent progress, the superintendent offered his own evaluation process as a way to test the committee's ideas and the process's workability. The plan was for staff at all levels to evaluate the superintendent, followed by teachers' evaluations of principals. Teacher evaluation revision was postponed until the following year. A subcommittee prepared a simple evaluation survey instrument. After review, it was circulated and the results were tabulated. The superintendent released the survey data to his cabinet and the school board and incorporated the results in his stated goals and objectives for the year. The principals, who were supposed to follow, balked.

During the year the principals had become increasingly suspicious of the trust agreement process, particularly since it involved evaluation, particularly their own evaluations. The process itself came under attack. Said one administrator, "What has evolved here is an inner circle developing meta policy, and people are beginning to ask, 'Who put them in charge?'" The problem was fueled by the relatively frequent meetings of the trust agreement team, which was largely composed of teachers and central office administrators, and the infrequent meetings of principals.

After school ended for the year, the trust agreement team, at the urging of the superintendent, staged a quiet retreat from the evaluation topic and agreed to work on something else during the next school year.

The problems experienced during the second year continued during the third. Decisional closure was difficult, even though the trust agreement team, whose membership remained largely stable, scheduled substantial blocks of time for meetings. Members quickly decided to move to a site decision-making agreement with a school renewal focus. Still, a specific agreement was not quickly forthcoming.

Meanwhile, the district received a series of traumatic system shocks. The veil of stability and community ethos, on which the participants prided themselves, was visibly torn. Early in the year a toxic contamination was found at one of the schools, requiring immediate closure and relocation of students. Then, a series of accidents and incidents of vandalism occurred. Finally, the serene political environment became contentious when a moderate incumbent was defeated in a school board election by dissident critics of the district and its administration. Trust agreement meetings continue, but the fundamental attention of district administrators is drawn toward its political and environmental crises. Meetings of the trust agreement team are reported to be times of comfort and camaraderie amidst the chaos.

Charlie District

The Charlie District had the earmarks of potential internal strife as it quite gingerly approached participation in the trust agreement project. There was a history of labor strife, and the old union leaders were still in place. The superintendent was relatively new. Although he was supported by the union, the associate superintendent, who had been the "inside candidate" for the superintendency, was symbolized by labor as the management devil. He returned the compliment. In addition, there was an ongoing administratively run committee of teachers and administrators working on evaluation—the very area that the union and management had considered viable ground for a trust agreement.

What followed was an extraordinary exercise in consensus and community building that occupied most of the next two years but which lay the foundation for a successful agreement on employee evaluation (see Table 3). Quite differently than in any other project district, there was a virtual referendum on the idea of a trust agreement. At the first session, school board members, administrators, and teachers were assembled. Lacking examples to cite, the author spoke about the underlying rationale of the trust agreement idea. Questions led to lengthy discussions. Other sessions followed, including a problem-identification session that was open to the public. Approximately 70 people wrestled with the problem-identification task in small groups writing on flip-chart paper.

Other large meetings were held, including one where the state union president endorsed the idea, and there were several smaller meetings at schools, which included discussion by teachers who had participated in the evaluation redesign. The process consultation involved was very informal and interpersonal—sharing food and drink, and discussing teaching, schools, what it's like to live in Charlie City, and what it's like to be a college professor.

Throughout this process, the union leaders and the superintendent were edging toward evaluation as the area of interest. Their attraction to evaluation was institutional in character rather than as a solution to a pressing problem. After a decade of decline, the district is expecting substantial enrollment growth in the next decade, and approximately 40 percent of the teaching staff will be replaced during those years. The two union leaders, who were hired during the last great enrollment boom, recalled the sink-or-swim beginnings they experienced and the consequent isolation of teachers in the district. They wished better for the next generation. Also, they visualized the trust agreement partly as a symbol that the union's position on educational policy questions had been legitimated. Trust agreements would mean that the union would be a party to district educational decisions.

Throughout, the superintendent was cordial, but he had not publicly, nor perhaps privately, committed to the idea. Only after

Table 3 Charlie School District

Year 1		**Year 2**	
Political and Organizational Environment			
New superintendent supported by union. Stable union leadership. Associate superintendent who was inside candidate for superintendency seen as union opponent; cool toward trust agreements.	Preliminary arena meetings: administrators, school board members, teachers, site administrators.	Meetings continue.	Meetings with principals and teachers to discuss agreement before it is finalized.
	Brainstorming about topics.		
	School board member attends retreat.		
Trust Agreement Negotiations			
Ongoing teacher/administrator committee to study the evaluation process. Studied several different new processes and developed new instruments and procedures.		Toledo staff tell about their experiences in evaluation.	
	Union leaders and superintendents move toward evaluation as area of agreement.	Informal meetings with interventionist and state union leader. Drafting starts.	
			Negotiations over drafts. Committee includes former opponent.
			Agreement language delegated to two persons.

there was an apparent consensus about "giving it a try" did the superintendent and the union president signal in a public meeting that they should move from exploration to fashioning an agreement.

It was at this point that the experience and work of the evaluation committee became of great value. Mary Helms, an assistant superintendent, had been staffing the evaluation committee. She had produced a wealth of information on evaluation systems nationwide, and many of these data had been discussed with teachers and union representatives. By the time consensus was reached about the idea of a trust agreement, there was a substantial base of information to provide direction.

As was the case in Able District, union and management representatives knew of the Toledo evaluation plan and had read about its operations. A decision was made to make the Toledo plan the baseline from which Charlie District would plan its own union-management evaluation system. Representatives from Toledo were invited to explain what they had accomplished—what worked and what didn't. But the visit also had a symbolic purpose. Like the initial community meetings, the Toledo representatives' visits were intended to make the evaluation project more knowable, concrete, and acceptable. In addition to several rounds of meetings at the central office, sessions with the union executive council and principals were scheduled at school sites.

Only when these processes were complete did serious discussions on the content of a Charlie District agreement begin. These discussions were handled by a small group—two union officers and three administrators with the superintendent and one school board member attending some meetings. Both the administration and the union produced draft texts, and the negotiations were over the merger of the texts. After the last meeting, one administrator was delegated the task of preparing a final draft.

The program went into operation during fall 1989 despite the superintendent's unexpected departure for a new school district.

CONCLUSIONS ABOUT CONSTRUCTING LEGITIMATE ARENAS, UNDERSTANDABLE AGENDAS, SECURE LEADERSHIP

These three cases are taken from a larger set of 12 districts and illustrate the central problem of bringing order out of ambiguity. If there is a clear lesson here, it is that successful Educational Policy Trust Agreement development requires clarification of two out of the three sources of ambiguity—the arena, the agenda, and leadership.

In the Able District, the peer assistance and review project moved forward despite the disagreement of the superintendent and union leadership over the legitimacy of the trust agreement as a labor-management setting. This seemingly odd result took place because support for the project and the project leadership were firmly in place before the trust agreement idea came into play. In the Baker District, there was no question of institutional acceptance for the trust agreement concept. In the staff development agreement, the project had clear definition from the start, and leadership for its implementation was apparent. But when the district moved on to other topics, continuing leadership in the trust agreement negotiations arena was always in question, and efforts to work out a decisional mechanism that was both consensual and productive proved frustrating. Moreover, the question of what to do was always in question. Team members perceived their schools as "special," different than most other schools. Models of successful ventures were not easily imported, and the lack of arena definition led to an inability to describe an action agenda in precise terms. In the Charlie District, leadership legitimacy and the legitimacy of the trust agreement concept were very much in doubt at the outset. Only the investment of substantial time and effort provided the support that allowed the parties to move toward reaching a successful agreement.

Constructing Legitimate Arenas

Trust agreements involve an extension of labor relations into areas that are commonly not negotiated, at least not explicitly. For a school district and union to enter such discussions requires abandonment, if not renunciation, of past, strongly held beliefs and adoption of new ones. We have posited the change in belief toward negotiating educational policy as a fundamental new idea in labor relations (Kerchner and Mitchell, 1988). New ideas in labor relations come as the product of revolutionary change and frequently are signaled by the displacement of old leaders.

In the three cases presented here, only in Charlie District were the symbolic changes firmly in place. The new superintendent, brought to the district by a school board supported by the teacher's union, was thought to be a person with whom the union "could work." Importantly, in the change of superintendents, union leadership saw a natural change in its own roles. Two changes were involved. One was an interpersonal change—from wanting to antagonize management, and drawing some pleasure from doing so, to wanting to be helpful. The other involved a growing sense of union support for the institution of public schooling in Charlie District. Union leaders began to talk about "leaving a legacy" for future teachers.

In Baker District, acceptance of the union as a participant in conversations about school policy presented no ideological problem on the surface. However, their dedication to process—working together—rather than instrumental change and written agreements makes it difficult to tell whether there was actually a shared ideology. It may be that rather than agreement over negotiated policy, the district and union share a belief in reincarnating meet-and-confer relationships.

It is in Able District that the lack of legitimacy for the trust agreement idea is most clear. The superintendent voiced difficulty in accepting the union as an instrument of teacher representation. This position is typical of what we call the *first integrational* period labor relations, rather than of individuals ready to embrace negotiated policy. But the superintendent's rhetoric and actions differed. He supported the project, run by union activists, as well as a governing board with official representation by the union and a voting majority of teachers. A pattern of dissonance had been established. We cannot predict the course of events in Able District, but it appears that a district retreat from the position of union involvement would build political resistance among the teachers.

Constructing a Project Involves Isomorphism

School districts copy one another, and it may be that invention, rather than necessity, is the mother of invention (DiMaggio and Powell, 1983). In Able and Charlie Districts, there was the clear imprint of the teachers' union in Toledo. Since 1981, they had involved themselves in peer review programs, including intervention with teachers against whom the district was preparing to bring dismissal proceedings. Clearly, teachers and union leaders in Toledo changed their concepts of loyalty and group solidarity. This change in belief was transmitted to teachers in Able and Charlie Districts, both in print and in person. Both districts brought teachers from Toledo to California to explain their programs. The Toledo intervention helped increase the ideological acceptance of teacher peer review, but equally important, it provided a concrete program that could be copied and modified. Toledo became the design standard for programs in Able and Charlie Districts. Conversations about how to visit a classroom or present a teacher's case were frequently prefaced by the words, "They do it this way in Toledo," or "This works in Toledo, but our situation is a little different."

A different type of isomorphism was present in the Baker District staff development program. It was building on the structure of an administrator-developed program already in existence in the district. What was new was the integration of teachers from different grade levels and the teacher-centeredness of the program. When the Baker trust agreement team left areas where there was some design parameters, they had more difficulty coming to agreement. Bakerites are proud, independent, and delightfully idiosyncratic, and this makes borrowing from other places difficult. There is, perhaps, a bit of the General Motors "not invented here" disease present—a pridefulness that recognizes only local intelligence. But it is clear that without skillful idea borrowing, progress is slow.

Constructing Secure Leadership

Entering into trust agreements challenges conventional definitions of authority. Conventional collective bargaining (during what we call the *second generation* of labor relations) perceives authority in layers or spheres of influence. In trust agreement settings, authority is much less automatically defined by organizational role or position. For instance, in the Baker District staff development setting, program implementation became the joint province of an assistant superintendent and a regular classroom teacher. At least two vertical authority layers separated the two, but in the context of the agreement, they were equals. The intermingling of authority can be seen in both the process of reaching agreements and in the contents of the agreements themselves.

Reaching Agreements. For more than a decade in California, labor leaders and administrators have been at opposite ends of the bargaining table. Their roles have been relatively clear—enough that superintendents and union presidents frequently delegate negotiating responsibility to others. Union and management representatives can negotiate secure in the knowledge that their role requires vigorous representation of self-interest. Taking and defending positions are relatively easily done, and skills in compromise and closure are obtained with experience and training. However, the beneficiary of a trust agreement is to be the clients or the public, and both union and management representatives are charged with the role of representing interests other than their own. In this context, the role requirements become cloudy.

Both superintendent and union president retain their historic roles of advocacy and defense. The union is still the union, but in this setting they are supposed to discover and represent the public good.

During the negotiations, we observed in Baker and Charlie Districts. The administrators and union presidents approached this new role largely by abandoning positional bargaining, at least at the outset. In Baker District, a strong bargaining norm developed. Very seldom did individuals speak of either their own office or of themselves as the representative of the district or the union. This solved the interest representation problem, but it created another problem. No one sat in the chair. No one was designated to lead and guide the meetings, and the union and management participants did not line up in orderly fashion behind their chief negotiator. As experienced negotiators know well, there is substantial negotiation within each side, and compromise toward agreement is facilitated by internal discipline.[3] In an effort to share negotiations leadership, no visible pattern of group leadership developed.

In Charlie District, a quite different group leadership pattern evolved, from all accounts, quite unconsciously. Throughout the year or more that the trust agreement idea was being publicly aired, meetings were often led by outsiders, members of the trust agreement project, or others. A meeting would be called by the superintendent and the union president but carried forward by others. However, when negotiations actually started, the union president and the superintendent resumed their complementary roles, each speaking for each side. Much of the idea aggregation and collection was done away from the face-to-face negotiations. Charlie District negotiations also benefited from a third-level administrator who functioned as a secretariat, writing position papers, collecting documents, and keeping the process going.

Agreement Content. Administrative authority is formally protected behind a wall of statute inpenetrable by the union. In California, as in other states, the scope of bargaining is narrowly constructed to "wages, hours, and other terms and conditions of employment." Acceptable "other terms" are innumerated in a short list. The state's education code reserves other substantial decisions, such as teacher evaluation, to administrators. In this context, entering into a setting where educational policy decisions are negotiable requires rethinking one's ideas of authority.

Personal authority in administration finds its highest expression in the giving of direct orders. As Mintzberg (1983) puts it, "At the limit, the manager can tell a subordinate exactly what to do. In effect, he makes decisions, and the subordinate executes the actions" (p. 143). Without doubt, trust agreements peck away at the authority barrier that separates the conception of work and its execution. This situation has not gone unnoticed in the three districts, and reaction ranging from anxiety to revolt has resulted. The reaction has been particularly pointed among principals, who, like first-line managers everywhere, are saddled with more responsibility than resources. (Principals in other school reform cities, such as Toledo and Rochester, have had similar reactions.)

What is often missed in this reaction is the increase in emphasis on other modes of expressing authority. Trust agreements establish new areas of action or decision making for organizational subunits. The teacher evaluation agreement in Able District, for instance, establishes a working area for each supervising teacher/new teacher relationship. At the same time, these agreements are highly value laden. They allow administrators (and teacher leaders) to "set the tune" for what is considered good and valuable. In Able District, the trust agreement required teachers and administrators to concretely define good teaching. Moreover, there is substantial evidence that the definition was shared by teachers other than those novices under the direct oversight of supervising teachers. In effect, the principal and supervising teacher jointly produced what Selznick (1957) calls "infusing the organization with value," a form of authority that extended beyond the individual order and response.

In addition, trust agreements also involve administrators in vertical job enhancement. Just as teachers are breaking the barrier between their jobs and educational policy making, so too are administrators. The most stressful events in our experience took place when administrators were not well represented in the evaluation negotiations in Baker District. The idea that teachers had gained policy access that they, themselves, lacked was particularly nettlesome. In contrast, the site administrators in Charlie District participated fully in shaping the agreement—at times guarding what they felt were prerogatives.

Policy involvement extended beyond the agreement-making stage, too. Every agreement we have seen so far involves a kind of joint operating committee to carry out the decisions. That is, there is something about the trust agreement setting that induces implementation by means other than the conventional hierarchy. Baker District's staff development committee has already been noted. In Able District, the evaluation review team involves central office administrators, principals, and teacher representatives. And the Charlie District evaluation plan includes several coordinating structures. All of these have the function of breaking down barriers between the central office and the sites, and of bringing authority much closer to that envisioned in a matrix-type management.

Endnotes

1. At the time this chapter was written, the project's directors were James Guthrie, Michael Kirst, Jerry Hayward, Wesley Apker, Deborah Edginton, Davis Campbell, and Miles Myers. Julie Koppich is the project director and Charles Kerchner is the principal consultant.
2. In California, public schools can designate up to 5 percent of their teaching force as Mentor Teachers who receive release time and a $4,000 annual stipend. Mentors can help train and socialize new teachers but may not legally evaluate them.
3. This is referred to as *intraorganizational bargaining.* Standard positional bargaining requires quite tight control of a bargaining team by a chief negotiator (see Walton and McKersie, 1965).

References

California Commission on the Teaching Professions. (1985). *Who will teach our children?* Sacramento: Author.

DiMaggio, P. J., and Powell, W. W. (1983, April). The iron cage revisited: Institutional isomorphism and collective rationality in organizational fields. *American Sociological Review, 48* (2), 147–160.

Kerchner, C. T., and Mitchell, D. E. (1986, March). Teaching reform and union reform. *Elementary School Journal, 86* (4), 449–470.

Kerchner, C. T., and Mitchell, D. E. (1988). *The changing idea of a teacher's union.* Stanford Series on Education & Public Policy. New York: Falmer Press.

Mintzberg, H. (1983). *Power in and around organizations.* Englewood Cliffs, NJ: Prentice-Hall.

Selznick, P. (1957). *Leadership in administration: A sociological interpretation.* New York: Harper and Row.

Walton, R. E., and McKersie, R. B. (1965). *A behavioral theory of labor negotiations.* New York: McGraw-Hill.

Chapter Fourteen

Traditional school systems have been managed through a set of hierarchical patterns, in "top-down" style, with the key management decisions being made at higher administrative and policy levels. In this concluding chapter, Cooper maintains that client-oriented organizations are a logical alternative—they would be designed to react to market pressures and client needs, and would be driven by demands from students and parents, with teachers acting on their (the students') behalf. Moreover, client-oriented organizations (called M-Form *organizations) would have a decentralized structure. Each school in the district would establish its own particular identity and be managed by a school-site group (of administrators and teachers) to address teaching and learning. For teachers, such a structure implies a stronger connection among teachers as well as between teachers and administrators.*

Changing Paradigms of School Organization: Implications of Teacher Collaboration on School Operations

Bruce S. Cooper
Fordham University
School of Education

> Teachers should be provided with the discretion and autonomy that are the hallmarks of professional work. State and local governments should set clear goals for schools and greatly reduce the bureaucratic regulation of school processes. Teachers should participate in the setting of goals for their school and be accountable for achieving agreed upon standards of performance (Carnegie Forum, 1986).

INTRODUCTION

Recent school reforms have finally recognized the key role of teachers in efforts to improve education. It seems obvious, since education occurs in classrooms under the control of teachers, that attempts to improve pupil attainment, adjustment, and life preparation must include teachers' involvement and cooperation. As obvious as it may seem, however, reformers for the last 15 years have concentrated efforts on working around or excluding teachers. This commentary on the way schools are organized and controlled is a theme of this chapter.

The "first wave" of national school reform, from about 1980 to 1986, concentrated primarily on educational "outputs," such as pupil achievement scores; graduation rates and, conversely, dropout rates; and literacy and numeracy, leading to demands for higher-order skills (e.g., critical thinking and problem-solving skills). Former President Reagan's first Secretary of Education, Terrence Bell, initiated the now famous "wall charts" showing state-by-state output measures and relevant "inputs" (per pupil expenditures, pupil-teacher ratios). At a glance, we were able to see our education failures and successes—state by state, datum by datum.

Teachers, as such, were visibly absent—other than the occasional complaint that they were poorly trained, scored badly themselves on most tests of intellectual attainment, and were weak performers on national and state tests of professional competence. Teachers, like students, had been reduced to blips on the screen of national school performance, just another "measure" to show that we had become "a nation at risk" (National Commission on Excellence in Education, 1983), failing to educate our children adequately. These findings were elegantly supported by works of the doyens of intellectual snobbery, Professors Allan Bloom's *The Closing of the American Mind* (1987) and E. D. Hirsch, Jr.'s *Cultural Literacy* (1987).

Teachers seemed relatively unimportant except as an object of comment or complaint in various reports. For example, a U.S. Department of Education study, *Two Years after High School* (1984), compared university students majoring in education in 1974 and 1982 and found a 10 percent decline in college students who had completed an "academic" high school program (down from 68 percent to 58 percent), matched by an increase from 32 percent to 42 percent in those prospective teachers who completed the (lower) "general" and "vocational" streams in high school.

Such data showed a continued decline in the quality of the background of those selecting teaching as a profession—a trend that led to the Holmes Group's (1986) recommendation that all prospective teachers should receive a liberal arts college degree, in part to attract more top students from the high school "academic" track into teaching and also to give compensation to those coming into college with weak secondary school preparation.

Thus, it was not until about 1986 with the so-called "second wave" of school reform that attention finally turned to teachers. Since this "wave" focused on schools, their organization, activities, and leadership, naturally teachers became key players in school-site management and budgeting, school improvement plans, and other efforts. Three approaches were used to assert the primacy of teachers in this reform effort.

First, teachers were seen as "workers," as commodities, particularly as shortages of qualified staff appeared in certain areas (e.g., mathematics, science, and special education). One reform, proposed by New Jersey's previous Governor Thomas Kean in the mid-1980s and supported in 1989 by President Bush, is access to public school teaching jobs for "unconventional" candidates—

liberal arts majors and business and military people who wish to enter the classroom directly, rather than through licensing in traditional teacher training programs (see the U.S. Education Excellence Act of 1989).

Second, reformers advocated "restructuring" the teachers' work place, the school and classroom, realizing that these "workers," this "comodity" in the classroom, could not function effectively without a greater decision-making role in the school. *A Nation Prepared* (Carnegie Forum, 1986, p. 3), for example, urges the following changes in education policy: (1) national teacher certification through a National Board for Professional Teaching Standards; (2) "Lead Teachers" with "proven ability," providing "active leadership"; and (3) performance incentives to enhance productivity—a euphemism for some kind of merit recognition and reward. As the report explains, "Teachers who routinely bring home students' papers and work on them late into the night are rewarded no differently from teachers who do not" (p. 89).

Finally, reformers came to realize that changing the work environment of teachers has important implications for the organization, management, and operation of the entire school system, not just the teacher in the classroom. In fact, this chapter argues that teacher restructuring (also called teacher *involvement, participation, collaboration,* and even "*empowerment*") reverses the reigning paradigm of school organization.

NEW MYTHS, NEW PARADIGMS

It appears obvious to observers of school systems that any real effort to include teachers in significant school decision making will require a reshaping of the way we understand and operate our school districts. Yet, radical rethinking is difficult, given our acceptance of current school structure. Furthermore, teachers and administrators have different myths, each supporting their own activities without overdependence on the other group.

One myth supports the theory that schools are run by those nominally in charge: boards of education, superintendents, assistants, and other top-level bureaucrats. The central office cadre, in this scenario, sets the direction for the schools; rules and directives come down from the top, and teachers, as subordinates, follow. The countervailing myth also exists: that schools are operated by those closest to the students and the teaching-learning process—the teachers, department chairs, and others who work with students. While top administrators may think they run things, teachers know that despite the memoranda, directives, policy statements, handbooks, and curricula guides, it is the teachers who make or break the system (see Cooper, 1989).

These two myths manage to coexist because they both serve the needs of their respective groups without undue interference. Teachers nod at top-down directives, while closing their classroom doors and doing mainly what they choose. Superintendents and staff hold meetings, promulgate policies, and set procedures, but much of what the central office mandates is irrelevant to teachers and can easily be overlooked. Even line administrators in schools tacitly agree to tread lightly, avoiding close and meaningful supervision of teachers, since it is very difficult to dismiss even incompetent teachers (Bridges, 1986).

This quiet compromise generally works well, with each side ignoring the other. Given the loose structure of schools and the reality that the zones of concern of teachers and those in the superintendents' offices (including board members, deputies, and even some principals) seem hardly to overlap, each group holds the belief that they have the final word, while giving lip service to the other group.

Yet, observers of school organization know that each party has radically different paradigms underlying their views. Those at the top believe in centralization, control, predictability, and standardization, whereas "bottom uppers" (teachers and their advocates) prefer spontaneity, autonomy, local decision making, decentralization, and professional discretion (see Lortie, 1968; Chubb and Moe, 1990). To superintendents, accountability and control must be retained at the top. To teachers, authority and discretion belong at the classroom level, where key and critical choices must be made if learning is to occur.

It is the classic struggle between managers' knowledge and workers' specialized skill, between central control and local autonomy, accountability and discretion, management and production. Gouldner explained, "On the one side, it is administration based on expertise; while on the other, it is administration based on discipline" (1954, p. 22).

Blau and Scott present it as a split between judgment "resting on technical knowledge and disciplined compliance with directives of superiors" (1962, p. 35). In fact, these scholars assert, managers are experts in administration, while it is the specialist who knows the particular production at hand. That is, teachers know the pupils, the class, and the demands of pedagogy in ways that a school board president, superintendent, or even a principal cannot.

School Organization and Management Theory

One of the major effects of the "second wave" of school reform has been to expose the myth of separate domains, making top and bottom decision makers (teachers and administrators) acknowledge that they alone do not make policy and that schools as organizations are undergoing a transformation. The bureaucratic paradigm, what William Ouchi (1984) calls the "U-Form" (unified) organization, is giving way to a more complex view. One way to understand these changes is to compare *organizational* theory with *management* theory, attempting to see the relationship between these two domains.

Teacher "participation," "involvement," "collobaration," or even "empowerment" challenge our concepts of both (1) how schools are structured at the district, building, and classroom level (an *organizational* concern); and (2) how these reconstituted "systems" are run by those at the various levels, a *managerial* focus. Both concepts—organizational and managerial—are essential in understanding the role of teachers in schools.

Often, theorists of organization have given too little attention to management theory and vice versa. Both groups have proceeded as though the other group was unimportant or nonexistent. For example, management scholars have long advocated forms of shared, democratic leadership (e.g., Rensis Likert's "System 4" [1967] or Reddin's 3-D [three-dimensional] theory [1970]). Theorists have advocated that leaders be more sensitive to the needs of followers and more intent on "involving" them in the management process (using rubrics such as "team management," consultation, participation, democracy, delegation, and high levels of human "consideration"). Yet, these analysts have sometimes ignored the organizational level, inadvertently pressing for shared power in a system where power is hierarchical, centralized, and "top-down." In education, too, few seem to recognize that leadership/management behavior and the structural paradigms of the organization cannot easily be separated.

For example, if reformers press for greater teacher participation in schools (a managerial concern), how might this change occur in a *system* that is highly centralized? We must recognize that the leadership behavior of teachers and the action paradigm of school system organization cannot easily be separated. Similarly, decentralized systems (an organizational reform) sometimes find that unit-level managers (principals and assistants) are so authoritarian that attempts to push authority "downward" to the teachers are stymied by heavy-handed, school-level leadership.

How can we truly devolve authority to teachers and make them partners, active leaders, and collaborators in school reform (an organizational strategy) when principals of schools will not share power with their staff (a managerial strategy)?

Thus, if decentralization stops at the schoolhouse door, substituting one form of control (district-level) for another (school-level), teachers may be more frustrated and no more involved. In fact, forms of false involvement—from either top-heavy school systems, authoritarian building principals, or both—can destroy teachers' trust and weaken what little confidence and autonomy they may enjoy.

As long as leaders and systems ascribe to the same basic paradigms (e.g., centralized or decentralized), little tension exists. But when the two areas, managerial and organizational, are out of sync, interesting problems may arise. Thus, proponents of teacher empowerment who ignore the close relationship between organizational structure and management behavior are at risk of confusion and failure.

David Clark (1988) has attempted to examine the behavior of leaders and organizations in much the same way, separating the traditional Theory X and Theory Y (McGregor, 1960) views of *management* from what he calls the X-prime (*X′*) and Y-prime (*Y′*) views of the *organization*. He finds, for example, that social systems (schools) often remain X′ (distrustful, watchful, controlling, and directive, to use McGregor's terms), whereas the leadership attempts to be Y′ (trusting, sharing, delegating, and seeking to help subordinates grow and improve). Clark's ideal, of course, is the Y/Y′ situation, where the system of education and the managerial philosophy are mutually supportive. Clark's example suggests some interesting innovations, including the election of principals by faculty—as in university departments—rather than appointment by the school board.

As shown in Figure 1, organizational and managerial orientations can be cross-matched to understand the combinations of structural and leadership styles that accompany teacher participation in schools. Across the top of the figure, one sees the two basic management styles: (1) *Centralized/Authoritarian,* in which principals run their schools in a controlled way and teachers are likely have little say in decision-making; and (2) *Decentralized/Participative,* in which leaders seek a participatory, democratic, and involving strategy, including the sharing of some power with teachers.

These two (horizontal) approaches are managerial in nature, whereas the vertical approaches are organizational and systemic, relating to the locus of control. Approach 1, *Centralized/Con-*

Figure 1 Cross-Matching Managerial Style and Organizational Structure

ORGANIZATION CONTROL	MANAGEMENT STYLE: Authoritarian	MANAGEMENT STYLE: Participative
Centralized	**Cell A** Traditional BUREAUCRATIC	**Cell B** Mixed "PATERNALISTIC"
Decentralized	**Cell C** Mixed "LOCAL TYRANT"	**Cell D** Autonomous Schools PARTICIPATIVE MANAGEMENT

trolling, relates to the way authority is distributed in the school district; in this case, decisions are made at the central office and imposed on schools in a bureaucratic manner. Hence, not only are teachers removed from the seat of power but so is the principal. Boards and superintendents make policy; schools carry it out in classic, "top-down" fashion.

Approach 2, in contrast, is *Decentralized/Autonomous.* Schools are given considerable freedom to manage their resources and make key decisions. As suggested in the "second wave" of reform, authority is devolved to schools, giving principals (at least) more opportunity to run their schools. In summary, the management and organizational dimensions range from controlling and centralized to delegating, participative, and decentralized.

- **MANAGEMENT APPROACH**
  1. *Centralized-Authoritarian.* Administrators set school goals and programs, and make key decisions with little teacher involvement. The traditional model.
  2. *Decentralized-Participative.* Administrators share authority with staff, seeking their counsel and pushing decisions down into subject and service departments; high reliance on team management.

- **ORGANIZATIONAL/SYSTEMS APPROACH**
  1. *Centralized-Controlling.* "Top-down" structure, with key central board making most decisions and controlling most funding. Directives and policies imposed on schools. Classic bureaucratic system.

2. *Decentralized-Autonomous.* Devolution of decision making and resources to the school site; encourages school-based management, budgeting, and programing. Principal of school is given wide discretion over staffing, curricula, and evaluation.

By cross-matching the organizational and managerial dimensions shown in Figure 1, we have an opportunity to analyze examples of teacher involvement embedded in a variety of paradigms and examples.

Cell A: Matching Centralist Paradigms

Teachers have traditionally worked in highly controlling systems, wherein superintendents often acted unilaterally in setting district policy, with board approval. Most teachers were not represented by a union, and the chances for meaningful involvement were limited by both a top-down organization and a strong, controlling building principal. In Figure 1, Cell A is what we call *Traditional-Bureaucratic* and shows a nice match between an authoritarian principal working in a system that stresses centralist values.

Further, each level is accountable, principal to superintendent, and teachers to principal, requiring strict monitoring and control. In school terms, congruence exists between the top-down structural paradigm of districtwide centralization and the top-down managerial approach of school administrators. One set of values reinforces the other. Expectations are that the hierarchy sends down directives, which are then imposed on subordinates. Blau and Scott (1962) describe this classic structure as focusing on "interpersonal discipline and rational expertness, and on control through directives originated at the apex of the authority pyramid and transmitted through channels down to its base" (p. 65).

This model of school organization and management is so common in the history of education that it was rarely challenged prior to the 1960s, with the introduction of teachers unions and collective bargaining. Yet, many of the qualities attributed to a chief school executives—drive, power, control, and ambition—are often qualities that reinforce the centralization of authority at the district level. Authority is something of a zero-sum game; if key decisions are made at the center, less opportunities exist for control at the periphery. And since principals are managed tightly by superintendents, they often use the same management philosophy with their teachers.

Larry Cuban, in his study of "urban school chiefs under fire" (1976), refers to a newspaper account that reports St. Louis school superintendent Willis "runs everything except tugboats" (p. 4). He centralized all decisions, robbing subordinates of the freedom and incentive to act on their own—including teachers. Cuban explains:

> Willis's aggressive, brusque personal style, with its grasp of detail and its enormous drive, drew from board members and subordinates responses ranging from unqualified admiration to strong criticism. One loyal assistant superintendent proclaimed, "He leads, we follow." However, one of Willis's aides, commenting on the general superintendent's desire to stay atop the decision-making process, pointed out a problem which this personality trait produced: "Sometimes a bottleneck develops in getting things done because Dr. Willis likes to keep his finger in everything" (1976, p. 5).

Cuban (1976) further reported that "by 1920, most big-city administrators could appoint and dismiss principals and teachers, determine new programs and policies in both curriculum and instruction, select textbooks, and prepare the budgets" (p. 45). It was not surprising, then, that teachers felt left out and turned to collective bargaining, strikes, and eventual contracts to gain at the negotiating table what they were denied in the organization—decentralized structure and sharing, supportive principals.

Cell A, the *Traditional-Bureaucratic* model, then, was the norm, until the 1970s and still is in many school systems. For teachers, it may seem a secure place to work, a setting that is highly regimented and controlled, where schools are part of a larger bureaucracy and principals see themselves as agents of the district, not advocates for teachers. But, as the 1980s have shown, teachers as professionals want a chance to become active participants in a system that devolves more freedom to schools and more options to classrooms.

Cell B: Mixed Environment—Paternalistic

Even in the most hierarchical of school systems, however, some principals boldly devolve and share authority with their staff. This "mixed-paternalistic" setting is one in which the management style is "participative," embedded in a highly "centralized-controlling" school system (Cell B, Figure 1).

We term this cell *mixed* because two different philosophies collide in this cross-match—a management approach based on sharing and delegation and a structural arrangement that is centralized and controlling. The term *paternalistic* expresses the likelihood that principals and other administrators who use Cell B styles run the risk of offering their staff "input" and options without the ability, at times, to deliver resources or choices.

For example, a principal who allows a faculty to design their own program in, for example, computer literacy without funds to buy computers or hire staff with computer training skills, could give teachers the sense that the principal is patronizing them—asking them to share in something that the principal does not have.

Considerable research (see Duke, Showers, and Imbers, 1980) shows that teachers do not trust superiors' offers to participate in school governance, mainly because the staff fear being "used" by administrators. Principals often coopt their teachers by making them feel that they are part of decision making without really taking their advice and acting on it. In part this "being used" is a testimony to the helplessness of principals in highly centralized systems (Cell B) and in part a strategy to disarm opposition amongst the teachers. Some teachers may feel that leaders are patronizing them when they offer chances to share power that principals do not really have or do not seek to share.

The net effect is to place administrators in untenable situations where they attempt participative techniques (sharing of authority) in a system where many critical decisions are already made at the district and state levels. At times, this "sharing" appears almost paternalistic, though handled skillfully, principals do have a considerable amount of discretion.

Hence, as shown in Cell B, Figure 1, the outcome is a mismatch between system ideology and managerial approaches, whereby on-site managers are admonished to accept more responsibility, be more involving, and to make their schools more responsive to local conditions and the needs of teachers. Yet the school system still retains control over (1) budgeting, (2) staffing, (3) programs, and (4) measures of success. The danger, then, of Cell B is that teachers may believe that they have an important role to play when in reality districts do not trust them.

Cell C: Mixed Model— Decentralization and Local Tyrant

Sometimes, too, the school system makes a serious effort to devolve authority, choice, and decision making to the school site, encouraging administrators to take control. Yet, for some administrators, sharing this authority does not come easily. In fact, in a few cases, principals actually use their own freedom to provide even tighter controls over their staff. (This situation is what David

Clark calls a Theory X style of leadership in a Theory Y′ organization.)

In a decentralized system, unions (bargaining, contracts, and grievance) may be seen as a central and standard way of protecting the rights of teachers from principals who might abuse their authority. The catalyst for unionization in New York City in 1968, for example, was the perception on the part of teachers that "community control" would injure the rights of teachers. When decentralized school boards in Ocean Hill-Brownsville and other areas acted to remove and transfer teachers, the United Federation of Teachers called a strike and pressed contractual protection.

This "mixed" model (Cell C) depicts a decentralized system, with authority devolved to schools and principals not sharing this discretion. Research (see Humphrey and Thomas, 1986) in Britain, where a number of school-site management experiments were tried, found that in a large number of schools, teachers did not even know that the decentralization had occurred. Some principals continued to run their school in the same authoritarian manner they always had, making a mockery of the new-found "freedoms" that these schools supposedly received.

In defense of "local tyrants," some principals may not trust the intentions of the central board when it says it will "decentralize" the system. These leaders seek to retain their authority, rather than sharing and delegating it, out of concern that the central board will watch the administrators fail and then "hang" them on their shortcoming. This ambivalence—"go ahead and fail" or "take enough rope to hang yourself"—makes some principals even more controlling, rule-bound, and Theory X, further undermining the efforts to decentralize authority to schools. When the system was highly centralized, principals could always blame the superintendent, school board, and other central office leaders. Now, however, with devolution to schools, some principals may feel "on the spot," inadequate to take command themselves and to share this power with their teachers.

Teacher empowerment under these circumstances, Cell C, is bitter fruit, for teachers know that their school has great latitude of action but they cannot quite get into the game. Like other "mixed" situations, where management styles and organizational structures are out of phase with one another, it is difficult for teachers and administrators to know quite what to do. Unfortunately, much of the recent school reform movement has given off just such mixed signals. Either the superintendent and board talk about giving schools more autonomy, and principals are ill-prepared or unwilling to share; or principals see the logic in getting their staff involved but cannot move very far because of tight controls and stringent conditions imposed from outside the school.

Cell D: Autonomous Schools—Participative Management

At the point where management and organizational paradigms are based on many of the same assumptions and behaviors, the chances for teacher collaboration, even empowerment, are greatly increased. Under such circumstances, the central board gives sufficient authority and autonomy to school units to make planning and implementation possible; in turn, leaders share this authority with their teachers, involving them in setting goals, distributing resources, and shaping programs. In a real sense, the philosophy of shared empowerment permeates the system, from top to bottom.

Figure 1 shows the cross-tabulation of these two dimensions, labeling Cell D managerial *Participative* and organizationally *Autonomous*. Clark (1988) would deem this a Theory Y style in a Y-prime (Y′) organization. McGregor (1960) typifies Theory Y as people working together in a trusting and supportive environment, with leaders who understand their needs and provide chances for advancement, growth, and involvement. Clark's derived Y-prime organization is one in which structures support caring, trust, and growth through various forms of consultation and involvement. Theory match Y/Y′ comes closest to the professional organization that schools during recent reforms seek to be.

For our analysis of models of teacher involvement, we could argue that good managers in Cell D wish to be effective, work through and with their staff, seek to fulfill the needs of staff and program, and identify with the needs of their school units. Similarly, Cell D organizations are based on these assumptions:

1. People closest to the core activities of the school organization (teachers, for example) need and require the greatest control.
2. School staff and managers, if given the chance, will work extra hard to make their school successful.
3. Effective schools control resources, programs, and staff in unique ways, based on local school needs, constituents, expectations, and problems.
4. The role of central management is not to control but to set priorities and standards, provide resources, facilitate improvement, gather data, and reward productivity.

When management systems and organization structure are working in concert, presumably, trust is enhanced. Principals need not act paternalistically, since their schools do truly have the resources and autonomy to act in significant ways. Teachers trust their superiors, since staff realizes that decision-making power does indeed reside at the schoolhouse and that Theory Y principals are willing to share it.

APPLYING MODELS TO TEACHER WORK ENVIRONMENTS

The recent reform effort has focused on teacher job enhancement, including peer supervision (Alfonso, 1977; Garmston, 1987), career ladders, teacher career development, merit pay, and other forms of "empowerment" and change. We have argued in this chapter that these enhancements are dependent, to a large degree, on the managerial and organizational arrangements in the school district. In Cell A, where direction is top-down and management is centralized, teachers fall in line, becoming employees in a hierarchical system.

In Cells B and C, the "mixed" management/organizational arrangements, a fair-to-low level of teacher participation is possible, though such involvement is problematic. The difficulty with the highly centralized school system (Cell B) is that principals run the risk of offending or disappointing teachers if they try sharing authority. Administrators also chance political problems with their own superiors if they don't "carry out" and enforce the policies and regulations of the central board. And the problem with Cell C is that authoritarian principals can thwart the effort of systems to devolve authority downward, robbing the teachers of a chance at codetermination around key issues.

Cell D, wherein schools are given a fair amount of autonomy and principals share those rights and resources with staff, seems the most promising. Mary Anne Raywid, in her chapter on "Paradigm High School" (see Walberg and Lane, 1989), puts all the pieces together in an interesting way:

> Paradigm High School has many of the features currently sought through restructuring: extensive personalization, a strong and distinctive ethos, an emphasis on the school as a community, and a continuing concern with the quality of work life within the school. . . . These attributes are sustained by a school-within-a-school organization, increased school site autonomy, strengthened collaboration and collective responsibility among teachers, and

> expanded, more flexible roles for all those within the school. These organizational features—the structure, culture, and the climate—have in turn yielded programs that truly engage students and teachers far more effective than most (p. 50).

This "paradigm" school has many of the same characteristics of the setting for teacher participation: *social* (personalization, ethos, community), *organizational* (school-site autonomy and "sub-schools"), and *managerial* (flexibility and collaboration) qualities. Arrangements in this ideal school put the teachers in the positive position of participating in key decisions rather than the traditional negative, destructive, recalcitrant role of "ignoring" or undoing external directives. Conley, Schmidle, and Shedd (1990) put the "organic" quality of supportive district and school work environments this way:

> The case for changing this division of labor—for involving teachers in the management of school systems—rests partly on the impact of participation on the quality of school and district decision making; partly on the impact of participation on the work of individual teachers; and partly on its impact on relationships among teachers themselves. Ultimately, it rests on the need for a closer, more organic integration of strategic and operational, technical and managerial decisions throughout a school system (p. 6).

Other key elements are missing, however, from this analysis: the definitional, practical, and logistical arrangements in particular schools to make collaboration among staff and administrators possible. It is one thing to talk about teacher "involvement," "participation," "teamwork," and "empowerment," but it is another to make it happen, even in "Cell D" schools where all the elements are in line: (1) a significant decentralization of power and resources to the school site and (2) management team members in the school itself who seek the opinion and involvement of teachers.

Definitions. The first issue is definitional: What is teacher "collaboration"—shared planning, decision making, support, governance? From the growing literature on the role of teachers in school, a range of qualities emerge. At one extreme, teachers would share fully in decision making, a form of involvement best defined as "governance." Teachers in schools might become like professors in universities: hiring, promoting, and tenuring their own colleagues; setting their own program requirements and standards; and so on. In fact, at one level, teacher governance of schools might make the permanent principal a thing of the past. Instead, teachers might rotate as principal, as university department chairs now do. In less radical form, shared governance might involve teachers serving on the management team and consulting on key issues.

For some principals, this level of teacher authority is highly threatening. As New York City superintendent John Iorio (1988) says, teacher-style shared governance might lead to union takeover of the schools. "If they [teachers] eventually succeed in their endeavors," Iorio continues, "there will be no role for supervisors as we now know them. They will be replaced by lead teachers, a new brand of supervisors created by and placed within the control of the union" (p. 10).

At the other end of the continuum is personal teacher "empowerment," defined as a much milder form of teacher involvement. Rather than having a strong political component, like shared "governance," "empowerment" is defined in human, individual, psychological, and professional terms. Or, as Garmin (1986) explains:

> "Empowerment" means helping people to take charge of their lives, inspiring people to develop feelings of self-worth and a willingness to be self-critical and reflective about their actions. Moreover, personal empowerment is the essential ingredient for a professional orientation. Without a feeling of responsibility for the profession and the sense of importance of empowerment, the educator becomes a kind of civil servant in a large community (pp. 12–13).

In this definition of *empowerment,* note the terms such as *self-worth, self-critical and reflective,* and *professional orientation.* These are the concepts of human growth, not political power. Teacher involvement that threatens the control of schools is very different from involvement on personal and professional levels. Some teachers will see the changing work environment—and the Cell D (decentralized/autonomous)—as a chance to seize some control ("governance," to use Iorio's definition); other teachers will concentrate mainly on the pedagogical and professional aspects of "empowerment" and will work within the given system.

Perhaps the first step in actually implementing a teacher participation scheme is to decide which working definition will be used. Principals who are secure enough will be willing to share the power, whereas others will prefer to empower teachers mainly to help themselves. A bit of both will likely occur.

Practice and Logistics. Collaboration, whether political, pedagogical, or both, cannot happen easily in the traditional school regardless of who is in charge and how much school-site control is enjoyed. Take the example of "peer supervision," a rather mild program where teachers "in peer coaching situations instruct, train, and tutor one another" (Garmston, 1987, p. 18). Peer supervision is hardly full-blown team management of schools; but Alfonso (1977) found that these kinds of teacher-to-teacher efforts are extremely difficult to accomplish in traditional schools, given teachers' schedules, work settings, and resources. He explains:

> It [peer supervision] is an understandably appealing idea, but professionally quite naive in that it fails to recognize the nature of formal organizations. . . . To attempt to implement a peer-supervision model in schools that are cellular and in which teachers carry out their work in splendid isolation would be to impose a model that is as uncomfortable, incongruous, and as ineffective as the isolated and routine classroom visits that still characterize the style of many supervisors (p. 597).

Take This Situation. Teachers are invited to join a schoolwide team to plan next year's program and staffing. But certain questions arise: Given their schedules, when will joint planning take place? Since students' needs continue despite this collaboration, who will cover classes, and who will provide or pay the necessary substitute teachers? How will the school ensure that all staff become part of the self-improvement effort since not all teachers will participate in all phases of joint planning? How will teachers—long accustomed to working alone—learn the skills of collaboration and group process? Who will manage the cooperative effort to see that democratic rules are followed *and* that things are accomplished? And where will experts come from, should the school embark on new projects?

These and other questions bring us from the central office to the classroom, from the superintendent to the classroom teacher. Research indicates three dimensions of effective school-site collaboration among teachers and administrators. These might be called the 3 Rs of teacher participation: Ratification, Resources, and Restructuring. Using the schools in New York City as examples, we shall examine these qualities of teacher involvement.

THE 3 Rs OF TEACHER COLLABORATION

Ratification

The first step in any effort to bring staff together for mutual planning and support is gaining the assent of central, school-level, and classroom professionals. Once the superintendent and school board devolve significant authority to schools, this delegation becomes a kind of ratification of the concept of teacher participation. In New York City, the district and central offices put forward the idea of collaborative consultation among teachers, and selected a school, Public School 19 (P.S. 19) in Queens, to be the site.

Resistance to such a plan often comes from all sides. Unions find the idea attractive, as long as the teacher involvement effort has the following qualities: (1) the attempts at collaboration are genuine and not just another trick—cooptation, control, disappointment; (2) teachers are paid for the extra time and effort required to plan the collaborative effort, train the teachers and leaders to work together as peers, and to carry out the joint decision making; and (3) access to the program is open and fair, that is, all teachers who wish to participate in joint planning and other forms of self-determination are eligible. This openness will overcome fear that the principal's "pet" gets to serve in participative decision making but not the teacher with strong contrary opinions.

Ratification can begin at any level. In some cases, teacher involvement is the result of teachers' banding together to help one another, and to run their own programs. In other settings, the school board might "restructure" the district to give principals (and their staff) greater information and control. In still others, principals change their schools to give teachers more latitude. Once the parties agree to let teachers participate, the issue becomes one of making the program work.

Resources

Participation takes time, money, and energy. Resources of all kinds—monetary, human, and technical—must be directed if teachers are to learn, improve, share, and take a lead in making schools better. Warren and Goldsberry (1983, p. 106) devote considerable attention to the new and redirected resources that schools must obtain to make these programs work. Such changes as having colleagues consult with one another, a first step in expanded responsibility, "demands the investment of a great deal of time and some money."

Districts and schools often have excess resources to garner, including combining classes and using nonteaching staff (librarians, nurses, guidance personnel) to free teachers to consult, plan, and help govern. And, Warren and Goldsberry (1983) explain that "using money allocated for in-service teacher education to hire substitute teachers is another alternative" (p. 106). The Collaborative Consultation Support System in New York City was determined that children would not suffer from having weak substitute teachers while the regular teachers were consulting, visiting classrooms, and providing peer assistance. Extra "floating" teachers were hired to relieve regular teachers, providing teachers with the time to work together effectively.

Restructuring

Finally, and most importantly, schools must be reorganized to allow teachers to participate more fully. For example, if teachers are to engage in joint planning, whether curricular, pedagogical, or organizational, the school day must somehow be rearranged so that planning groups have similar schedules. If teachers are to devote 10 percent of their time to nonteaching activities, for example, enough "slack" must be found in the work day and the work environment to allow staff to participate without undue strain. Teachers who work a six-period day in the classroom will have little energy, time, and inclination to engage in serious school leadership on any of the following levels:

1. *Self-Improvement.* Staff need time to grow as professionals, whether this means taking a sabbatical, attending a university for continuing professional education, or participating in shorter, inservice work. Opportunities to work on one's own professional development is critical, if teachers are to improve. A number of states and districts are moving toward individual professional development plans, which are supported by the school and district through time off, funds, and activities. Instead of the traditional top-down forms of staff development (where everyone attends a workshop on a topic selected by the superintendent's office), this form of staff development is bottom-up, driven by the needs of each individual teacher.

2. *Peer Professional Support.* A mounting body of research indicates that teachers, working in pairs, triads (see Iorio, 1988), and groups, can do much to assist one another in improving teaching. The New York City program, the Collaborative Consultation Support System Program (CCSSP), for example, puts a veteran, a newcomer, and a midstage teacher together in a "triad" to work on better teaching techniques—through peer observation, sharing, and teamwork. Such arrangements are made possible by taking teachers from the same elementary school grade (or high school discipline), scheduling similar periods free, and giving them opportunities to tackle common problems. The CCSSP has completed its second year, with six triads in each year. In 1989–90,

the model will be expanded to four more schools in District 24, Queens, New York.

3. *Shared Governance.* Most controversial, perhaps, are attempts to engage teachers in key school-level decision making. Such plans require that discretion be given to each school and shared by principals with staff. The model might be mainly consultation, where the principal controls the process by including the staff as advisors and consultants; or true shared leadership might be attempted, with an executive committee of teachers—like university faculty—who make many key decisions, such as hiring staff, evaluating peers, and jointly managing.

Currently, however, the vast majority of schools are not structured to allow time and interest in true joint management and control. A compromise might be some form of decentralization of schools into subschools, mini-schools, or "schools-within-schools," where teachers—led by a head teacher—make many decisions jointly, and the principal becomes more of a coordinator and facilitator than a director and controller. Whatever form of restructuring is attempted, we know that teacher participation is difficult without change in the way schools are organized, scheduled, and structured, as Arthur Powell (1985) explains in *The Shopping Mall School:*

> It is more important to organize school time so that such conversations [about curriculum and learning] can occur, than to impose an ideal curriculum on schools from outside. Rearranging school time in this manner empowers teachers by placing them in the center of educational decision-making rather than on the periphery. It empowers good teachers by removing protective isolation that allows the mediocre to survive and the competent to remain impotent. And it underscores that an effective school for students and a desirable one for teachers is a genuine community of learning for both (p. 35).

CONCLUSIONS

Teacher involvement in their schools is a valuable but difficult process. Already, reformers are recognizing the importance of teachers as central to any effort to foster school effectiveness. Somehow, innovations in education, whatever they may be, must reach the classroom, its teachers, and its students. But breaking the wall of "splendid isolation" has not proved easy.

Teaching itself has been made a solitary activity. Teachers have become accustomed both to working away from other professionals in their classrooms and to being manipulated in the total school environment by administrators and systems designed to control rather than enhance them. This chapter has argued that two very different factors—one managerial, the other organizational—affect the ability of teachers to participate as partners in school decision making and programs.

In this four-cell model, Cell A depicts the traditional school bureaucracy, wherein teachers fall at the bottom of a centralized, top-down kind of system. In turn, school principals interpret their job as mainly one of carrying out district policy; hence, the organizational structure and the management style are congruent, controlling, centralized, rule-bound, and authoritarian. Teachers in such settings have failed to be treated or to act as professionals. One might argue, in fact, that it was the Cell A mentality (or Clark's Theory X/X′) that led teachers to form unions, strike, and seek collective power (see Kerchner and Mitchell, 1988)—to overcome the destructive discretionary power of the centralized system.

Cells B and C, "Mixed-Paternalistic" and "Mixed-Local Tyrant" are more typical of U.S. schools. In Cell B school systems, the district is centrally controlled, but principals, at their own peril, share their authority and control with staff. As teachers realize that such principals really have little independent power, staff begin to see these efforts to "share" and "give input" as a charade and view such principals as paternalistic. In Cell C, where systems have devolved major authority to principals, these administrators may refuse to share the power they have—and may, in fact, use their new-found discretion to be even more controlling and authoritarian (hence, the term *tyrant*). Here, the philosophy of delegation and sharing is twisted by principals into ever stronger control.

Finally, in an increasing number of districts, significant authority is being delegated to schools, and principals, in turn, are engaging their staff in meaningful decision making. Under Cell D circumstances, what we've called "Participative-Autonomous," opportunities for teacher empowerment and governance emerge, since the system trusts the schools to make the right local decision, and the principal trusts the staff to respond to local needs and conditions.

Yet, in schools where teachers want to be engaged in professional development and shared decision making, logistical problems still exist. How, for example, can school empowerment plans incorporate the 3 Rs of teacher involvement: Ratification, Resourcing, and Restructuring? How can we overcome the reality that the teacher's work environment was designed to prevent real opportunities for collegial growth and support? Teachers teach alone. Their schedules prevent regular interaction with other teachers. Extra resources are necessary to allow teachers to do things as simple as meet with a fellow teacher. And few real structures exist to give teachers a meaningful, collective voice in school operations. It's no wonder, then, that teacher empowerment experiments have gotten off to a rocky start.

Several alternatives exist. Give schools greater individuality and choice, thus freeing up the teachers and administrators to respond to the changing demand of parents and community. Put teachers back in the center of school reform. Once teachers acquire greater professional discretion and control, their leadership will force change throughout the system. Such bottom-up reform will influence how schools are organized and function, will challenge the paradigms of schools as large bureaucratic structures, and, most important, will get America's teachers intimately involved in school reform and improvement.

References

Alphonso, R.J. (1977). Will peer supervision work? *Educational Leadership, 34,* 594–601.

Blau, P. M., and Scott, W. R. (1962). *Formal organizations: A comparative approach.* San Francisco: Chandler.

Bloom, A. (1987). *The closing of the American mind.* New York: Simon and Schuster.

Bridges, E. M. (1986). *The incompetent teacher.* New York: Falmer Press.

Carnegie Forum on Education and the Economy. (1986). *A nation prepared: Teachers for the 21st century.* New York: Carnegie Forum.

Chubb, J. E., and Moe, T. (1990). *Politics, markets, and America's schools.* Washington, DC: Brookings Institution.

Clark, D. (1988). *The theory Y leader in the Y-prime organization.* Paper presented to the Danforth Foundation, Arizona State University, Tempe.

Conley, S., Schmidle, T., and Shedd, J. (1990). Teacher participation in management. *Teachers College Record, 39* (2), 34–48.

Cooper, B. S. (Fall, 1988). Bottom-up authority in school organization: Implications for the school administrator. *Education and Urban Society, 21* (4), 380–393.

Cuban, L. (1976). *Urban school chiefs under fire.* Chicago: University of Chicago Press.

Duke, D. L., Showers, B. K., and Imbers, M. (1980). Teachers and shared decision-making: The costs and benefits of involvement. *Educational Administration Quarterly, 16* (3), 93–106.

Garmin, N. B. (1986). Reflection, the heart of clinical supervision: A modern rational for professional practice. *Journal of Curriculum and Supervison, 2,* 1–24.

Garmston, R. J. (1987). How administrators support peer coaching. *Educational Leadership, 44,* 18–26.

Gouldner, A. W. (1954). *Patterns of industrial bureaucracy.* New York: Free Press.

Hirsch, E. D. (1987). *Cultural literacy: What every American needs to know.* Boston: Houghton Mifflin.

Holmes Group. (1986). *Tomorrow's teachers.* East Lansing, MI: Holmes Group.

Humphrey, C., and Thomas H. (1986). Delegating to schools. *Education,* May 10.

Iorio, J. (Summer, 1988). Empowerment and governance as revolutionary and evolutionary processes. *SAANYS Journal,* 10–15.

Kerchner, C. T., and Mitchell, D. E. (1988). *The changing idea of a teachers' union.* New York: Falmer Press.

Likert, R. (1967). *The human organization: Its management and values.* New York: McGraw-Hill.

Lortie, D. (1968). The balance of control and autonomy of elementary school teachers. In A. Etzioni (Ed.), *The semi-professions and their organization.* Glencoe, IL: The Free Press.

McGregor, D. (1960). *The human side of enterprise.* New York: McGraw-Hill.

National Commission on Excellence in Education. (1983). *A nation at risk.* Washington, DC: U.S. Government Printing Office.

Ouchi, W. (1984). *The M-form society: How American teamwork can recapture the competitive edge.* Reading, MA: Addison-Wesley.

Powell, A., Farrar, E., and Cohen, D. (1985). *The shopping mall school.* Boston: Houghton Mifflin.

Reddin, W. J. (1970). *Managerial effectiveness.* New York: McGraw-Hill.

U.S. Department of Education. (1984). *Two years after school.* Washington, DC: U.S. Government Printing Office.

U.S. Education Excellence Act of 1989. (SB 221, 1989).

Walberg, H. J., and Lane, J. J. (1989). *Organization for learning: Schools for the 21st century.* Alexandria, VA: The National Association of Secondary School Principals.

Warren, D. E., and Goldsberry, L. F. (Spring, 1983). Developing teacher collaboration through colleague consultation. *Texas Technical University Journal of Education, 9* (2), 101–109.

Index